The Heart of a Pastor

The Heart of a Pastor

A Life of Edmond Lee Browning

Sheryl A. Kujawa-Holbrook

Forward Movement
Cincinnati, Ohio

Cover design by Robert Grove

First Edition

Library of Congress Cataloging-in-Publication Data

Kujawa-Holbrook, Sheryl A.
 The heart of a pastor : a life of Edmond Lee Browning / Sheryl A.
Kujawa-Holbrook. —- 1st ed.
    p. cm.
 Includes bibliographical references and index.
 ISBN 978-0-88028-324-3 (soft cover)
 1. Browning, Edmond Lee. 2. Episcopal Church—Bishops—Biography.. I.
Title.
 BX5995.K85 2010
 283.092--dc22
 [B]

                                        2010033154

                            Printed in China

FORWARD MOVEMENT
412 Sycamore Street
Cincinnati, Ohio 45202-4195
800-543-1813
www.forwardmovement.org

Table of Contents

Acknowledgements

This book was a collaborative effort from the start, and its completion is due to the work of many people. The project team—Peggy Beers, Brian Grieves, and David Perry—stayed with the project from the idea stage through the fundraising stage, and beyond that through the manuscript stage to the finished book. This book would not have made it into print without the encouragement of the publisher, Forward Movement, and Richard H. Schmidt, Carole Miller, Janet Buening, and Jane Paraskevopoulos, and the assistance of Mission Graphics and Peter Ng and Jimmy Cheng of the Episcopal Church of Our Savior, New York City. Jim Solheim worked with the project in its earliest stages and provided many of his own source materials. Brian Grieves wrote much of the chapter on the Hawaii years, as well as excerpts from other periods. David Perry, Pat Mauney, and the Episcopal Archives in Austin offered photos. David Beers offered his legal advice and recollections of key periods in the Browning administration. Margaret Larom, Elma Blair, and Scott van Pletzen-Rands of the Episcopal Church Center Staff provided administrative assistance. Larry Kirchner graciously conducted interviews in Okinawa, and

Carolyn Francis translated those materials from Japanese into English for the author. John Ratti gave his editorial expertise throughout the project, as well as his own stories from his years at the Episcopal Church Center.

Our patrons, Katharine Jefferts Schori and Frank Griswold, along with Phoebe Griswold, believed in the importance of the project from the beginning.

This project was generously funded by many donors across the Episcopal Church whose financial support made this work possible. Donors (in alphabetical order): Ed Bacon; David and Peggy Beers; Donald Berg; Fred and Barbara Borsch; Bobbie Brodhead; Donald and Carol Anne Brown; Jon Bruno; Dick and Delia Chang; Pamela P. Chinnis; Herb and Mary Donovan; Don and Helen Douglas; Peter and Mimi Freeman; Carl Gerdau; Clark Grew; Brian J. Grieves; Betty F. Hirozawa; Harold and Nancy Hopkins; Sam Hulsey; Carolyn Tanner Irish; William and Linda Jenkins; Bob and Mary-Page Jones; John Jubinsky; Preston and Virginia Kelsey; Charles and Christine Keyser; Rustin and Gretchen Kimsey; John and Nancy Lockwood; Coleman and June McGehee; Charlie and Alice McNutt; James Montgomery; Alfred and Ruth Ono; Denis and Lyn O'Pray; James and Lillian Ottley; David and Ricki Perry; William Persell; John and Kirsten Peterson; Nathaniel and Gail Potter; The Procter Fund and Thomas Breidenthal; George Regas; Gene Robinson; Hays and Linda Rockwell; Cynthia M. Salley; Tom Sekimura; M. Thomas Shaw, ssje; Arthur and Lynette Williams; Geralyn Wolf; Pattie Woodbury.

The Browning family opened their lives and their hearts to make this book possible: Robert and Marylee

Acknowledgements

Browning, Mark and Ella Browning, Paige Browning and Steven Winkle, Philip and Lisa Browning, Peter and Melissa Browning, and John and Tammy Browning were all generous supporters of the project.

Lastly, the project team and author offer our profound thanks to Ed and Patti Browning for allowing their story to be told. Their integrity and ability to trust that their story would be well told is yet another of their many gifts to us all.

— Sheryl A. Kujawa-Holbrook,
Claremont, California
July 2010

Preface

Ed Browning, soft-spoken and gentle, can give the impression of a pushover. Anyone thinking such thoughts would be in for a rude awakening for he would discover a man of steely determination, not easily shaken from reaching the goal he had set himself, whatever the barriers. But I must say I cannot imagine Ed ever being rude to anyone. I crave the reader's indulgence if I speak from the perspective I know intimately—the perspective of someone whose people had languished long under the yoke of apartheid: South Africa's vicious racist policies so long condemned by the world.

Ed came to South Africa in 1986 accompanied by, among others, Bishop Rusty Kimsey of Eastern Oregon and Bishop John Walker of Washington to attend my enthronement as Archbishop of Cape Town. They were shocked by what they saw of the squalor, poverty, and deprivation in the black segregated residential areas. It is to exalt them no end to call them residential areas, for most of the houses were thoroughly inadequate so-called matchbox dwellings, the rest lean-to shacks. All this poverty existed cheek by jowl with the affluence of the salubrious white suburbs with their imposing mansions. The archbishop's official residence, Bishopscourt, was in one such suburb to which it had given its name. When I became archbishop it was still a criminal offense for me and my family to occupy Bishopscourt, which was out of bounds for blacks according to the Group Areas Act. I had declared publicly that as I had been duly elected archbishop my family and I would occupy the archbishop's official residence and I was not asking the government for permission to do so. Mercifully, the apartheid government was smart enough to turn a blind eye to this act of blatant defiance.

All of this was not lost on Ed. It served to reinforce his determination to join in the anti-apartheid struggle with vigor. Injustice of any sort made this mild-mannered man bristle with a controlled anger. And thus it was that he committed the Episcopal Church to a policy of supporting the divestment campaign that sought to persuade U.S. corporations to divest from South Africa. It was hardly a popular stance, as a significant part of our church in the United States derives its membership from the segment of society that had significant shareholdings in these companies. Ed was quietly and courteously determined to stick to his guns to help overturn a vicious system as nonviolently as possible, if we can be pardoned the mixing of images. He is a wonderful exponent of the incarnational sacrament of presence, and thus it was hardly surprising but wonderfully affirming that he should want to attend the very first Provincial Synod (equivalent of the General Convention of the Episcopal Church) over which I presided as archbishop and metropolitan in 1989. His presence was a visible sign of his commitment to support us, and a message to those inside or outside our church that we had a formidable ally on our side not to be trifled with. One cannot compute what contribution that made to assist in making my own ministry more effective than it would otherwise have been.

It was all really a seamless robe. One could understand Ed's unwavering support of the unhindered ministry of women in the church and his stance on human sexuality, and it was all of a piece. And so it was that his very strong pastoral instincts drove him to invite three other archbishops (of Canada, the West Indies, and South Africa) and their spouses to accompany him and his dear, devoted, and equally committed Patti on a pastoral visit just before the 1988 Lambeth Conference to the dioceses of Panama, Nicaragua, and Honduras to encourage and support the churches there at a very trying time in their own histories.

I think it was at the funeral of Bishop John Walker in the National Cathedral that I saw another side to Ed. We were in the vestry just before the service, and I was so deeply impressed, indeed moved, by how he related to one of the bishops whom he could have avoided, someone who opposed Ed's stance on human sexuality and the place of women in the church. Ed did nothing of the sort. He was as affable with that bishop as if with someone with whose views he concurred completely. It was a touching scene to see just how friendly and welcoming Ed was to someone whom he might have considered rather a pain in the neck.

I was sad about all the unpleasantness regarding the distressing conduct of the Episcopal Church's finance officer. That is one of the problems with delegating and trusting your colleagues to fulfill their responsibilities and to have integrity and be conscientious, not needing to be wet-nursed like novices. Ed's trust seems to have been abused and taken advantage of, and the whole sorry business took a heavy toll on him and Patti. He looked haggard and wan. It has been so wonderful to see how he has bounced back in retirement, thankfully looking like his old gentle and caring self.

Just when one would have thought that after his grueling term as presiding bishop he would concentrate in his retirement on quiet pastimes such as gardening and fishing far from the maddening crowd, Ed has shown just how committed he is to working for peace and justice and supporting underdogs by taking on the North American chair of Sabeel, an organization that is quite vocal in its call for justice and equity for the Palestinians. This is no sinecure, since there are a few powerful organizations and individuals in the United States that accuse those who advocate justice for the Palestinians of anti-Semitism. Such groups have often succeeded in persuading, for instance, universities to withdraw invitations to targeted individuals to speak on their campuses, as I know from personal experience. They are formidable adversaries. But this has not cowed Ed and Patti from doing what they believe to be right. Thank God for them.

I have been very favorably impressed by the graciousness of the Episcopal Church's stance on the issue of human sexuality that has shaken our Anglican Communion to its foundations in the face of an aggressive intransigence, and have been amazed at its gentle, accommodating spirit despite the extreme provocation. We give thanks for this, knowing just how much it has contributed to holding the Anglican Communion together. God be praised for this wonderful attitude. I believe Ed contributed significantly through his ministry as presiding bishop to this splendid ethos in the Episcopal Church.

I have no doubt that one day our Lord will proclaim to Ed: "Well done, good and faithful servant." It will be an accolade richly deserved.

— Desmond M. Tutu
Archbishop Emeritus

The Heart of a Pastor

EACH OF US CARRIES a piece of God's heart within
us. And when we love one another, the pieces of
God's heart are made whole. [1]

— Desmond M. Tutu

Ask anyone who has traveled with Edmond Lee Browning
and you will be told it is impossible to get anywhere fast
when in his company. Both as the twenty-fourth presiding
bishop of the Episcopal Church and in retirement, Ed
Browning's accessibility and his way of making anyone he
talks to feel important draw people to him wherever he
travels in the church, and beyond. If Patti Browning, his
wife and partner in ministry for over fifty years, is also
there, it takes even longer. Patti, too, has the gift of putting
people at ease and helping them open their hearts.

The 2009 General Convention in Anaheim, California was no exception. Although initially leery of attending the General Convention after many such memorable
gatherings in the past, Ed and Patti Browning agreed to
be there in 2009 and to spend time in the Forward Movement booth signing book plates for *The Heart of a Pastor:
A Life of Edmond Lee Browning*. The line formed down

the exhibit hall for two days and included many people who had met the Brownings somewhere in the Episcopal Church or in the world and never forgotten the quality of that encounter. There were several priests who were in high school when they met the Brownings at an Episcopal Youth Event and decided then and there to minister in the church. There were women active in the Episcopal Church Women who remembered a Browning visit to their parish or conference. There were missionaries and missionary children and grandchildren who had met the Brownings somewhere overseas. There were retired bishops and even one other retired presiding bishop who came to the booth, many thanking Ed Browning for his ministry to them. Each of these people told their own story of how Ed and Patti Browning had touched their hearts and changed their lives. And once again they experienced a love and interest so genuine that they will not forget the encounter. As I sat in the booth handing Ed Browning bookplates to sign, many people whispered to me, conspiratorially, "You know, he will always be my PB."

Kay Collier McLaughlin, a communications professional in the Diocese of Lexington, is one of those persons for whom Edmond Lee Browning will always be "my PB," as he remains for a great many people across the church. McLaughlin had her first encounter with the twenty-fourth presiding bishop minutes after he was elected in Anaheim in 1985. McLaughlin was in the crowd when Browning said, "There will be no outcasts in this church." She later wrote, "The communications person in me recognized not only the most important line he would ever utter, but the path he had set for himself and the ruthlessness with which he would be reminded of its truth and impossibility again and again...The very human wounded person in me grasped his words with my whole being, and hung on with all my might."[2]

McLaughlin remembers when Browning visited her diocese with the Executive Council. There was the usual presentation of diocesan programs and ministries. The bigger and more substantially funded endeavors nearly overshadowed the ministries of the smaller parishes. After the presentations, Browning rose from his chair and graciously thanked all who had participated. Then looking past all the "casts" of the larger churches, he walked to the mission representative and asked the man if he would join him on the platform to speak more about his work. "I will never forget the expression on that man's face as he went to stand beside his presiding bishop, seeming to stand inches taller and prouder as he accepted the gracious invitation. For me it was an incarnational moment—straight out of the heart of the pastor who always dwelt inside the primate." McLaughlin broke with journalistic precedent and had her picture taken with Browning at the General Convention in 2009. Journalists are generally reticent about getting in photos. But this was different. "You made a great difference in my spiritual journey," said McLaughlin to Browning. "He touched his heart. As he touched mine and this church," she wrote.[3]

The Office of Presiding Bishop

Roland Foster's book *The Role of the Presiding Bishop* is one of the few modern works to examine the role of presiding bishops in the Episcopal Church in detail, though there are biographies of individual presiding bishops. In the earliest days of the Episcopal Church, shortly after the American Revolution, the rules of the House of

Bishops called for the senior bishop to preside at meetings. This limited canonical role grew under the influence of William White, the first and fourth presiding bishop, who served for a total of forty-one years, to encompass the role of chief liturgical officer of the church and president of the new Domestic and Foreign Missionary Society. While gaining authority, White also set a standard for the office as someone moderate, impartial, and above conflict and dissent. Philander Chase, bishop of Illinois, took the office in a different direction when he became presiding bishop in 1843. Chase saw the role of presiding bishop as a spokesman for the church, to "speak God's words to the church and to the world." [4] Throughout its history one of the underlying tensions within the office has been between the ideal of the presiding bishop as an impartial presiding officer and the ideal of the presiding bishop as a spokesman of the gospel and, at times, a controversial figure. [5]

Like most mainline denominations in the early twentieth century, the Episcopal Church grew as a bureaucracy and became increasingly centralized in its efforts to best support its mission. The office of presiding bishop was reorganized along with other church structures. The 1919 General Convention in Detroit created an elected, full-time presiding bishop on the model of a chief executive officer, along with a unified and ongoing national body. The charter of the new board was written into a new canon 60: "The presiding bishop and council, as hereinafter constituted, shall administer and carry on the missionary, educational, and social work of the church, of which the presiding bishop shall be the executive head." [6] At the time the changes were hailed as epoch-making and the most important structural changes of the century.

"An older, classic view had been significantly altered, and a conception of the presiding bishop which is still fundamentally operative had been enthusiastically written into the canons and, more importantly, into the national life of the church."[7]

After the 1919 General Convention, subsequent conventions modified and expanded the office of presiding bishop. At the 1925 General Convention in New Orleans, when John Gardner Murray, bishop of Maryland, became the first elected presiding bishop, the Committee to Consider the Election of a Presiding Bishop affirmed the administrative and executive aspects of the office, yet stressed that "its supreme opportunity is spiritual." As the committee noted, "To interpret the church's growing consciousness of her unity and of her mission to the world, to interpret it to both the church and the world, to lead and inspire, to carry confidence and faith and develop devotion and loyalty, your committee believes that such is the chief responsibility which will rest upon the presiding bishop."[8] Murray lived less than three years after taking office, yet his devotion to the office of presiding bishop made a deep impact. He was applauded as a figure of unity for the church, and announced early in his term his intention to travel to every diocese and missionary district, to demonstrate "that every bishop's problems lay on his heart and every piece of work had his loving thought and prayer."[9]

Despite the brevity of John Gardner Murray's term of office, he set the stage for consideration of the presiding bishop as "chief pastor" for the church. "He is father in God to the whole church," wrote the editor of *The Living Church* at the election of Murray's successor.[10] One problem that soon became clear was the tension between the full-time duties of the office and the fact that the presiding bishop was also supposed to serve his diocese. By the 1930s the role of "chief pastor" was formally articulated. The General Convention introduced the idea of a prophetic role when the Joint Committee on the Status and Work of the Presiding Bishop called the presiding bishop a "spiritual leader," "a witness-in-chief to Christ" called "to make known to the world the gospel of Christ in application to the problems of the age." [11] It was not until 1943 that the tension between the presiding bishop's responsibilities to the national church and his home diocese was fully addressed. The General Convention that year decided that future presiding bishops would resign their diocesan jurisdiction. [12]

There was almost continuous debate and legislation concerning the office of the presiding bishop from 1919 until the election of Henry Knox Sherrill in 1946. Sherrill, who served a twelve-year term, combined the ideals of a spiritual leader with his administrative expertise as chief executive officer and ability to raise large sums of money. Uncompromisingly dedicated to the mission of the church, he saw his primary role as "chief missionary," his son later recalled. [13] Faced with the daunting task of naming Sherrill's successor in 1958, the General Convention elected someone with a more prophetic idea of the office of presiding bishop, Arthur Lichtenberger, bishop of Missouri. "The note which stands out more clearly than any other as a new one in Arthur Lichtenberger's term is a prophetic one; more than any previous presiding bishop, he was concerned with relating the gospel to the great issues of justice and freedom which were beginning to dominate this country's internal life." [14] In 1963 Lichtenberger appointed a Committee on "Mutual Responsibility and

Interdependence," known throughout the church as MRI, which brought together the various strands of tradition found in the office of the presiding bishop into three roles: chief executive officer, chief pastor, and prophetic witness. [15]

The election of John E. Hines, bishop of Texas, was viewed as an affirmation of the prophetic vision of Arthur Lichtenberger. Hines had fought racism and segregation in Texas and was thus considered a controversial figure. Determined that the Episcopal Church respond to the crisis in American cities, Hines was often viewed as the architect of the controversial General Convention Special Program (GCSP), begun in 1967 as an effort to engage the Episcopal Church in the struggle for racial justice in America.

At the 1967 General Convention in Seattle the church also enshrined in the canons the three roles of chief pastor, chief executive officer, and prophetic leader responsible for initiating and developing the policy and strategy of the church. "Far more than any other presiding bishop in our history, Hines sought to engage this church directly in great social issues of race, poverty, and justice. His ability to do so in the dramatic moments of the convention at Seattle was a remarkable testimony both to his witness and to the power of the office of the presiding bishop. And his inability to persuade the church to continue in that kind of advocacy role with that kind of involvement was an equally remarkable testimony to the limits which are inevitable in the office." [16]

Unlike the transition from Arthur Lichtenberger to John Hines, the election of John Maury Allin in 1973 was not perceived as an affirmation of the previous administration. "John Hines must have felt trepidation that the bishops had elected the most conservative candidate on the slate and a frequent critic of his administration of the church." [17] Though more influenced by the theology and style of John Hines, Edmond Lee Browning worked with both of his immediate predecessors, and as presiding bishop attempted to reconcile the goals and vision of the past two administrations into a unified vision for the church. One canonical change to the office of the presiding bishop during the Browning administration was the reduction of the term of office from twelve years to nine. At the time Browning himself affirmed the change. Interestingly, his successor, Frank T. Griswold, who served as presiding bishop for nine years, thought the longer term would have been advantageous. [18] Undoubtedly, the office will continue to evolve and the Episcopal Church will change over time, as will the gifts and perspectives of those called to the office.

The Heart of A Pastor

The title of this book is meant to suggest something of the nature of pastoral care in general and the ministry of Edmond Lee Browning in particular. The physical heart holds the body together and pumps blood to every cell of the body. In the body, the heart is responsive to the needs of the whole: to pain and injury, to passion and beauty, to physical needs, and to the environment. In times of crisis, the heart sends extra support to parts of the body most affected and sometimes beats harder in anger and in sorrow. It is also the heart that receives into itself depleted blood for replenishment. The heart is always connected and interdependent, always in relationship with other organs, and always part of a system. The circulatory system is organized, but at times the heart has to be adaptive and respond to the unexpected. The heart of a pastor is interested in holding the body together and nourishing every cell. The heart of a pastor is always in relationship, always mindful of the diverse needs of the body. In Latin both "compassion" and "courage" are matters of the heart, and they are interrelated: compassion is one's heart suffering with other people; courage is the strength of one's heart to stand with and up to people. [19] It is the heart that calls the pastor to have compassion, to have the strength and courage to stand in solidarity, and to stand up for those trapped in unjust systems.

The late Henri Nouwen, a Dutch priest and theologian, is one of Browning's favorite theologians. Much of Nouwen's work speaks to the need of the faithful to greet the world with a loving heart, despite pain and suffering, even when their hearts invariably get broken. "The more you have loved and have allowed yourself to suffer because of your love, the more you will be able to let your heart grow wider and deeper," writes Nouwen. "When your love is truly giving and receiving, those whom you love will not leave your heart even when they depart from you. They will become part of yourself and thus gradually build a community within you." [20] Patti Browning says that her husband's ability to respond with love to the suffering of others, even when he was very young, is what has characterized so much of his life and his ministry. As a team it was always how they hoped to live among the people they served. "The wider the community of your heart, the wider the community around you," writes Nouwen. [21]

Franciscan theologian Margaret Eletta Guider examined the characteristics of the "prophetic heart" and what it means in terms of spiritual leadership. She believes those with prophetic hearts are able to draw others in, "to effectively enchant and 're-enchant' others," whether friends or adversaries, as they bear witness to God. Those with prophetic hearts attend to God's vision for the world despite the cost to themselves; they allow for greater flexibility; seek to uphold human dignity; announce the Good News of Jesus with integrity and boldness; and, in the context of community, bear witness to solidarity and hope in times of fear, awe, and wonder. [22]

The heart of a pastor. The stories collected during the course of writing this book are a testament to the hearts of Edmond Lee Browning and Patricia Sparks Browning. The Brownings are a "true union" and some say that their hearts beat as one. [23] I attempted to use as many of the stories as possible in this book, and yet, I know there are many more out there than one book can hold. Anne C. Fowler, a priest of the Diocese of Massachusetts, and a longtime advocate for lesbian, gay, bisexual, and transgender people in the Episcopal Church, remembers seeing Browning at Gene Robinson's consecration in New Hampshire. There, Fowler thanked Browning for "helping to make this day possible." To which he sighed and said, "Oh, somebody remembers." In researching this book I discovered, although I did not doubt it, that *lots* of people remember. Fowler says she still has her "No Outcasts" T-shirt from 1985. [24]

Jim Creasy, a priest of the Diocese of Alabama, remembers working with Browning during the celebrations for the 75th anniversary of the Diocese of Southwestern Virginia. Browning and a bishop from the Church of England were part of a festive eucharist. Creasy was the bread steward, and one of his duties was making sure the bishops had enough loaves during the Holy Communion.

He said that he had to supply Browning with four loaves before the other bishop exhausted his first loaf. "Bishop Browning was always more than generous with his time, talent, and treasure," he reflected. [25] Frank Boyd Crumbaugh III tells a story about preparing a young man for confirmation in his home parish, St. John's Episcopal Church in Ramsey, New Jersey. At the time Crumbaugh worked at the Trinity Institute and met Browning in a sacristy before a service at Trinity Church, Wall Street. He told Browning about the young man and about the Prayer Book he was preparing, signed by the young man's parents, diocesan bishop, and other folks as witnesses of all baptized people. Upon hearing about the Prayer Book, Browning's face brightened, and he got that characteristic crooked grin, and said: "*I* want to sign *that* book!" "Ed Browning got it," said Crumbaugh. "That Prayer Book became and remains today one of the now-not-so-young man's treasured possessions. A book he actually uses, I am grateful to say. Ed touched me as well as my 'mentee,' and I shall never forget it." [26]

When searching for a title for this book, I was deep into research and interviews. Past writing has taught me to search for a title as it emerges from the work, and I cannot remember a project where that did not happen. Not far into the research I realized that the word *heart* kept emerging in the documents, in interviews with Ed and Patti Browning, and in the words of the many people I talked with who worked with them and who count themselves as family and friends. Even people who disagreed with the Brownings also commented on their kindness and the depth of their hearts. Then one day it happened. It was a day when I had three interviews scheduled, all with *very* different people with little in common, but they all said

that Ed Browning has "the heart of a pastor." Beyond the
Holy Spirit sending me an email with a suggested title, I
am not sure how more clearly I could have received the
message. Moreover, Browning said the title brought tears
to his eyes, which I took as a test of its authenticity. To be
sure, Browning is a most tender-hearted man. At this stage
of his life he is very porous, and tears come more easily to
him now than before. His children joke that he cries even
during Hallmark Card commercials. But more often than
not, they are tears of grace, of reverence, of thanksgiving;
and sometimes they are tears of anger at flagrant injustice
or senseless violence.

Desmond Tutu wrote that Ed and Patti Browning
have a "special and particular concern in their hearts for
victims of injustice, oppression, poverty, and homelessness;
they found themselves reaching down to the presence of
God within their hearts and reaching out with their hands
to give to the voiceless." [27] The Brownings have kept the
heart of their partnership and their family whole, and it
is that and their abiding hope which fuels the strength
that emanates from them today. A close friend of Ed and
Patti Browning believes that their sense of hope comes
from reflecting on their past lives, their own "miracle"
stories, and their many travels. This looking back and
acknowledging God's presence in the past, and projecting
it into the future, is the wellspring of hope. As the psalmist
says, "My heart, therefore, is glad, and my spirit rejoices;
my body also shall rest in hope" (Psalm 16:9).

Part of the challenge of writing a biography of a
presiding bishop is the reality of ecclesiastical titles. For the
most part I have not included titles throughout this book,
for the sake of accuracy and to avoid confusion, because
titles changed over time for both Ed and Patti Browning,

as well as for their friends and staff. Staff and many friends referred to Ed Browning as "Bishop Browning" in professional contexts. However, in informal settings the Brownings were mostly known as "Ed and Patti" and that is what most of those interviewed call them today. Part of the attraction of the Brownings to people all over the church was their accessibility and ability to put people at ease. Yet this informality should not be misconstrued as a lack of respect for the office of presiding bishop. Michael Peers, retired primate of Canada, made the following observation about Ed Browning: "In the Episcopal Church the primate wears a purple clerical shirt and is referred to as 'Ed.' In the Anglican Church of Canada, the primate wears a sweater and is referred to as 'Your Grace.' Yet if anyone deserved to be called 'Your Grace,' it was him." [28]

This book is an invitation to reflect on the life and ministry of some extraordinary people during an extraordinary time in the history of the Episcopal Church. It is an opportunity for those who were present during the Browning administration, as well as those who benefited from those years of hope and struggle, to reflect and to remember, to acknowledge God's presence in the past and project it into the future. It is a challenge to all of us to live more courageously, more compassionately, and more hopefully. It is a life story of a man who gave his heart to the Episcopal Church.

Introduction Notes

1   Desmond Tutu and Douglas Carleton Adams, *God's Dream* (Cambridge, Mass.: Candlewick Press, 2007), n.p.

2   Kay Collier McLaughlin, "The Heart of a Pastor: A Tribute to Presiding Bishop Edmond Browning," Diocese of Lexington, July 12-17, 1969.

3   Ibid.

4   Roland Foster, *The Role of the Presiding Bishop* (Cincinnati: Forward Movement, 1982), 23.

5   Ibid.

6   Ibid, 65.

7   Ibid, 69.

8   Ibid, 76.

9   Ibid, 77.

10 Ibid, 78.

11 Ibid, 86-87.

12 Ibid, 93-95.

13 Ibid, 100.

14 Ibid, 104.

15 Ibid, 114.

16 Ibid, 122.

17 Kenneth Kesselus, *John E. Hines: Granite on Fire* (Austin: Episcopal Theological Seminary of the Southwest, 1995), 388-389.

18 Frank T. Griswold, interview by Sheryl Kujawa-Holbrook (hereafter cited as SKH), March 2009.

19 A close friend of Ed and Patti Browning reminded me of my long-ago Latin and reflected with me on the pastoral "heart."

20 Henry J. M. Nouwen, "Love Deeply," taken from *The Inner Voice of Love* (New York: Doubleday, 1996).

21 Ibid.

22 Margaret Eletta Guider, osf, "The Heart of Prophetic Spirituality: Insights and Challenges from the Franciscan Tradition," unpublished paper, n.d.

23 Judy Mathews, interview by SKH, March 2009.

24 Anne C. Fowler, letter to SKH, March 3, 2009.

25 James A. Creasy, letter to SKH, February 3, 2009.

26 Frank Boyd Crumbaugh III, letter to SKH, March 3, 2009.

27 Desmond Tutu, "A Testimony for Ed and Patti by the Archbishop of Cape Town," Primates' Meeting, Jerusalem, March 15, 1997.

28 Michael Peers, interview by SKH, May 2009.

Finding Home
1929-1959

W<small>HEN</small> I <small>WAS IN SEMINARY</small>, we had a controversy that tore our community in two. During my first year, the seminary wished to admit an African American man into the incoming first-year class. When the University Trustees found out about the seminary's desire, they demanded that the seminary withdraw their desire. This sounds crazy now, but those of us who were around in the 1940s remember many more egregious things than that. You can imagine the turmoil in the community when this happened…

A number of faculty members and many of the students left. I left. But during the summer came word that the University Trustees and Seminary Trustees had reached a new agreement. African Americans would be admitted to the seminary if desired. Of all the students who had left, I was one of the few who returned.

I know some of my classmates thought I was wrong to go back, to reward a concession that must, in some cases, have been only a grudging one. But I wanted to be there to help make it work, I wanted to be there for any new colleague as he would begin what could only be a stressful period in life's journey. I had been part of the protest, and now I wanted to be a part of the reconciliation. And I knew I could not be part of a reconciliation if I were not around. Controversies come to an end. They come to a resolution. And then our common life has to go on. [1]

— Edmond Lee Browning,
A Year of Days
Revised by ELB, February, 2010

Edmond Lee Browning is the only presiding bishop of the Episcopal Church who was named after a hardware store. It was Flato's Hardware Store in Corpus Christi, Texas, to be exact. At the time of his birth, on March 11, 1929, Ed's father, Edmond Lucian Browning, worked for Mr. Flato and thought it would be "just dandy" to name his first child after his employer. Fond as the Brownings were of Mr. Flato, Ed's mother, Cora Mae Lee Browning "went beserk" and thought better of giving her newborn son the moniker "Flato Lee Browning." She was a determined woman. The couple struck a compromise and decided to name their son "*Edwin* Lee Browning," using Mr. Flato's first name instead of his last. But this was a name that did not stick. When he was twelve years old, the red-haired boy who would become the twenty-fourth presiding bishop of the Episcopal Church rode his bike to the courthouse and changed his legal name on his own, using money he had earned from a variety of part-time jobs. He named himself "Edmond Lee Browning," after his father, although much to his chagrin the more popular spelling "Edmund" would surface many times in the years to come.

The Early Years

The family of Edmond Lucian Browning and Cora Mae Lee Browning eventually grew to include three sons: Ed, the eldest, followed by Robert born in 1932, and years later a "surprise" son, Ben, born in 1944. Ed Browning's godfather was South Texas political boss George Parr, the infamous "Duke of Duval County." [2] The boys were raised in Corpus Christi, Texas, amid an extended family of grandparents, aunts, uncles, and cousins. It was very much a Southern upbringing. Ed Browning excelled in fishing and played most sports. He and his brother Robert shared friends around the neighborhood, including Bobby Beale, Bob Bonner, Bill Graft, and Chico Mason. "He played football in high school and was a very competitive person," said Ed's younger brother, Robert Browning. Bob called his elder brother "Bubba," and the two forged a strong bond that lasts to this day. "I was a typical younger brother and looked on Bubba with great admiration," said Robert. "He was always a step ahead of me." [3] Ed was also busy with school and the Boy Scouts. "I never made Eagle Scout," said Ed Browning wistfully while reflecting on his days in the Boy Scouts, "but I did get Life Scout rank!" [4]

The Brownings lived in a house on Furman Avenue in Corpus Christi, three blocks from Ed's paternal grandparents. Ed's father was the third of twelve children, so there were many cousins. Ed was particularly close to his paternal grandmother, "Granny," a politically savvy woman who taught piano, was an expert seamstress, and took care of several of her granddaughters. One of Ed's paternal aunts, Anna, was a professional musician, and his Uncle Philip, the youngest in the family, was a graduate of the United States Military Academy at West Point.

Growing up, Ed saw his mother's family less often. Cora Lee Browning's father was the sheriff of Nueces County in Texas for sixteen years, although as his grandson Ed Browning recounts, the man never carried a pistol. Ed was also close to two of his girl cousins on his mother's side. The Brownings and the Lees rarely socialized together, seeing each other mostly at funerals.

Every Friday night for a special treat Cora Mae took her sons out to a nearby Mexican restaurant for dinner, while her husband stayed at home. "Mother was the strong force," said Robert Browning. "We never did get any particular direction or discipline from Father."[5] Ed remembers that the family brought their own butter to the Mexican restaurant. Given the rationing during World War II, butter was especially costly for a small business like the family-owned Mexican restaurant near the Browning home. Today, one of Ed Browning's favorite meals is a Mexican "combination plate."

Although Ed was too young to fight in World War II, it captured his imagination. He listened to radio accounts every evening. The family saved every scrap to give to the war effort, such as balls of tin foil and used motor oil. Ed remembers not receiving new shoes for two years because the leather was needed for combat boots and worrying about what would happen if his feet grew and there were no shoes to fit him. "I never said anything to anybody, though," he wrote. "I didn't want to give aid and comfort to the enemy by seeming to begrudge our soldiers the boots they needed to win the war."[6] Ed was profoundly moved by listening to the Nuremburg trials on the radio. "I had no place in my experience to fit people who could put living babies in flaming ovens in the morning and listen to a symphony in the afternoon. I felt as if I had been a fool, believing that the world in which I lived was a good place."[7]

Although Ed Browning has many happy memories of his childhood, especially of his mother's abiding love and support of all her sons, his childhood was overshadowed by his father's addiction to alcohol. Alcohol controlled Edmond Lucian Browning's life, as it had his father's life before him. Although Ed remembers periods during his childhood when his father was sober, he relapsed often and secluded himself in his room for weeks at a time, unable to speak. "I would hear his door open from my room, and hear his uncertain footsteps down the stairs. I would hold my breath until I heard him reach the bottom without falling. I remember how hard it was on my mother. The sorrow of this resided permanently in our house. We were never without it."[8] During those times of seclusion Edmond Lucian Browning stopped working, and Cora Mae and the boys provided for the family. Mostly, the family soldiered on, accepting the stress and upset as part of life. Ed remembers his mother's tears during the worst times, like when his father seriously cut his hand on a broken glass in the bathroom, and he was determined to make things better for her and his brothers.

As the eldest son, Ed matured beyond his years and felt responsibility for his mother and brothers. He even went to the hospital and paid for the delivery when his youngest brother Ben was born. Although Ed Browning had a "deep relationship" with his troubled father and sometimes went fishing with his dad, Edmond Lucian Browning gradually became removed from his sons' lives, and it was Cora Mae who stepped into the gap to raise their children and support the family, with help from her eldest son. Ed Browning remembers poignantly that his father missed the most important milestones of his life—his graduations, his ordination, and his wedding. Still, he feels mostly sadness, not anger, when he reflects on his father's life. "I don't feel any anger toward my father, and although some people don't understand it, I can't say that I feel anything but sadness," said Ed Browning. "He was a very kind man, but very sad."[9] At the same time, Ed never denied the impact of his father's battle with alcohol on the family. "I'm very aware of the potent effect that early experience had on me. I know my scars. I remember them all, and I burn with longing for the healing of others' pain."[10] Closer to his mother who relied on him, Ed loved his father deeply but did not always agree with him. For instance, it never occurred to Ed Browning that an African American friend, Dillard Robinson, could not stay at the family home when he invited him, yet his father said no. Although Browning recognized that "my dad was in another place" on race relations, at an early age Ed set patterns of inclusivity for his own life that were beyond the norm for his place and time. Robert Browning suggested that Cora Mae Browning may have influenced Ed in this regard. "Growing up we were raised to believe that everyone is equal," said Robert Browning.[11]

The kitchen was the most important room in the Browning household, and Ed remembers the wonderful smells that permeated it as his mother cooked. Ed remembers the evenings when he and his brother Robert talked to their mother as she cooked. Eventually the hungry boys would set the table, and the family ate together. Ordinarily, the family ate supper in the kitchen, unless it was a Sunday or a special occasion. Sometimes, when Ed complained about something he didn't want to eat, Cora Mae reminded her sons of the starving Armenian people, although then, as now, the impact of that suffering did not seem to make a big impression on little boys. After dinner the boys did their homework on that same table, by the warm yellow light of a lamp. Ed remembers one dinner, just after his father had returned from a hospital stay, when the family sat around the table enjoying a special chicken dinner. "Seeing him in his chair, right where he belonged, I thought, 'Dad's going to be all right now.' I thought that every time he went," wrote Ed. "But it was never true." [12]

Ed's father was a gifted artist and high school quarterback who had turned down three college scholarships in order to help support his parents and eleven brothers and sisters. "I have a photograph of him as a teenager, returning victorious from a football game," wrote Ed Browning. "Such a broad, sweet smile—it's jarring to me now, seeing that innocence on a face I would later know only as sad...I long for the healing of one who has victimized another with a fervency I probably would not feel if I had not been forced to confront the need for reconciliation every day in my own home. Bitter things for a young person to know, but I am glad I know them." [13]

"The situation with Ed's father was heartbreaking," said Gerald McAllister, retired bishop of Oklahoma and a friend of Browning's since the early days of his ministry. "But it made him the caring, loving, sensitive person we have known." [14] Edmond Lucian Browning eventually died of alcoholism at the age of sixty-three in 1964, while his eldest son was a missionary in Okinawa. Because of the distance, Ed did not return home to Texas for his father's funeral. "I didn't go home for the funeral. I told my mother that she didn't need him. It was a huge mistake," Ed Browning later said with regret. [15] "The death of his father further deepened his relationship with his mother," said McAllister. "His mother was head of the family, and after he left home Ed saw her as often as he could."[16]

While Ed Browning still lived at home in Corpus Christi, the United States government opened a naval station and his dad got a job as a civilian manager for one of the firms connected to the station. Later, he went into the army surplus business. In 1947 the elder Browning started a furniture store, Browning Brothers, where Robert Browning worked until his retirement in 2007. Cora Mae and her sons all worked in the family store at one time or another; she also worked at Lichtenstein's department store, where the boys worked summers.

Red-haired like Cora Mae, and "the apple of his mother's eye,"[17] young Ed was interested in finding any way possible to help the family, and took a variety of odd jobs. He started work at the age of seven when he peddled *Liberty* magazine door-to-door without his mother's knowledge. His favorite customer was Mrs. Furman, who tipped him generously when he told her that she reminded him of his granny. "I learned early in life how to be nice and the importance of being a gentleman," he later reminisced.[18] "Bubba always had a job," said Robert Browning.[19] Ed Browning also worked as a delivery boy, a soda jerk, a used shoe salesman, and a drive-in laundry clerk, as well as working in the family store.

As a boy and young man, Edmond Lee Browning said he wanted to be three things when he grew up. The first two were a circus clown and a Marine, and the third, nurtured in his local parish and diocesan summer camp, was to be a priest. "When he came home from camp and said that he decided to be a priest, that's what I wanted for him," said Cora Mae Browning.[20] Both Edmond Lucian, a lapsed Methodist, and Cora Mae Browning, an

Episcopalian, believed that their sons needed a religious upbringing. They dutifully sent Ed and Robert to the church two blocks away, The Church of the Good Shepherd, Corpus Christi. "It was home," said Ed Browning.[21] The church was one of the most prominent in the diocese and had a long history of outreach and mission.[22] At Good Shepherd Ed was known as "the little red-haired boy that carried the cross," and he took on parish life with enthusiasm. He was a faithful acolyte at a very young age, although during his first experience carrying the flag in church he hit a light and it exploded. For Ed and Robert the Episcopal Church was a mentoring community: their faith was nurtured by the people of the church. The rectors of Good Shepherd during Ed Browning's childhood and youth, particularly Ben Minifie and David Rose, became important mentors throughout his young adulthood, helping fill the gap left by an absent father. In addition to nurturing Ed's vocation to the priesthood, The Church of the Good Shepherd also mentored Robert Browning, who continued in life as a husband, father, businessman, and devoted churchman. Robert has also served the Episcopal Church as deputy from the Diocese of West Texas at several General Conventions.

Ed was active in his parish youth group and was a popular camper and counselor, known as "Red Browning" at Camp Capers, in the Diocese of West Texas. Browning was also active in and for a time president of the West Texas youth program. James "Jimbo" Garland remembers Ed Browning from diocesan youth conferences in the mid-1940s. He first met "Red" at the 1944-1945 Winter Conference of the diocesan youth program. Ed ran for president that year, and was defeated by Agnes Barnes. He was elected president the following year, however.[23]

He attended the 1949 General Convention as a youth delegate. Years later, as presiding bishop, Browning would say with confidence that it is a mistake for the church to consider young people "the church of the future," when in fact they are "the church of today." He believed this not just because it was a catchy thing to say in the 1980s and 1990s, but because of his own experience as a young person who found his vocation within the church as a child and as a young man. Ed Browning credits the laity and clergy of his home parish for mentoring him in his nascent vocation. It was also at Camp Capers that "Red" Browning came to the attention of the diocesan bishop, Everett Jones, who confirmed him. Jones was another mentor and father figure to Ed Browning during his seminary years and in the early years of his ministry in West Texas.

The Church of the Good Shepherd was one of the earliest congregations in the Diocese of West Texas to pursue interfaith relationships. Ed remembers visits from Rabbi Sidney Abraham Wolf to the parish and believes they were an integral part of his religious experience as a child. In 1935 William Caper Munds, rector of The Church of the Good Shepherd, believed it was time for all Christians and creeds to band together against the rise of National Socialism in Germany. He invited Rabbi Wolf and members of Temple Beth El to join with the church in an interfaith Thanksgiving Day service. The Women's Guild of the church and the Sisterhood of the Temple participated. On the day of the service the rector, the rabbi, and the church choir processed down the aisle bearing a menorah. Munds read from the *Reformed Jewish Prayer Book,* while Rabbi Wolf read from the King James Version of the New Testament. Jews and Episcopalians sat side by side in the pews. At the time, the interfaith service was newsworthy enough to be featured in the November 30, 1936, issue of *Time* magazine with a photo of Munds and Wolf under the heading, "Love in Corpus Christi."[24] Years later, when Browning was presiding bishop, he had dinner in New York with his chancellor, David Beers, and his wife Peggy Beers, along with their daughter and new son-in-law, David Shenk. During dinner, while talking about Ed's days in West Texas, Shenk asked Ed if he had ever met his grandfather, Rabbi Wolf. "I loved your grandfather!" exclaimed Ed Browning.[25]

The Church of the Good Shepherd was known throughout the diocese for its emphasis on mission. It was considered the "mother church" of the region. In addition to its innovative interfaith outreach, the congregation started numerous rural mission congregations and funded outreach programs. Munds, rector when Ed Browning was a little boy, "was determined to extend the work of Good Shepherd as far beyond the actual parish as he was able. It was the beginning of the renewed missionary movement which was to characterize the last decade of the century in the history of the church."[26]

While enrolled in Corpus Christi Senior High School, Ed Browning and his friend Chico Mason attended a traveling revival that came to town. Under a great tent, women fanned themselves with fans, painted with Bible scenes, from the funeral parlor, while the men sweated in their shirtsleeves. The enthusiastic preacher held his Bible in the air and shouted and cried emotionally. By that time Ed Browning had heard quite a few sermons, but he had never witnessed a scene like this. When the preacher called for people to come up to the front and be saved, Ed was swept up in the spirit of the occasion, accepted the altar call, and walked down the aisle, surrendering his life to Jesus Christ. As true as his dedication to Christ was at the time, after the excitement wore off, Ed Browning sat at home and wondered if he was going to be kicked out of the Episcopal Church for a moment of religious enthusiasm. "I thought of the night before, of the heavy hands of the preacher on my head. And then I thought of the rector of my parish church, a man who was like a second father to me, and I pulled the covers back up over my face. Why on earth had I gone up there?" The next day Ed received a letter from the rector telling him how proud he was of him. Instead of admonishing the young man, the priest congratulated him on his experience and offered his continued support. "I was safe calling upon the name of God, no matter where I did that. Nothing has been lost. I had not ceased to be myself. God is large enough to be met in some pretty out-of-the-way places." [27] It was a pastoral lesson in compassion and support that Ed Browning never forgot. He reflected on the experience in his sermon to open the Decade of Evangelism in 1990 while he was presiding bishop:

> Someone asked me the other day about my *own* faith journey, how I came to Christ. I thought about that night in the tent meeting. But that wasn't where I came to Christ. That was just a step along the road. I couldn't really give you a time and a place, because for me it was a gradual kind of thing. I learned about Christ from my wise rector over the years of my childhood and adolescence, but I also learned from my parents. And from my wife, even before she *was* my wife. I also learned in seminary. And I am still learning about it. The knowledge that I belonged to Christ was formed in me by many, many things over many years, and

I think that's true of a lot of people. The meaning of Christ's love for everyone else also grew in me as my world grew wider. [28]

The University of the South

Ed Browning graduated from Corpus Christi High School in 1947 during the height of the polio epidemic. School officials, parents, and students were concerned that the school would have to close before the end of the year, and it did indeed close for Ed's last semester. Ed Browning enrolled in Del Mar Junior College for two years, to save money and to work in his family's store. It was through the intervention of David Rose, rector of The Church of the Good Shepherd, that Browning got a scholarship to the University of the South, more popularly known as "Sewanee" for its location in Tennessee. Rose was an alumnus of the institution, and since it was an Episcopal school, he was able to procure the necessary funds for Browning to complete his degree there. "It did not take me long to discover that Red Browning was highly respected both by his peers and the adult members of the congregation—for good reason. He was an eager, all-American type young man, responsible and personable, enjoying everything in life and fun to be around," wrote Rose. "His interest in sports was avid—and still is—and his social life was always full. The boys liked to be around Red, and the girls swarmed, a situation to which he was not averse." [29]

During the first decades of its existence, the University of the South functioned as a military school; until 1892 all students were required to wear gray Confederate uniforms. "It was a small college, in wooded mountains, its students drawn from the impoverished Episcopal gentry of the South, its boarding houses and dormitories presided over by widows of bishops and Confederate generals. Great Southern names were thick—Kirby-Smith, Elliott, Quintard, Polk, Gorgas, Shoup, Gailor. The only things it wasn't rich in were worldly goods, sociology, and science. A place to be hopelessly sentimental about," wrote William Alexander Percy. [30]

Known as the "Oxford of the South," the Sewanee community of the 1950s differed little from the previous decades, and would seem very formal to college students today. The young gentlemen—women were not admitted to the university until 1969—dressed in coats and ties and dinner was a formal affair. Dean Lancaster and Dean Webb, the deans of men, presided over "a benevolent but no-nonsense system of student life." [31] There were weekend parties, Sunday night visitations, and Saturday classes. Nine fraternities were the center of most of the social life. There were trips to Miss Clara's in Monteagle, and meals in Gailor with occasional food fights. Chapel was required (thirty weekdays and six Sundays for gownsmen, and thirty-five weekdays and seven Sundays for non-gownsmen.) There was plenty of beer but hard liquor was forbidden. [32] "The founding of the University, over the years, was a dedication to the faith of a great tradition," wrote Charles T. Harrison in 1957. "Actually it is not difficult to define this faith. It is the faith that nature, reason, and virtue are divine in origin and in sanction; that human life is ideally capable of attaining beauty and dignity; that the cultivation of knowledge, wit, and good manners is a worthy human interest." [33]

Ed Browning loved college life and he loved Sewanee. He found the mission of the school very meaningful and responded to the "church-centered" community. While at Sewanee Browning became a member of the Order of the Gownsmen, a form of student government, the student vestry, the acolytes' guild, and the Blue Key, an honorary service fraternity. He was also active in intramural sports, was a runner on the track team, and was a member of the Phi Gamma Delta social fraternity. Jim Garland, Ed's friend from Camp Capers, recruited "Red" to join. "A college fraternity also may be likened to a workshop in brains, actions, and emotions where a man may serve a four-year apprenticeship to life," states the Phi Gamma Delta pledge manual. [34]

An English major, Ed Browning remembers the excellent faculty at Sewanee, inculding Professor Long who taught English, Professor Gass who taught Greek, and Professor Burton, a phenomenal math teacher. His father was not overjoyed that Ed decided to go on to seminary— the elder Browning had wanted his son to stay at home and work in the family business—yet Ed was recognized as a young man with seminary in his future. He graduated from the University of the South in 1952 with a Bachelor of Arts degree and returned to St. Luke's School of Theology at Sewanee to complete his education.

Like his father, other people back home also feared that seminary would have a negative effect on Ed Browning. "When I went off to seminary some people in my town were concerned I might be educated out of my faith," he wrote. "School would make me question things I had no business questioning. Faith was best untainted by critical scholarship. I might lose my relationship with God if I questioned too far...but God is just not that small." [35]

It was during seminary that Ed Browning started the practice that has anchored his prayer life ever since. "Into your hands I commend my spirit." It is from the Orthodox practice of the "sentence prayer." It is his first utterance as Ed Browning awakens in the morning, and after over fifty years of prayer, it is as automatic as opening his eyes and seeing the new day. [36]

Like most seminarians, Browning participated in field education. He wanted to learn more about the people of the region and every Sunday drove "off mountain" to a small Appalachian church. Most of the people in the congregation were poor and unable to buy enough food or fuel. Browning remembers that they stuffed newspapers in the cracks of the church to keep warm during the winter. At that small church Browning had a pastoral ministry that was moving and rewarding. While other students sought out more middle-class and affluent congregations, Browning was drawn to those people who had the least in the material sense but who opened their hearts. His own experience with austerity equipped him to understand what the people of that small church needed to do just to stay alive and to feed their children. His approach to ministry in an Appalachian congregation was essentially the same as his later approach in South Texas, Okinawa, Europe, Hawaii, and eventually as presiding bishop. "Just as with my earlier experience in my home parish, Camp Capers helped me to see that the primary role of the church is in building relationships and establishing community," he said. [37] There Ed Browning learned to listen deeply to the people, to build relationships, and to nurture the community—all skills that have characterized his pastoral ministry ever since.

Given the history of the University of the South, conflict became inevitable once the Episcopal Church began to stress the need to desegregate in the post-World

War II era. John E. Hines, bishop coadjutor of Texas and later presiding bishop, was one of the first Episcopal leaders in the South to advocate for desegregation. Between 1947 and 1949 most Southern dioceses granted equality to African American laypeople and parishes, but it was not until 1952 that black and white participants were seated together for a meal at an annual convention. A year earlier, in 1951, the provincial synod had discussed the closing of the Bishop Payne Divinity School for African Americans in Petersburg, Virginia, and decided that rather than opening another segregated seminary, existing seminaries in the South should be opened to students of all races.

It was in June 1952, the summer before Ed Browning's seminary "middler year," that the Board of Regents of the University of the South decided not to admit African American students to the seminary. Although one bishop among the trustees feared the loss of financial contributions should the seminary desegregate, the board's decision to reject the resolution was made largely on practical grounds—to admit African American students would create a contentious atmosphere for both races and violate Tennessee state segregation laws. Trustees also believed that further study of the effects of desegregation on Sewanee was needed before the matter could be settled. [38]

The decision was a bitter disappointment to many students and faculty at the School of Theology; the majority of the faculty and over half the student body, including Edmond Lee Browning, decided not to return the following school year. The theology faculty charged that the trustees' position was "untenable in the light of Christian ethics and of the teaching of the Anglican Communion." [39] At the same time, the larger Sewanee community was shocked that the theology faculty made segregation a public issue; 80 percent of the undergraduates signed a statement in support of the chancellor and trustees, and affirming the traditions of the school. Some feared that the admission of African Americans would destroy "the Sewanee ideal" for the sake of a few applicants. The situation escalated when James Pike, dean of the Cathedral of St. John the Divine in New York City, heard of the decision and publicly refused an honorary degree based on the school's "apartheid policy." Pike's media campaign pushed the issue and assisted those trustees in favor of desegregation. In June 1953, after a year of delays, the largest group of trustees gathered in the school's history met in special session and reversed the 1952 decision. Eighteen out of twenty diocesan bishops present supported desegregation; fourteen committed to keeping their students out of the school if it remained segregated. Segregation remained the de facto policy of the undergraduate school at the University of the South until 1961. [40]

Ed Browning had already made plans to transfer to the Episcopal Theological Seminary of the Southwest in Austin, Texas, when he learned that the Board of Regents at Sewanee had reversed their previous decision. Most of the faculty and students decided not to return; the majority of bishops asked their students to transfer elsewhere, and about one-third of the students enrolled at the Virginia Theological Seminary. [41] After conversations with his rector, David Rose, and Bishop Jones, Ed Browning decided to return to Sewanee to support any African American students who might be admitted to the seminary and to serve as a force for reconciliation in the fractured community. The decision to return was by no means an easy one, but required much soul searching. It also made Ed Browning's final year of seminary traumatic. Years later Browning said that the only "saving grace" in the situation was the leadership of the acting dean of the seminary, Edmund Pendleton Dandridge, retired bishop of Tennessee. Although the seminary community agreed with the cause of desegregation, there was also anger and disapproval with the tactics of those who had resigned. Not only did Dandridge preside over the rebuilding of the community, he paved the way for the appointment of a new dean and faculty and for the eventual accreditation of the school. [42]

The confrontation over desegregation in his seminary changed Ed Browning's outlook irrevocably and provided a framework for the way he would confront controversy in years to come. Firm in his belief in desegregation, Ed Browning refused to disassociate from the community. His principled decision to return to the school despite the conflicts and hardships ahead was anchored by his belief in the need for reconciliation. Rather than avoid controversy or leave the community, he stood with all parties and worked for reconciliation. The controversy also provided Browning with some stunning examples of bishops and diocesan trustees of the Episcopal Church who worked from the inside of an institution to change it in a decisive way. "In this instance the Anglican position on race relations overcame other legal, cultural, and conservative preferences." [43] It was a powerful example of the Episcopal Church's ability to impact societal change. The incident at Sewanee also revealed Edmond Lee Browning's determination in the face of injustice and his willingness to risk criticism to work for reconciliation.

True Love in Taft, Texas

Although Ed Browning's final year in seminary was difficult in many respects, it also included life-changing events of a happier nature. "Marriage saved me," he said. [44] Salvation came in the form of Patricia Alline Sparks, an art student at Stephens College in Columbia, Missouri, and a native of Taft, Texas. In addition to study and sports, the Southern gentlemen of the University of the South participated in another great pastime, the college dance. Ed Browning was no exception and danced with many young college women brought to Sewanee for the occasion. At one such event, he danced with a young woman from Stephens College, who asked him if he knew Patti Sparks from Taft. Browning did what any proper Southern gentleman would do when he wanted to impress a young woman: he lied. He said, *of course* he knew Patti Sparks. He had never met the woman. What's more, when the dancing partner returned to Stephens and told Miss Sparks about meeting her "friend" Ed Browning, Patti responded that she had never heard of *him*. After another chance encounter with a friend of Patti Sparks, Browning decided it was time to try to meet her.

Ed Browning and Patti Sparks finally met on a blind date over the Christmas holidays in 1951. Another mutual friend tried to set them up, but at first Patti demurred. Then her plans fell through and she decided she would go out with Ed Browning after all. The destination was a debutante ball. For Ed it was love at first sight. "I fell in love with her in a minute," he said. [45] For Patti it took a little longer; her first thought was, "I have never seen him before!" [46] It also took longer for Patti to admit her feelings for Ed because her mother fell in love with him immediately and blatantly encouraged his ardor for her daughter. No teenager likes to think she will end up with someone selected by a parent. Lyra Sparks also enlisted Patti's sister in the cause. She said to her older daughter, "I want you to tell Patti what a wonderful person he is," before Cathleen had ever met Ed Browning.[47]

An industrious young man, Browning wasted no time. He visited Patti at Stephens College after the holidays and invited her to come and visit him at Sewanee during spring break. Patti remembers that she refused his fraternity pin on several occasions but relented and they were officially "pinned" when he dropped her off at the train station after a visit to Sewanee. Over the summer months they spent time together every day or evening. By the time they had known each other for about a year, they made the decision to visit Bishop Jones over the Christmas holidays to request permission to marry.

Ed did not actually ask Patti to marry him until after he had asked her father's permission. Like any responsible father of the 1950s, Walter Sparks grilled Ed Browning and asked how the couple would support themselves financially. After Ed responded that he and Patti were going to "live on love," Walter Sparks responded with the predictable, "I *thought* you had a lot to learn," but gave his blessing anyway. "It all happened very suddenly," recounted Patti. "I remember telling him [Ed] that I wanted to go paint and live in Greenwich Village, and the next I knew we were sitting in the bishop's office!"[48]

Patricia Alline Sparks was born on September 30, 1932, to Walter Charles Sparks, Jr., a banker, and Lyra Millicent Haisley, a poet. Patti was the couple's second child; another daughter, Cathleen Lyra, had been born twenty months earlier. The two sisters remain close, although Patti says they seem nothing alike. Cathleen got the red hair and took more after their father, and, according to Patti, "was closer to their parents."[49] Patti's sister, now Cathleen Gallander, a retired art museum director, says Patti was "the dreamier" of the two girls.[50]

Patti's father Walter Sparks came from a Southern family that had some means until the Great Depression. A staunch Republican, he was a practical man who managed several small banks in South Texas. He was known for his sense of humor, his drive, and his relentlessness. A "man's man" and the life of the party, Walter Sparks overwhelmed his sensitive, youngest daughter, who often experienced him as domineering. As is often the case, Walter Sparks's efforts to control his children had the opposite effect, and by the time Patti met Ed Browning she was eager for some independence.

Patti identified more with her mother Lyra Haisley, a descendant of a Quaker family. Patti's maternal grandfather had attended Earlham College, a Quaker school in Indiana. Lyra was quite different from many South Texas mothers. The Haisleys were birthright Quakers who came from Pennsylvania and Iowa before they bought land in South Texas. Lyra Haisley lost her mother to rheumatic fever when she was sixteen and was then sent to boarding school. She was a Democrat, bookish, beautiful, and serious. Lyra studied for two years at Earlham College and for another two years at the University of Texas before eloping with Walter Sparks. Her father was furious; he had hoped that Lyra would complete a doctorate. After her marriage, Lyra Sparks was active in the American Association of University Women and wrote the book column for the local paper. A woman with an independent spirit, Lyra took occasional trips on her own. "Mother had some determination," said Cathleen Gallander. "She raised us to always feel equal to men." [51] Patti remembers her mother as philosophical with a touch of sadness—someone who never quite fit in with her environment. Two miscarriages also added to her sorrow. Although Lyra and her daughter Patti remained proud of their Quaker roots and the faith's quiet spiritual tradition, there were not many Quakers in South Texas, so the family joined the Presbyterian Church. Later Walter Sparks considered the Presbyterians too liberal and switched to the Methodist Church.

Patti and Cathleen remember having their friends over to play but urging them to be quiet as their mother worked on poems. Patti and Cathleen loved to read their mother's poems, and were thrilled when she mentioned them in her work. Although Lyra Haisley Sparks had a reputation of being "different," she had a powerful positive impact on her daughters. "The way their mother wrote about her world gave them a powerful sense of the significance of things which seem on the surface to be ordinary." [52] Patti loved to read—comic books, Nancy Drew, the Bobbsey Twins, "any sort of bad literature." [53] She started piano lessons at the age of five and could play by ear by the time she was nine. Patti was an animal lover as a girl. She raised lots of cats and rode horses. She eventually enjoyed attending a girls' camp during the summer, but her sister says she was very homesick at first. By the time she was ten, Patti had found art, and thereafter spent a lot of time in art lessons and painting, doing portraits and pencil sketches and making paper dolls. Patti followed Cathleen to Stephens College. Their father approved of the school, particularly the good football team across the street at the University of Missouri. Although not yet an

Episcopalian, Patti remembers that Roger Blanchard, who later became an important figure in college chaplaincy and the bishop of Southern Ohio, was at the church in town. Patti thrived at Stephens College, spiritually, artistically, and intellectually, because of the independence afforded her there. She had originally wanted to attend Antioch College, a school with a five-year program, and also considered working at an orphanage overseas, traveling to Europe to rebuild bridges ruined during the war, and studying art in Florence. But her father had said no to those more adventurous options.

Cathleen Gallander believes that her sister Patti was always a profoundly spiritual person who would spend time on her knees in prayer every night. While at Stephens College, Patti Sparks was one of ten young women elected to the Burrall Cabinet, a prestigious group on campus charged with deepening the spiritual lives of college women through community service. Patti was social chair for the group and volunteered in a psychiatric facility. "It turned out to be great on-the-job-training for a bishop's wife," she later said. [54] Membership in the cabinet included a special training period in June after classes ended and a retreat at Estes Park, Colorado. The mission of the Burrall Cabinet was grounded in the idea "that religion is worthless if it isn't expressed through seeing other people's needs and acting promptly upon one's good intentions." [55] After she met and decided to marry Ed Browning, Patti was confirmed in the Episcopal Church at school by another presiding bishop, Arthur Lichtenberger, then bishop of Missouri. Ed and Patti did not share the news with her family until several months later. "After the religion of my childhood, I felt that the Episcopal Church was a breath of fresh air," recalled Patti. [56]

Bishop Everett Jones of West Texas was an influential mentor of Ed Browning's and took an active interest in the young man's seminary career. Jones did not allow his seminarians to marry, so although Ed Browning and Patti Sparks had information about others who had married and successfully completed seminary, Bishop Jones told the couple that he would not allow them to marry until Ed's grades improved. Ed hit the books and they received permission. In fact, Browning's grades and attitude soared so remarkably during his first year of marriage that Everett Jones lifted the marriage ban.

Ed and Patti spent the summer before their marriage working at Camp Capers. They were married on Thursday evening, September 10, 1953, at The Church of the Good Shepherd, Corpus Christi. The service was conducted by Bishop Jones and the rector, David Rose. Ed and Patti spent their wedding night driving to San Antonio (Ed slept while Patti drove), and their honeymoon consisted of the drive back to Sewanee for Ed's senior year of seminary.

Ed Browning said that throughout his long ministry, he never officiated at a marriage without remembering his own. "Patti was a beautiful bride," he wrote while he was presiding bishop. "Our daughter used to love to look at that picture of her mother, small and young and surrounded by lace, splendidly adorned for our wedding. But her real adornment was not that complicated dress, however magical it was. It was her own rock-bottom goodness and strong sense of self, those things that caused me to love her in the first place…I think that's probably why Patti seems to me not to have changed at all. She is still wearing it." [57] The day after their wedding, Ed Browning sent a telegram to his new in-laws, Walter and Lyra Sparks: "Thank you for the beautiful wedding and lovely things that went before but more especially, thank you for your beautiful daughter. I only hope that I can take care of her as well as you have. God bless you both." [58] "I never saw a man love his wife more than Bubba does," said Robert Browning. [59]

Married life at Sewanee was an adventure. Later, Patti reflected that their year together at Sewanee was about learning what it meant to be married. Although the word "ministry" was not used to refer to marriage in those days, the Brownings believe they learned about marriage as a ministry. At Sewanee the married student housing consisted of Quonset huts with walls so thin that it was possible to hear the snoring in the bedroom next door. Everyone knew when Patti and Ed had an argument because their voices could be heard through the walls; they remember being greeted by awkward looks as they emerged from their rooms in the morning. There were few modern conveniences and no washing machines, so Patti washed everything by hand. Patti's father had hoped they would finish seminary in Austin, so she could complete her college degree. In Sewanee, Patti worked as a substitute teacher at the elementary school and helped around campus offices.

A major preoccupation for Patti Browning while at Sewanee was to attend teas given by faculty wives. The occasions were designed to offer support to the wives of students bound for parishes in the near future. While the wives of the older students seemed to take it in stride, Patti, at the age of twenty, found it frightening. During one tea, when it was her turn to pour, she spilled coffee on Mrs. Simpson Atmore, a formidable campus matriarch. The goal of these gatherings, according to Patti, was to help her become an "LPW," a lovely priest's wife. Never comfortable with that interpretation of her role, Patti tried to be as cooperative as possible while searching for other ways to define herself. She took notice when one faculty wife implored the seminary spouses to be careful about the amount of work they did at a parish. This same woman recalled that at one of her husband's parishes it took eleven people to replace her when they moved. "Now that got my attention," said Patti.[60] While at Sewanee, Ed and Patti Browning met other young couples, such as Bill and Margaret Stough, who became lifelong friends and colleagues. Stough would later become bishop of Alabama. Ed Browning received his Bachelor of Divinity degree from the University of the South and was ordained to the diaconate in July 1954 and to the priesthood in May 1955.

Ministry in South Texas

After seminary, The Church of the Good Shepherd wanted Ed Browning back and he returned to his home parish. David Rose wanted Browning to come home for his first job, and he felt loyalty to the mentor who had done so much to support him. The decision left Patti in tears. The Brownings had the opportunity to go to a parish in San Antonio, which Patti would have loved. In retrospect, moving back to Corpus Christi was probably not the best choice, though the young couple made the most of it. Moving close to home meant they would be near their parents' homes and expected to spend their holidays with them rather than form family traditions of their own. The Brownings and the Sparkses were cordial to each other but did not socialize together, and thus there were hard feelings when Ed and Patti spent time with one family and not the other. (Later, when their own children married, Patti was adamant that they should have the freedom to establish their own family traditions and not be expected to return home for every holiday.) Then there was the reality for Patti that The Church of the Good Shepherd was really Ed's home territory. He was their little red-haired acolyte who came back as "Mr. Browning," and she was not a part of that history. Sometimes when Patti went to church she was even asked to sign the guestbook.

Ed Browning was the third and most junior member of the clergy at The Church of the Good Shepherd in 1955. He was in charge of Christian education and youth ministry and preached whenever a month had five Sundays. In many ways it was a typical first clergy job, and Browning's background at Camp Capers served him well in working with children and youth. One summer the parish sent him to Union Theological Seminary in New York to take a course in Christian education. He also attended a "Life Lab" conference on group process. Browning felt that he learned a great deal from David Rose about parish administration and pastoral ministry as a newly ordained deacon and priest. He also appreciated the team aspect of the ministry at Good Shepherd, rather than being on his own for his first two years in ordained ministry. The Church of the Good Shepherd was the largest and most prosperous parish that Ed and Patti Browning would ever serve. Browning learned about the difference that resources can make in the ability of a parish to meet the needs of the people. Early experiences of ministry often have a powerful impact on the future ministry of a clergyperson, and Ed Browning was no exception. He learned during those years at Good Shepherd that "you don't have to go out looking to do something to become a prophet, but you have to respond to the context. You're dealing with the dignity of all human life. Sometimes, most of the time, the pastoral and the prophetic are linked."[61]

One of Ed Browning's funniest stories comes from his early ordained ministry in Corpus Christi. One day a funeral home called the parish to request the services of a priest for a burial in Rockport, Texas. Browning, the only one available, was scheduled to do the burial. His first response was similar to that of many a recent ordinand on such occasions—sheer terror. While certain that he had learned something about funerals at Sewanee, in his nervous condition he didn't remember much of it, except an admonition by one of his professors not to stand too far away from the grave lest the dirt thump on the lid of the coffin as it was lowered. So Ed Browning got to the cemetery and opened his Prayer Book to the Burial Office. He got as close to the edge of the grave as possible. What he did not anticipate was the sandy soil and the slippery surface around the grave. Fully vested and intoning the Burial Office from the 1928 Prayer Book, Browning felt himself going down, slipping slowly into the grave. Luckily, the undertaker grabbed his arm and pulled him out of the grave before he slipped out of sight. Experienced or not, Browning never missed a beat, continuing to read as he was pulled out of the hole.

In addition to the humor in the vision of a young curate falling into the grave while conducting a funeral, that story is an indication of Ed Browning's self-effacing humor. Their sense of humor was a main source of support for both Ed and Patti Browning during tumultuous times. "I always felt very blessed to have Patti in my life," said Browning, "because no matter where we were, she was so positive and so helpful. Our biggest joys are our shared experiences and our children." [62] Browning also said that he learned during his first years of ministry that he did not have to be perfect. "I longed to image Christ to my people, and to serve Christ in my people. But I didn't know then, as I know now, how important it was to let other people be Christ to me. Or how effective people would be in being Christ to one another." [63]

"It was interesting to see Ed Browning, who left for seminary as 'Red,' return as 'Ed' or 'Mr. Browning,'" said David Rose, who was later elected bishop of Southern Virginia. "His relaxed manner, his love for people, and his contagious joy never left him." Rose remembers asking Ed, after his ordination, to call him by his first name, as they were now colleagues at the parish. Ed cast his eyes down, swallowed, and said, "It's going to be hard to get used to that." [64] The Brownings stayed with the Roses while looking for an apartment in Corpus Christi and gave them a gift of a vase shaped like a pair of cupped hands with red fingernails. At first the Roses were too polite to comment. With great hilarity Ed and Patti finally confessed. The hands had been a wedding gift to them. After that the hands moved between the two families, across the country and the world every Christmas, until they met their demise somewhere in the Pacific. [65]

Two years after his ordained ministry began at The Church of the Good Shepherd in Corpus Christi, Ed and Patti Browning moved to The Church of the Redeemer, in Eagle Pass, Texas. Eagle Pass, the county seat of Maverick County, is located on the Mexican border. The town received its name from the eagles that nest in a pecan grove on the Mexican side of the Rio Grande and fly back and forth across the river, hence the name "The Pass of the Eagles." [66] Cattle and sheep ranching were the region's leading industries. For Patti the move was "a breath of fresh air" and an opportunity for the family to be more on their own.

Ed Browning's arrival at The Church of the Redeemer also meant he had some big shoes to fill. Earl Dicus, the rector there for the previous nine years, had been elected the first suffragan bishop of the diocese. "Ed did such a good job as our next priest that I don't think anyone even made a comparison," said Patsy Thomson McGaughy, who was a young girl in the parish.[67] McGaughy said that it was not uncommon for young people to stop by Ed and Patti Browning's house in the evenings. One Saturday evening Patsy remembers asking Browning what he was going to preach on the next day. He admitted that he had some ideas but had not decided yet. The two exchanged some ideas. "Imagine my surprise the next morning when I heard Ed incorporate some of my ideas into his sermon," she said.[68]

Browning continued in youth ministries during his years at The Church of the Redeemer. He was the director of the Senior Young Churchmen's Conference at Camp Capers, a ten-day summer program for youth ages fifteen to eighteen. Patsy McGaughy worked as a counselor with Browning. "He treated us counselors as his equals and was a great leader and guide for us," she wrote.[69] One summer Browning made arrangements for three boys from Dallas to join the camp. Long before gangs were prevalent in South Texas, there was activity in the northern part of the state, and these young men had gotten into some trouble. Although suspicious of Browning and the campers at first, the boys gradually began to participate in the community. McGaughy credits Browning's acceptance and support as the key element in the camp's success. One of the young men had long hair as part of his identity with a Dallas gang. By the end of the camp, he asked to have his hair cut and to be baptized. Browning arranged a special service of Holy Baptism just for him.

During Ed and Patti Browning's ministry in South Texas, three of their children were born. The Brownings welcomed their first child, Mark, in 1955 while they were at The Church of the Good Shepherd, Corpus Christi. Patti said that during those years they navigated the transition from being a "fancy free" young couple to "responsible parenthood." [70] Patti was five months pregnant when they moved to Eagle Pass. Paige was born there in 1956 and Philip in 1958. "I will never forget my shock at how small they were—it didn't seem possible that a person could be that little and still be all right! I was nervous about holding them at first," wrote Browning. "I was afraid I would do something wrong and the baby would break! People had to talk me through it until I got the hang of it." [71]

The Browning family multiplied at a fast rate even for the 1950s, to the extent that Walter Sparks would ask his daughter when she answered the telephone, "Did you have any more children?" Ed and Patti Browning and their small red-haired children lived in a rectory next to the church and the church school. The family's living space was the center of parish activity. "We were beginning to realize how much spouse support needed to be a part of this ministry during these times of transition," said Patti. [72]

Eagle Pass was a bicultural community on the Mexican border. Always a town with a Hispanic majority, it was populated by European Americans, Mexican Americans, and Mexican nationals who worked there. The population was about 85 percent Hispanic and

15 percent Anglo. Many of the Anglo families were related to immigrants from Britain and most were Episcopalians. Most of the town leaders were Anglos, as was most of the membership of The Church of the Redeemer. Eagle Pass was about four hours from San Antonio. "It really had the feeling of a Western place," said Jim Garland. "There were fewer than 5,000 Anglos in a town of 30,000 to 50,000, depending on the time of year. Some wealthy Mexicans kept homes in Eagle Pass in order to send their children to high school there. The white families would often send their children to boarding school and away to college. The circumstances were almost colonial." [73]

The area near the border was divided into large ranches, and members of ranching families belonged to The Church of the Redeemer. At the time, intermarriage between those of European and Mexican descent was rare. Just across the border in Mexico were American and Mexican zinc smelting and coal mining operations. As rector of The Church of the Redeemer in Eagle Pass, Ed Browning frequently visited the families at the American colony at Nueva Rosita in Coahuila and nearby ranches in northern Mexico. Monna MacLellan, a former staff member at the Episcopal Church Center, remembers visiting the parish during summers when the Brownings served there and recalls that many older parishioners called him "Mr. Browning," although other parish leaders called him by his first name. [74] MacLellan's cousin, Jeanette Sanford Frazier, a widow, lived with her parents and three children on the Hacienda de Cloete, a few miles from Nueva Rosita. The hacienda was a lush and verdant oasis in the midst of dry land. [75] When visiting northern Mexico, Browning usually stayed at a family home overnight, rather than drive back the sixty miles to

Eagle Pass. The families of ranchers took turns hosting him. Most were Protestants, although some were Roman Catholic. The gatherings were opened to all and featured prayers, hymns, and a talk by Browning.

Although both Ed and Patti had spent most of their lives in South Texas, the three years they lived in Eagle Pass was an opportunity for a deepened cross-cultural exposure. Richard Aguilar, who served as the rector of The Church of the Redeemer after Browning, said that Ed and Patti were on the "ground floor" of what became an intentional mission to the Hispanic community in the Diocese of West Texas. [76] Although Browning says that his Spanish never was very good, the parish experience there made him familiar with cross-cultural ministry and the impact of colonization on people and their religious heritage. Patti believes that living in Eagle Pass helped her later adjust quickly to life in Okinawa. "They are both developing countries," she said. [77]

The hardship and stark poverty faced by many people who lived on the border awakened Browning's compassion and empathy for the suffering. His experience there also awakened his interest in missionary service. After serving The Church of the Redeemer for three years, Browning began to reflect on the years ahead. He had been too young to enter the military during World War II and had a seminarian's deferment while he attended Sewanee. He shared with Patti his desire to enter some kind of specialized ministry. "It was in our dining room in Eagle Pass," recalled Patti, "that Ed told me he always thought he was deferred for military service to be a missionary or to do a military chaplaincy." [78]

From the beginning of their discussions about the shape of their future, Patti was clear that she wanted to go along, and not stay home in Texas with their family as Ed entered the chaplains' program or missionary service. Both attended a presentation at the Civic Auditorium in Corpus Christi for a thousand people from The Church of the Good Shepherd given by Harry "Honolulu" Kennedy, bishop of Hawaii. Kennedy spoke about the new mission field opening in Okinawa and the need for people to minister in the church there. Ed and Patti were at Kennedy's welcome dinner that night, hosted by Gerald and Helen McAllister. The McAllisters and the Brownings were friends and had children about the same age. The two men sometimes went dove hunting, as their wives picnicked with the babies, although neither man remembers ever actually shooting a dove.[79] Gerald McAllister served at The Church of the Incarnation in Corpus Christi, was the litanist at Ed Browning's ordination, and was eventually elected bishop of Oklahoma. But on that night in South Texas the talk was about the possibilities of missionary service.

After Harry Kennedy's visit to Corpus Christi, Ed and Patti Browning researched the missionary placements available, including Saudi Arabia and the Philippines, and concluded that Okinawa seemed the most practical for their young family. Harry Kennedy wasted little time in urging them to go. The Brownings were to serve a large English-speaking congregation in Okinawa for three years, and thus no extensive language instruction was needed. After a training conference at Seabury House in Greenwich, Connecticut, the family was on their way. At the conference was a professor from the General Theological Seminary, H. Boone Porter, who had just rediscovered the work of an early twentieth-century English missionary, Roland Allen. Ahead of his time,

Allen was disparaged in his own day for advocating the raising up of indigenous leadership in missionary districts. Although impressed with this message at the time, little did Ed and Patti Browning know the depth of their call to Okinawa and the life-altering ministries that lay ahead. When Ed Browning returned to South Texas after seminary, he thought that he and Patti would minister and raise their family there for the rest of their lives, "but the spirit had other plans..." [80]

Chapter One Notes

1   Edmond Lee Browning (hereafter cited as ELB), *A Year of Days with the Book of Common Prayer* (New York: Ballantine Books, 1997), February 12. Revised by ELB, February 2010.

2   Joyce Saenz Harris, "Edmond Lee Browning: Presiding Bishop Guides a Diverse Episcopal Flock," *The Dallas Morning News,* December 25, 1994, 3.

3   Robert Browning, interview by Sheryl Kujawa-Holbrook (hereafter cited as SKH), March 2009.

4   ELB, interview by SKH, January 2009.

5   Robert Browning, interview.

6   ELB, *A Year of Days,* June 27.

7   ELB, *A Year of Days,* July 18.

8   ELB, *A Year of Days,* February 24.

9   ELB, interview.

10   ELB, *A Year of Days,* August 15.

11   Robert Browning, interview.

12   ELB, *A Year of Days,* February 22, February 24, July 28.

13   ELB, *A Year of Days,* September 20.

14   Gerald and Helen McAllister, interview by SKH, March 2009.

15   Ibid.

16   Ibid.

17   Patricia Sparks Browning (hereafter cited as PSB), interview by SKH, January 2009.

18   ELB, interview.

19   Robert Browning, interview.

20   J. Michael Parker, "Mom to Pray for Strength for Bishop at Investiture," *San Antonio Express-News*, January 11, 1986.

21   ELB, interview.

22   The Episcopal Church of the Good Shepherd, "A Short History," The Church of the Good Shepherd, http://www.cotgs.org/history.htm.

23   James Garland, interview by SKH, March 2009.

24   The Texas State Historical Association, "Sidney Abraham Wolf," *The Handbook of Texas Online*, http://www.tshaonline.org/handbook/online/articles/WW/fwomj.html.

25   David Booth Beers, interview by Brian J. Grieves, December 2009.

26   Hortense Warner Ward, *A Century of Missionary Effort: The Church of the Good Shepherd, 1860-1960* (Austin: Von Boeckman-Jones Co., 1960), 95.

27   ELB, *A Year of Days,* July 10.

28   ELB, "Christ for a New Century: A Sermon to Open the Decade of Evangelism," Episcopal News Service, May 10, 1990.

29   David Rose, "Edmond Browning Is a Man Whose Life and Prayers Are Inseparable," n.d., Browning Collection.

30   Quoted in William Butt and William Strode, *Sewanee: The University of the South* (Louisville: Harmony House, 1984), n.p.

31 Samuel R. Williamson, Jr., *Sewanee Sesquicentennial History: The Making of the University of the South* (Sewanee: The University of the South, 2008), 297.

32 Ibid.

33 Quoted in Butt and Strode, *Sewanee.*

34 Robert H. Alexander, *The Purple Pilgrim* (Washington, D.C.: Phi Gamma Delta, 1965),13; James Garland, interview by SKH, March 2009.

35 ELB, *A Year of Days,* May 29.

36 Leonard Freeman, "Personal Interview with Presiding Bishop-elect," Convention Video News Program, transcript, September 10, 1985.

37 ELB, interview.

38 Gardiner H. Shattuck, Jr., *Episcopalians and Race: Civil War to Civil Rights* (Lexington: University Press of Kentucky, 2000), 45-50.

39 Ibid., quoted on page 45.

40 Ibid., 47-50.

41 Ibid.

42 Williamson, *Sewanee Sesquicentennial History,* 274.

43 Ibid.

44 ELB, interview.

45 Ibid.

46 PSB, interview.

47 Cathleen Gallander, interview by SKH, April 2009.

48 PSB, interview.

49 Ibid.

50 Cathleen Gallander, interview by SKH, April 2009.

51 Ibid.

52 ELB, *A Year of Days,* April 19.

53 Ibid.

54 Ibid.

55 "Miss Patti Sparks Is Member of Burrall Cabinet at Stephens," Taft, Texas newspaper, n.d., Browning Collection.

56 Ibid.

57 ELB, *A Year of Days,* December 29, June 10.

58 Telegram, September 11, 1953, Browning Collection.

59 Robert Browning, interview.

60 Ibid.

61 ELB, interview.

62 Ibid.

63 ELB, *A Year of Days,* June 15.

64 David Rose, "Edmond Browning."

65 Ibid.

66 Eagle Pass Chamber of Commerce, "Eagle Pass," from the collection of Monna MacLellan; The Texas State Historical Association, "Eagle Pass," *The Handbook of Texas Online*, http://www.tshaonline.org/handbook/online/articles/EE/heel.html.

67 Patsy Thomson McGaughy, letter to SKH, March 2009.

68 Ibid.

69 Ibid.

70 Patricia Sparks Browning, "Clergy and Spouses Retreat Address," Diocese of Delaware, n.d., Browning Collection.

71 ELB, *A Year of Days,* September 9.

72 PSB, "Clergy and Spouses Retreat Address."

73 James Garland, interview by SKH, March 2009.

74 Monna MacLellan, letter to SKH, January 24, 2009.

75 Monna MacLellan, letter to SKH, March 18, 2009.

76 Richard Aguilar, interview by SKH, September 2009.

77 PSB, interview.

78 Ibid.

79 Gerald and Helen McAllister, interview by SKH, March 2009; ELB, interview by SKH, March 2009.

80 Freeman, "Personal Interview with Presiding Bishop-elect."

Born Again
1959-1971

W E W E N T T O O K I N A W A for many reasons—
some good and some not so good. Certainly one
of those reasons was to be in some way a means
by which God in Christ could be introduced to
the Okinawans. The understanding that I would
like to share with you—that I believe is a key to
understanding mission—is one that I learned
gradually as I came to know the Okinawan people.
Their lives were lived in beautiful simplicity,
always with a deep caring and concern. You could
see this in the way they emphasized the family, for
they saw it as the cornerstone of society. You could
sense it in the way they related to children and
the aged. You could feel it as you watched them
struggle for justice and dignity when they were
being tossed to and fro politically. You knew it in
the way they related themselves to nature and in
their appreciation of their environment.

I came to understand that I was not there to
introduce God to the Okinawans or the Okinawans
to God. I came to realize that he was there before
I arrived—before any missionary reached those

shores—and that I was there because he had called me to join him in one of the places in which he was already at work. Again, the key to understanding the church's mission is to seek to discern in this confused, suffering, and starving world where God is at work and how we might join him. [1]

— Edmond Lee Browning,
"Our World Mission," 1976

During his years in Okinawa, Ed Browning regularly visited a community of lepers. They lived isolated from all the other people on the island. Although leprosy, or Hansen's disease, as it is properly called, can be arrested, many of the people lived with terrible disfigurement and had grown old in the colony. It was fear that kept the lepers there, not medical necessity, for the spread of leprosy in Asia was not a threat. The lepers could have lived among the general population without medically endangering anyone else, but they could not live with the fear projected upon them as the bearers of sin and death. "And so they went to the colony, leaving their worlds behind. Parents leaving children, husbands leaving wives, families broken apart at the entrance to the compound, never to be together again...There are not many things I have seen that taught me more about Christ than that which I saw in the leper colony on Okinawa," said Ed Browning. "I will never forget it." [2]

Among those in the leper colony, some had missing features, eyes or noses wasted away. Others were missing fingers or had disfigured limbs. Yet despite the suffering, the leper colony was far from a hopeless place. Ed Browning loved to visit there, and he took his children there on pastoral visits. "They were joyful people. Generous and joyful, looking out for one another in emergencies, seeing to the children," he wrote. [3] Browning was the first bishop to tell the people in the leper colony that they did not need to use the traditional white linen head coverings for confirmation. "We finally have our bishop," was their response. "I did so because Jesus taught me to touch the lepers," said Browning when he was presiding bishop. "It is Jesus, not me, who said—there will be no outcasts." [4]

Browning's compassionate presence forged a deep pastoral bond with the people of the leper colony, and his ministry to them was reciprocated as they also ministered to him:

> I remember that one man insisted on giving me twenty dollars to take my mother out to lunch once when I was going to visit her in the States. Twenty dollars was a lot of money in that time and place. I kept protesting about the gift, that it was too generous for me to accept. I can still see his ruined face, with its big smile, as he told me how lucky I was to be seeing my mother. No wife, no children—but he nurtured as well as any father I ever knew. He still nurtures me. He confirms in me the central tenet of my faith: hope in every situation. God in unexpected places, grace and power from unexpected people. Joy conquering despair. [5]

Transformation and Change

Their years as missionaries in Okinawa were transformative for the Brownings. Ed and Patti left South Texas in 1959 with three small children, on an arduous air journey via Oakland, Honolulu, Wake Island, and Toyko, arriving in Okinawa in the wee hours of the morning on August 1, 1959. Their destination was All Souls' Church, Machinato, Okinawa, where they committed to a three-year term serving the English-speaking community. Although the trip took many days, both were excited at the prospect of ministry in Okinawa. The Brownings were in their twenties and ready for some time as a family on their own, away from South Texas. "In some ways it was tough," said Patti, "but it was also like being 'born again'—we became who we are in Okinawa." [6] It was in Okinawa that Ed and Patti were formed together for their ministry in the years to come. Soon after arriving there, they both felt they wanted to spend the rest of their lives in Okinawa. Although it was not to be, the spirit of their years in Asia pervades the Brownings' home today, and their love for the people there remains strong. Ed and Patti Browning lived in Okinawa from 1959 until 1971, with the exception of two years in a Japanese language school in Kobe, Japan (1963-1965).

Those years were a time of great change in the Episcopal Church. A year earlier, in 1958, Arthur Lichtenberger succeeded Henry Knox Sherrill as presiding bishop. In the same year, the Episcopal Divinity School in Cambridge, Massachusetts, admitted the first women to its Bachelor of Divinity program. In 1959 the Episcopal Society for Cultural and Racial Unity (ESCRU) was founded in Raleigh, North Carolina, and three years later, in 1962, John Burgess was elected bishop of Massachusetts, the first African American to be elected in a predominately white diocese. In the same year, construction was completed on the new Episcopal Church Center at 815 Second Avenue in New York City. In 1963 the Third Anglican Congress in Toronto produced "Mutual Responsibility and Interdependence" (MRI), a document calling for every Anglican to measure every activity by the test of service and mission. The MRI movement had a deep impact on Ed Browning and other church leaders of his generation. Then the 1964 General Convention elected John E. Hines presiding bishop, and the House of Deputies heard an address by Martin Luther King Jr. At the next General Convention in Seattle in 1967, when Edmond Lee Browning was elected bishop of Okinawa, John Bowen Coburn was elected president of the House of Deputies; a plan for revision of the Prayer Book was approved; women were approved as deputies for the first time; and the General Convention Special Program (GCSP), a plan designed to provide funding to organizations working with the poor and people of color, was created. A Special General Convention in 1969 updated the missionary strategy of the Episcopal Church. The following year, the General Convention in Houston approved the ordination of women to the diaconate and seated the first women deputies. In 1971 the bishop of Hong Kong, with approval from his synod, ordained two women to the priesthood. [7]

During their years in Okinawa, Ed and Patti Browning were aware of the issues facing the United States and the Episcopal Church, but were more involved with the social and political issues affecting the people of Okinawa and life in the Pacific. Philip Browning said he remembered how his father wept when they learned of the assassination of Martin Luther King Jr., and held a special memorial service on the military base. [8] Yet because of their location in the Pacific, Ed and Patti Browning viewed the issues of the church and society of the mainland, such as the impending Vietnam War, through a different lens.

They witnessed the negative impact of U.S. and Japanese foreign policy and actions of the Episcopal Church on the people of Okinawa. Browning's ministry in Okinawa gave him opportunities to "speak truth to power" in a manner that was unparalleled in his earlier ministry. "Those years were as important as any in preparation for the rest of my ministry," he said. [9]

Origins of the Church in Okinawa

For much of its history, Okinawa, a small island of the Ryukyu Islands located between Japan and Taiwan, had been occupied by an outside power. First occupied by China, Okinawa was later under Japanese rule for one hundred years and then occupied by the United States military from the end of World War II until 1972.

This military presence was the source of considerable tension between Okinawa and Japan. In the years leading up to World War II, the Japanese government sought through conscription, mobilization, and nationalistic propaganda to reinforce the national identity of Okinawans, who at that point had been full Japanese citizens for a generation. The Japanese military also conscripted high school age girls to serve as battlefront nurses. When Japan became a dominant power in Asia, many Ryukyuans were proud of their Japanese citizenship, although there was an undercurrent of dissatisfaction and prejudice against the Japanese. The Battle of Okinawa was one of the bloodiest of World War II, with an estimated 72,000 American and allied casualties, with at least 12,000 dead or missing. In addition, 100,000 Japanese troops were killed, many through suicide. At least 130,000 indigenous Okinawans were also killed, wounded, or committed suicide rather than face capture.[10] The Ryukyu Islands were the only inhabited part of Japan to experience a land battle. Some military historians believe that it was the fierce fighting of the native Okinawans that persuaded American strategists to look for means other than direct invasion to conquer Japan, thus leading to the use of the atomic bomb on Hiroshima and Nagasaki. After the war Okinawa was occupied by the United States military until the islands were ceded to Japan in 1972. The American military still controls 19 percent of the island's land area today, and although it provides needed jobs, crimes committed by American soldiers against Okinawans have caused ongoing tension.

Keyia Aoki, an Anglican layman, started the Episcopal Church in Okinawa.[11] Aoki had leprosy and came to Okinawa to evangelize other victims of the disease there. In 1938, with the aid of the Anglican Church in Japan, the Nippon Sei Ko Kai (NSKK), and the Japanese government, Aoki founded the Airakuen Leper Colony. In 1967 Keyia Aoki was ordained deacon to serve the leper colony chapel. The Episcopal Church first assumed responsibility for ministry in the Ryukyu Islands in 1949 at the request of the presiding bishop of the NSKK, Michael Yashiro. Bishop Harry Kennedy was appointed bishop-in-charge. The first American missionaries to Okinawa, Norman Godfrey and William "Bill" Heffner, started a worshiping congregation in 1949 and founded the Church of St. Peter and St. Paul in Naha on March 21, 1951. In 1958 the United Thank Offering funded the Nazareth Kindergarten there. In the same year, All Souls', Machinato, was built to serve the English-speaking community and dedicated to the nearly one-quarter-million Okinawans, Japanese, and Americans who died in the battle of Okinawa. Other work soon followed. With Peter Shinjo's arrival in 1960, mission work began on the island of Miyako, 200 miles south of Okinawa. Shinjo was also involved in the founding of St. James' Church, Hirara, and St. Michael's Church in the Ryukyus' second leper colony. St. James' was the site of an orphanage for children of leprous parents and a dormitory for junior high school girls from the outer islands. In 1964 the Nazareth Order of Tokyo at All Saints, Shimabuku, founded St. George's Convent. In 1967 mission work began on the Ryukyus' southernmost island, when Matthew Takara went to Ishigaki City, Yaeyama.

Early in 1967, after consultation with the NSKK, the Episcopal Church's Overseas Mission Department created the Missionary District of Okinawa. At the House of Bishops' meeting in Seattle that same year, Edmond Lee Browning, then the archdeacon of the diocese, was elected the first bishop of Okinawa. Browning's work as bishop included forming a community, creating the necessary diocesan structures, developing needed ministries and institutions, and strengthening the relationship with the NSKK in the hope that the diocese would be transferred to the church in Japan within ten years. When Ed and Patti Browning first arrived in Okinawa in 1959, they did not envision the road their ministry would eventually take, nor were they aware of how their vision would be expanded in the process. Yet they arrived ready for the challenges ahead and embraced the tasks at hand.

First Years in Okinawa

When the Brownings arrived at All Souls', the parish had just finished building a new church, paid for in full within a year. The Brownings moved into the vicarage next door to the church and the parish house. The vicarage was small but well-designed and completely stocked by the parish; the parish also provided for the landscaping. Although the first missionaries to Okinawa were reluctant to establish an English-speaking congregation because they were sent to be missionaries to the people of Okinawa, they eventually relented and decided on the site in Machinato on the main highway because of its convenience for military families. The Marines helped clear the snake-infested hill for the new church. The church faces the sea to the west and offers some of the most beautiful sunsets on the island. Across the highway, looking east, was the scene of the terrible Battle of Okinawa in 1945.

The money to build All Souls' was donated by Grace Church, Utica, New York, in honor of the 75th anniversary of its founding. A bishop from the NSKK heard about the construction of All Souls' and decided that they would donate a beautiful hand-carved Christus Rex as the cross above the altar. [12] In the Brownings' time, the congregation consisted of approximately 600 people, most of whom worked for the United States' Defense Department and many of whom were military families, including the Army, Navy, Air Force, and the Marines. There were typically three services every Sunday. The members of the congregation included people from a wide range of cultural and racial backgrounds, including Anglo, Spanish, Chinese, Filipino, Japanese, and African American. Most lived within thirty miles of the church and were able to participate in parish life. There were also four Marine camps at the northern end of Okinawa where Browning held weekly services. Bishop Harry Kennedy from Hawaii visited twice a year; Bishop Michael

Yashiro, the presiding bishop of Japan, also visited the congregation regularly.

From their days in South Texas, Ed and Patti Browning were familiar with multicultural environments as well as the advantages and challenges of living in these communities. The ministry in Okinawa required the Brownings to move constantly back and forth between several worlds, the American military and civilian worlds and the Okinawan world. The politics were not easy to negotiate. The military were ambiguous about missionaries, and although many parishioners were on base, the Brownings did not have the same privileges of supplies, education, and medical care afforded to other American families. Among the Okinawans there was growing unrest and demand for reversion back to Japan. Although the Episcopal Church had urged the reversion of the diocese back to the NSKK, there was tension within the Japanese church about that decision and mixed feelings about welcoming back the Okinawans. Browning served an American, English-speaking congregation, but his heart was with the people of Okinawa, disenfranchised and treated as second-class citizens by their own country. "Ed, with real courage, moved back and forth between the two worlds, defending the legitimate rights of the Okinawans to the military leaders," claimed Bill Heffner. [13]

The Brownings welcomed their fourth child, Peter Sparks Browning, born in Okinawa in 1960. Peter was the smallest of the Browning babies, weighing "only" nine pounds at birth. The Brownings were not permitted to have the baby in the military hospital, so Peter was born in the new (and not yet completed) Seventh Day Adventist Hospital on the island. "Of course being here and not having been completed it lacks some of the things that one is used to, and has some things that one is not used to," wrote Ed in a letter home after the birth. "When they took Peter to the nursery I noticed a couple of lizards in the room and a couple of roaches in Patti's room—other than that it was lovely and the help was superb." [14] Paige Browning, who had hoped for a baby sister, was at first bitterly disappointed to have yet another brother, but soon came around and helped take care of the new addition.

When they married, both Ed and Patti had hoped for four children and now they had their wish; Ed was thirty and Patti was twenty-seven at the time. Because their children were raised mostly overseas, the Brownings feel that they became comfortable in the wider world and have today a worldview similar to that of their parents. As is the case with many missionary children, the Browning children had a culture of their own, sometimes referred to as "Third Culture Children." More welcomed by the Okinawans than the American military, the Browning children played with Okinawan children and quickly picked up the language. Because Ed and Patti were less fluent in Japanese, the family spoke English at home. Sometimes it was made obvious to the family that they were not considered a military family. Philip Browning remembers the time his little brother Peter was hit by a car while crossing the highway. He was first taken to a military hospital by a neighbor, where the staff refused to treat the boy. Patti worked her way up the chain of command in an effort to get treatment for her son, despite being told that, "Americans like you don't deserve to be treated." Eventually Peter was placed in an ambulance and treated at another hospital. [15]

In addition to dealing with frequent typhoons and flooding, the Brownings met the challenge of raising a young family and building a ministry in Okinawa with zeal. Unlike in Eagle Pass, where Patti was "always pregnant," and even with Peter Browning's arrival, Patti actively participated in their team ministry in Okinawa. Ed Browning started a prayer group, in which Patti participated. She also sang in the choir. Browning's ministry was chiefly devoted to evangelism, education, and pastoral care. "We find many seeking a deeper relationship with God—a relationship which they hope will provide a security and a hope that the world has yet to offer," said Browning in the parish newsletter. [16] Because of the size of the congregation, Browning made pastoral calls for most of the day, including regular visits to the leper colony. He also developed a strong relationship with the diocese and, as priest-in-charge of one of the largest and the only English-speaking congregation, began gradually to take on a leadership role there. All Souls' participated in all the diocesan activities; the Brownings believe the congregation served an important role as a "bridge" between the Okinawan and English-speaking communities.

Bill Heffner wrote that Ed and Patti Browning, from the onset of their ministry on the island, went out of their way to get to know the clergy of the Okinawan churches and their families. Ed was at the forefront of bringing young people together from All Souls' and the Okinawan congregations for programs. "Though he understood not a word of Japanese at that time, he radiated a love that spoke to the heart and made all who met him feel that he was their friend." Ed Browning was also a regular participant in diocesan clergy conferences, usually held at St. Peter and St. Paul in Naha. "He sat there patiently, waiting for shortened translations of what was being said," wrote Heffner. "And he contributed. It is hard to want to be so much of a group and to find yourself on the outside because of the language barrier. Ed Browning never complained, but I'm sure it was hard, especially when the group would erupt into gales of laughter and he couldn't share in it until the translation. In a very short period of time, people forgot that there was a language barrier. They came to know him as a friend and to trust him as one of their own." [17]

One of the Brownings' most popular ministries at All Souls' was their Sunday brunches for servicemen and women, many of whom were lonely. In particular, the pain experienced by a gay soldier there moved Ed Browning deeply and sensitized him to the treatment of gay and lesbian people in the larger church and society. The young man was a frequent visitor to the Sunday brunches and eventually grew comfortable enough to pour his heart out to Ed Browning.

The Brownings' home was a social center on the island and they routinely gave up their privacy to welcome anyone who came to their door. Some stayed for a few hours, some overnight, and some longer. Every Sunday Ed and Patti had lunch for two or three dozen people, as they tried to create a family atmosphere at the parish. By 1962 the Sunday brunches grew into a full-fledged servicemen's center, including recreation, books, classes, and other activities. The center sought to provide support and "wholesome activities" for young men in the services, in local Western businesses, and in local Okinawan communities in an effort to enhance friendships. [18] Clyde Jones, a Navy physician, regularly attended All Souls' and the brunches at the Browning home while he was stationed in Okinawa. "Ed has never been overly impressed with himself," said Jones. "Whenever I returned from Ed and Patti's, I felt joyful," he said. [19]

The Brownings tenure at All Souls' coincided with the onset of the Vietnam War, and there were many families living on the island with spouses and fathers in combat. "It was a tense and uncertain time," said Patti Browning. "We tried to create an atmosphere of family within the church, where each person could share these feelings and have a sense of belonging while living in a foreign country on the edge of a war zone." [20]

Janet Surrett, whose husband was a military pilot, remembers the years her family was stationed in Okinawa when the Brownings were also there. "Ed and Patti had a deep sense of caring and they gave it to all of us in the parish. They had a real gift for hospitality," she said." Surrett said that the Brownings and their children sometimes came to their home during typhoon warnings, as the rectory sat on top of the hill and was a "magnet" for hurricanes. Surrett also noted that although her husband was not a churchgoer, he appreciated Ed Browning, and the feeling was mutual. "He is a wonderful man and father, he does not have to be Episcopalian," said Ed about Surrett's husband. Surrett, who also knew the Brownings later in Germany, said she still feels a pastoral connection with Browning from the days she attended All Souls' in Okinawa. "He is just so great about making a connection with people," she said. Surrett recalls Browning's installation as presiding bishop as one of the highlights of her life. "I saw him there just for a moment in the midst of thousands of people, and he called me by name," she said. "I thought, what a special priest he is to be able to do that." [21]

Neither Ed nor Patti really had a day off during their first years of ministry in Okinawa. They embraced the opportunity of their first furlough in 1962 with zeal. On their way to Canterbury, the Brownings and their children traveled around the world, stopping in Hong Kong, Thailand, Beirut, Tehran, and Jerusalem. In the 1960s, air travel around the world meant hours on turboprop planes and landings on remote airstrips. Before 1967 Jerusalem was part of Jordan and fraught with tensions. For both Ed and Patti it was a first opportunity to become acquainted with the plight of the Palestinian Christians who so strongly figure in their later ministry. (Their next visit to Jerusalem was in 1986 after Ed Browning had become presiding bishop.) In 1962 they felt they could identify with the Palestinians as inhabitants of an occupied land. The family arrived in Jerusalem a week after a nun had been shot. Despite the dangerous atmosphere for Palestinian Christians at the time, both Ed and Patti recall the warm welcome they received. They began to study the issues of the region. From Jerusalem the family traveled to Rome and Frankfurt and then decided to skip Paris and go on to Zurich and the Jungfrau to rest for several days. The family eventually arrived in England for a six-week stay in Canterbury. The Brownings concluded their furlough with six weeks with family in Texas.

Although arduous in some ways and filled with the antics of travel with small children, the furlough served to strengthen Ed and Patti Browning's ministry as world citizens. Although articles on Ed Browning's missionary years written after he was elected presiding bishop mostly focused on his ministry, Ed and Patti saw themselves as an integrated team. In Okinawa, their deep faith matured and deepened. It was expressed in a buoyant love for all humanity, their commitment to a ministry of servanthood, and their courage to witness when the circumstances demanded it. [22] "There have been times during the course of our lives when we have been called to difficult witnessing, which has strengthened our support for one another," said Patti. "Ed's sensitivity to needs and issues which should be spoken to have sometimes led us in scary directions. We never knew what the consequences would be, but upholding one another through these times has been a ministry we both have needed to give and to receive." [23]

Language School in Kobe

By January 1961, a year and a half after their arrival in Okinawa, the Brownings were considering staying on past their original three-year commitment. "The way I feel about it now," Browning wrote to his mother, "and this could change in another year and a half, but if I leave Okinawa it will not be just to get away from something, but I will have to feel that what I am being called to will be equally as important as far as my ministry and abilities are concerned." [24]

After four years in Okinawa, the Brownings felt called to work more intentionally with the Okinawan community. That would require training in the Japanese language. The Brownings received support from the bishop-in-charge, Harry Kennedy, and moved to Kobe, Japan, for training at a Canadian language school in 1963. Once there, Browning also served as assistant to the bishop of Kobe. It was a busy but happy time for the Brownings, for the first time freed from parish responsibilities as a young family. Every day Ed and Patti studied together and then jointly shopped, cooked, cleaned, and cared for the needs of their four children, at that time ranging in age from three to eight. The family lived in a small Japanese-style tatami house; the walls were made of mud thatch and they slept on pallets. The simple quarters proved comfortable and low-maintenance until the boys knocked one of the walls down while imitating sumo wrestlers. In Japan Patti took up painting again. It was "a period when our concept of joint ministry grew to an even deeper level," she said. "We realized we needed not only to work as a team for the church, but for our family as well."[25]

The Brownings' decision to study the Japanese language so they could work more closely with the Okinawan people was a deeply spiritual one. "It was a time to search ourselves," said Patti. It was also a time to dream of directions for the future. "We returned as new creatures," she said.[26] A family friend believes that the Brownings' spirituality was indelibly influenced by their years in Japan. "They have a sense of dignity and a way of embracing kindness that comes from Japan, as well as a sense that they will be missionaries for life. The experience enlarged their theology and their hearts. At times the suffering and the strain broke their hearts open. Little did they realize just how big their mission field would become."[27]

Fred Honaman, an American missionary who worked for the NSKK, first met the Brownings in Kobe. Part of his responsibility was to provide logistical support for missionaries, and he helped the Browning family secure housing. Eventually both the Brownings and the Honamans had cottages in the mountains near Kyoto; another missionary family, John and Elizabeth Lloyd, were also in the area. In the mountains the missionary families went on vacations and had the opportunity for some family refreshment and a respite from the demands of parish life. "Ed and Patti's ministry was 24/7," said Honaman. "Whatever helped the people, they were involved in it." Honaman also noted that Ed Browning's adaptability enhanced his ministry around the world. "Ed adjusted to living and working on islands, and not everybody can do that," he said. [28]

As the Brownings were on their way to Japanese language school in Kobe, events that were to have a wide-ranging impact on mission within the Anglican Communion were underway. In August 1963 the Advisory Council on Missionary Strategy and the Consultative Body of the Lambeth Conference met in London, Ontario, immediately before the Anglican Congress. The focus of the talks was on the changing world and the Anglican Communion. Conceived by missionary leaders and endorsed by the primates under the title "Mutual Responsibility and Interdependence in the Body of Christ" (MRI), the focus shifted away from thinking of some churches as "mother" churches and others as "dependent" or "younger" churches. Touted as "the rebirth of the Anglican Communion," MRI suggested a new understanding where all were equal in responsibility, serving God and humanity in one missionary task. "The church that lives to itself will die by itself," said Archbishop of Canterbury Michael Ramsey. [29] Steven F. Bayne, executive officer of the Anglican Communion and eventually bishop of Olympia, was instrumental in the consultation and in the drafting of the MRI report. Key to Bayne's thought was the idea that mutual responsibility and interdependence is what should drive Anglican mission, and that through this spirit the whole world would be transformed. No longer should churches be locked into individual issues, but rather, Bayne reasoned, Anglicans needed to embrace the world with a larger vision. He wrote:

> It is now irrelevant to talk of "giving" and "receiving" churches. The keynotes of our time are equality, interdependence, mutual responsibility. Three central truths at the heart of our faith command us in this: *The Church's mission is response to the living God who in his love creates, reveals, judges, redeems, fulfills. It is he who moves through our history to teach and to save, who calls us to receive his love, to learn, to obey and follow. Our unity in Christ, expressed in our full communion, is the most profound bond among us, in all our political and racial and cultural diversity. The time has fully come when this unity and interdependence must find a completely new level of expression and corporate obedience.* Our need is not therefore simply to be expressed in greater generosity by those who have money and men to spare. Our need is rather to understand how God has led us, through the sometimes painful history of our time, to see the gifts of freedom and communion in their great terms, and to live up to them. [30]

Rustin "Rusty" Kimsey, retired bishop of Eastern Oregon, remembers the impact of the Anglican Congress in 1963, in particular MRI, and especially in Province VIII of the Episcopal Church, the American West. "Steve Bayne was a powerhouse for world mission," said Kimsey, "and his study program appealed to the frontier spirit in Province VIII." [31] Kimsey noted that he, Ed Browning, and other clergy of their era were "deeply immersed in MRI" and that it "pulled people together in a different way" than mission had done in the past. "MRI was so powerful because it diffused authority and instilled it in the people," said Kimsey. "We believed we could make a difference, a deep difference, in the Communion of Christ." Ed Browning remembers hearing about MRI from the primate of Japan. "It was one of the most moving things I had ever heard," he said. "The line I shall never forget was, 'We are no longer a receiving church. We have something to contribute to the whole [Anglican] Communion.'" [32]

Rusty Kimsey believes that it was the spirit of "Mutual Responsibility and Interdependence in the Body of Christ" that fueled Ed Browning's future ministries in Okinawa and Europe, at the Episcopal Church Center in New York, in Hawaii, and eventually as presiding bishop. "When it comes to mission he does not get the credit he is due," said Kimsey in reference to Browning. "He sees the authority of the church in terms of mission, not in terms of bishops. Some saw his openness as the cause of turmoil in the church, not realizing that is where we ought to be." [33]

Ministry in Oroku

Upon his return to Okinawa in 1965, Browning was appointed priest-in-charge of St. Matthew's Church, Oroku, in the capital city of Naha. In the same year, Bill and Margaret Stough, friends of the Brownings from seminary days, went to Browning's former post in Okinawa, All Souls', Machinato.

Although it is a difficult language for many Westerners to master, the Brownings had left school proficient in what missionaries call "kitchen Japanese," or enough of the language to be able to communicate with people in their congregation. Although the Browning children learned to speak Japanese fluently, Ed found the experience of trying to learn the language one of the most humbling of his adult life. Yet he was able to celebrate, preach, and communicate in Japanese. St. Matthew's Church was located in an economically depressed area surrounded by open sewers; children and pets were always falling in and staph infections were common. "We were really glad when we were able to get a real first aid kit so we could avoid some of that," said Patti. [34]

The Brownings lived in a house attached to the church—so attached, in fact, that one of their bedroom doors opened right into the sanctuary. The house bathroom had a swinging door with a hole cut into it. When the Brownings arrived the only way to get to the church was over a rickety bridge. "You really had to have faith to go to church," said Browning. [35] The first service in Oroku was a family affair: Ed was the preacher and celebrant, Patti played the organ, Mark was the acolyte, Paige handed out Prayer Books, Philip handed out the slippers, and Peter turned the pages in the hymnal for his mother. When the Brownings arrived, there were approximately five members in the congregation. "We doubled the congregation the first Sunday because there were six Brownings," Ed joked. [36]

Although in culture shock after two idyllic years in Kobe, Ed and Patti took hold quickly and immersed themselves in the lives of their new community. One of the most visible needs was for services for children. Soon after their arrival, the Brownings started a kindergarten in their home. Half the children met in the church and the other half met on a tatami mat that doubled as the Brownings' dining room. A large portion of the church property was sunken and flooded after every rain, so Browning enlisted the help of friends at home, filled the area with soil, and installed playground equipment. The area became a community gathering place for children, teenagers, and young adults. When a child or a pet fell into one of the sewers, the Brownings' utility room served as a washing room. The kindergarten started out with forty children and grew to include over one hundred children in two years. With the assistance of a grant from the United Thank Offering, a separate building was built to accommodate the growing number of children in the school. "As I look back on this period, I believe that the specific things that we did were not as important as living together as a family with this community and becoming gradually a part of it," said Patti. "This meant becoming involved, as much as they would let us, with their joys, sorrows, and struggles, and sharing ours with them." [37]

In addition to the kindergarten, Ed Browning undertook the pastoral ministry of the growing congregation while also active in many diocesan activities. He was appointed archdeacon of the diocese in 1967. Fred Honaman remembers visiting the Brownings one Christmas before Ed became bishop. Honaman drove with Browning while he made some pastoral visits. "It is easy to forget what a good parish priest he was," said Honaman. "He was so gentle and caring, and he met people where they were. That's why so many people knew him and welcomed him." [38]

While at St. Mathew's, Patti Browning undertook a myriad of ministries she never thought she would do. She played the pump organ at worship, taught English, gave first aid for playground casualties, drove people to hospitals for treatment, participated in festivals and school activities, and was the sales and production manager of a cottage weaving industry. Patti was particularly interested in Okinawan weaving and in building up the Nago Crafts Center, started there by a priest as a way for women in need to support themselves. [39] "The beautiful skirt lengths which Father Hio started the women weaving have been transformed into beautiful and stunning creations. The women are really excited and they are selling like hotcakes," wrote Patti. [40] There were few ways for Okinawan women to support themselves financially at the time, and many war widows were forced into prostitution. Under Patti Browning's leadership and with her design skills, 125 weavers diversified their products and were able to sell them in Okinawan villages and to American military clients to great acclaim. Patti also worked with twenty basket weavers in Miyako, many of whom were lepers, with the craft as their only source of income. Although weaving was a natural outlet for her artistic gifts, Patti also found great satisfaction in doing a ministry that so directly benefitted Okinawan women and children.

A Family-Centered Culture

Ed and Patti Browning's family thrived while they were in Okinawa and Kobe. The living conditions were often trying, and in their early years of ministry their missionary salary was about $300 a month. Nonetheless, they appreciated the family-centered culture. Two Okinawan women lived and worked with the Browning family and remain extended family members to this day. Keiko Matsuda lived with the family from 1959 until 1964 while they were at All Souls'; Yoshiko Miyagi from 1965 until 1972 in Naha and for a year in Germany after the family moved to Europe. They worked as "mother's helpers" to meet the needs of the household and help watch the children. As local women and survivors of the war, they offered the Browning family a perspective into the lives of the Okinawan people.

Both women were amazed when they were so graciously welcomed by an American family. Neither expected Ed Browning, the man of the house, even to speak to them, much less to treat them with kindness. "When I first went to work for them they asked me to do ironing and I didn't know how," said Keiko. "I made a mistake and cried and apologized to him [Ed Browning], and he forgave me." [41] The Brownings eventually arranged for Keiko to attend business school. "It was a miracle that I met them," she said. [42] Yoshiko Miyagi remembers the many dinner parties hosted by the Brownings and confirms that they were wonderful hosts. She also remembers how the Browning family ate the same food as the Okinawans, including the locally grown vegetables, a practice unthinkable to other Westerners at the time. Yoshiko thought the family fit in with the Okinawan lifestyle very well. "They always expressed gratitude for everything they received in a very humble way, " she said. "I think if I had not met them my life would have been very different." [43]

Everyday household chores were daunting in 1960s Okinawa, and tasks such as shopping for food, doing laundry, and cleaning the church and rectory took a large amount of time. There was no refrigeration so food needed to be purchased and prepared for a large household daily. The electricity was uncertain, and often the lights went off in the middle of supper. Then the family brought out the candles and ate by candlelight. After the children went to bed, Ed and Patti would sit and talk quietly in the dark. "The children just loved this," wrote Ed. "Sometimes they'd beg to have candles at supper time even when the electricity was working...We were always a little sorry when the lights flickered back on later in the evening." [44]

The Brownings' letters home from their missionary days in Okinawa chronicle the experiences of a young family living in a new culture. One of the first, written within days of the family's arrival, tells the story of Patti's dismay at finding six men taking a bath in the backyard, until she learned that was common practice since many people lacked running water in their own homes. In the same week Ed had his checkbook stolen and flunked his driver's test. [45] Typhoons were frequent and Ed and Patti gradually learned to carry on in inclement conditions. "Paige and Philip were sick during the deluge, and Paige was all but out," wrote Patti about a month after their arrival in Okinawa. "I walked around the house in rain boots trying to dose medicine, cook meals, rock babies— Ed had most of the bailing to do but I helped out when I could." [46] In one letter home, almost two months after their arrival in Okinawa, Ed boasted that his first confirmation class comprised twenty-six people, including two colonels, one major, captains, lieutenants, privates, and a woman who owned the local Teahouse of the August Moon. [47]

As Ed and Patti Browning grew more at home in Okinawa their letters became more reflective. Although their correspondence always included news about children and pets, the Brownings also wrote of significant church events. For instance, within the first year of his arrival Ed attended the ordination of two Japanese priests, Michael Yamamoto and Peter Shinjo. The service was very moving to Ed Browning, particularly because Shinjo, an Okinawan, had slight birth defects. Browning tells the story that at the time of Shinjo's birth, his father, as was the custom of the day, instructed his mother to do away with the baby. The woman disobeyed her husband and instead hid the child. "During the ordination I had the thought that even though the world and her customs cannot tolerate imperfections, here God was taking one for his very own and had called him to the sacred order of priests—that he had been saved for something very sacred, and through the loving care of a mother this had been accomplished." [48]

As is the case with long family separations, the Brownings' letters show how difficult it can be for a missionary family, even one that is thriving, when life-changing events occur back home and it is impossible to be physically present. One of Browning's cousins and his beloved grandmother died soon after the family arrived in Okinawa. In a moving letter to his father, Ed offered his thoughts and consolation on Granny's death: "In becoming sorrowful I had forgotten that she was now in the presence of God—the place that all of us strive to be in—the ultimate purpose of every creature of God, and what more could we ever want for our loved ones?" he wrote. "One thing that we know is that she is no longer burdened down with her worn-out body—that she no longer suffers and that she is at peace with God." [49] On a happier note, the Brownings rejoiced at the news of Ed's brother Robert's upcoming marriage; youngest brother Ben stood as best man. "I don't know of anything that I would rather do than be there for the marriage," wrote Browning to his family. "When I received the letter the other day telling about all the excitement and how Bob had asked and said how he wished that we could be there, it was all I could do to hold back the tears. That sounds sentimental, but it is the truth."[50]

Much to the Brownings' surprise, in 1967 they discovered that their fifth child was on the way. "I remember, in fact, that Patti was more than surprised; livid would be a better word to describe her feelings at that time," wrote Ed.[51] At the time she was pregnant with John Browning, Patti was thirty-five and thought she was done with diapers. Ed said she didn't speak to him for weeks, but then it turned around. "Our experience of an unexpected dividend was like that of most families who get one: a wholly gracious thing, another chance at a job we'd come to realize we were pretty good at....It seemed that every moment with him was dessert," wrote Ed after the birth.[52] Ed Browning believes that each of their children made him a different person from who he was before their arrival, and that each one transformed the whole family as well. "Every time, something precious and unique was added to the mix. And all of us were changed," he wrote.[53] The first four Browning children were born on a Sunday; John Browning's birth altered that tradition, when he arrived on All Saints' Day, a Wednesday.

During their years in Okinawa, Ed and Patti Browning's relationship matured and strengthened. They became a dynamic ministerial team; both were missionaries and both gave of their gifts and talents to the ministry as a whole. Patti in particular maintained the "team" concept of their relationship. When they began to grow out of touch with each other, or when she began to feel that her role was overshadowed by "his ministry," she called the situation into account so that they could get back on track. Despite her gentle demeanor, Patti

Browning was not one to acquiesce as far as her marriage was concerned, and the couple had a stronger bond because of it. Conversely, Ed Browning always felt that he was part of a ministerial team and cannot imagine his life and work apart from Patti. "Patti and I had the privilege of working in a number of out-of-the way places that helped us define who we really were, and what our ministries might be, by giving us the remarkable experience of evaluating them in the setting of cultures very different from the one that nurtured us," wrote Browning. "I don't think there was a single assumption about life and relationship that went unchallenged in those years of living and ministering in other countries. I wouldn't have traded it for anything. I cannot imagine us apart from the experiences of those years, and I cannot imagine us in those years without each other." [54] Samuel Van Culin, a longtime family friend and colleague in world mission, believed the enormous challenge of raising a family in a culture damaged by war strengthened the bonds among Ed and Patti and their children. "Of all their accomplishments, that family is the most significant," he said. [55]

Early in their marriage Ed and Patti Browning intentionally tended to their relationship with each other and with God, as a couple and as individuals. "We can spend ourselves facilitating other peoples' religious experiences in our churches, and unless we take explicit care of our own souls, we can find ourselves in a situation in which everyone gets fed but us," said Patti Browning at a retreat for clergy spouses. [56] "I recognized early in the forty-six years since I met Ed Browning that my walk with Christ was mine. That I wasn't going to be able to borrow Ed's. That I would be the most supportive of his ministry as he was supportive of mine, and that each of us had special gifts we could use to build and strengthen each other, wherever our ministry took us." [57] In Okinawa and elsewhere, one of Patti's chief assets was her ability to "go with the flow." This also helped as their family grew to include five children and other extended family members. "And somewhere, back there in the early years of our marriage, I realized that I would be able to find God in any situation in which I found myself. That I am called to this life in order that I may find God in it. So wherever I have gone I have made it my business to be alert. To listen for the presence of God. To watch for the signs. And, in forty-six years, there has never been a time when I did not find signs." [58]

Browning says that Patti taught him early in their ministry together that marriage is work and that their marriage was "a living thing that needed nurture. She refused to allow us to slip into the work pattern that was common in those days: the husband devotes himself solely to his career and the wife solely to the home, and once in a while their paths cross...I don't know how she became so wise so early." [59] Sunday was almost always a workday for the Brownings. After all the services were over and the last hand was shaken, both Ed and Patti looked forward to sharing some quiet time and perhaps a simple supper before going to bed. "Not much rest on our Sundays," Ed wrote, "but they are holy nonetheless." [60]

During their years in Okinawa the Brownings practiced the family values they maintained over the course of their lives together. While not poor according to Okinawan standards, neither was the family affluent. Ed Browning has always been careful with money, in a way that many Americans who lived through the 1930s and 1940s can remember. At the same time, both Ed and

Patti were unfailingly generous in their hospitality. Giving
delighted them both. Patti's sister Cathleen said that when
they were girls, Patti gave anyone anything off her back
without question, a trait the elder sister admired until
her own possessions came into play. [61] Ed felt that their
children innately understood and graciously accepted
when their parents could not give them the latest styles
and when they had to wait for some things their parents
could not get right away or at all. "They knew we were
a large family living on a clergyman's salary. And they
knew that we would have given them the whole world if
we could have," he wrote. [62]

Not surprisingly, Ed and Patti Browning's missionary
letters also contained political commentary. President
Eisenhower's visit in June 1960 was exciting, although
All Souls' was forced to cancel its 11:00 a.m. service
because 12,000 troops blocked the highway for eleven
miles on each side of the road. Marines were stationed
near the church with machine guns ready to protect the
president. "It was real exciting," wrote Ed in a letter to his
family. "He passed within fifteen feet of us, and just as
he drove by he stood up and waved. I think that we got
some good pictures, and when they are developed I will
send them on to you. After they passed by, Mark said,
'Daddy, when is the parade coming?' " [63] Not a supporter
of John F. Kennedy for the presidency, Ed Browning was
philosophical after the election in 1960: "It's now the day
after the election and I must say that both Patti and I are
pretty sick over the way it turned out. I sure hate to see
what Kennedy will do with his foreign policy—the little
that I have heard about seems very dangerous. Of course
we see it probably differently than you because we are
sitting but fourteen minutes from the mainland. I really

believe the indifference of the American people to the world situation beat Nixon as much as anything. Fretting won't get the job done—we must pray that we won't be led into another war and that the new administration will be able to lead us in peace." [64]

Ed and Patti Browning delighted in the simple pleasures of life and were conscious of the grace in simple moments. Perhaps it is because their lives were so busy and so focused on giving to others that they never took for granted the times they enjoyed with their own family. Ed compared the sight of their large family at the dinner table to a glimpse of the heavenly banquet, just as he remembered the love he felt at the dinner table as a boy in Corpus Christi. Although dinner at the Brownings' table was loud, Browning still speaks of "the joy of watching our children eat—I was acutely conscious of the palpable presence of love in the room....My flashes of heaven-consciousness only lasted a moment or two—until somebody knocked over the milk and I was on my feet, headed for the kitchen to get the dishrag." [65]

Not surprisingly, all the Browning children grew up with an international perspective. Although they lacked geographical roots, they formed a strong family bond. The family lore is laced with tales of the travel adventures of little Brownings, from elevator races in Stockholm, to diapers strung all over the room in Rome, to the time one little darling threw all of Patti's underwear out a hotel window. There was also the time Ed walked through a German guesthouse in his boxer shorts to quiet his children sleeping in another wing. "One of our claims to fame as a family is, we've been spanked in every major capital of the world," said Mark Browning. [66] "They followed their hearts and did what they believed," said Paige Browning.

"And with each move they made, their lives became richer. Their faith and trust in God is very strong, and I think they have touched a lot of lives," she said of her parents. [67]

The Episcopate

The House of Bishops, meeting in Seattle in 1967, elected Edmond Lee Browning as the first bishop of Okinawa. He was thirty-eight years old and had been serving in Okinawa for eight years. At the time of his election the Missionary District of Okinawa consisted of eleven parishes with just under 2,000 baptized persons, served by twelve clergy and six lay readers. Browning was ordained bishop of Okinawa in June 1968 and attended his first Lambeth Conference the following summer. His first regular House of Bishops meeting was scheduled for October 1968 in Augusta, Georgia. Browning arrived exhausted after a long flight. He was then asked to sign up to preach in a parish on Sunday, which intimidated him after he saw a sea of purple shirts in the lobby upon arrival at the hotel. Browning thought with dread, "Do I have to preach before all these bishops?" [68] By Sunday he was even more nervous. He was scheduled to preach at a parish twenty miles away, and luckily, he thought, no bishop would travel that far. Several bishops proved him wrong and were already sitting in the congregation. Two of them in particular, Bill Gordon of Alaska and Bill Brady of Fond du Lac, became his good friends.

Ed Browning remembers his first session of the House of Bishops as a meeting fraught with conflict. The House of Bishops of the Anglican Church of Canada was invited to foster collaboration and stayed in the same hotel, but the Episcopal House of Bishops was so conflicted that the two groups did not meet together for even an hour. The House of Bishops was struggling with racism. One black bishop got up to speak and the next speaker, a white bishop, completely ignored his line of thought. Another white bishop recognized the switch in topic and attempted to apologize to the black bishop, only to refer to him by the wrong name. Another black bishop then said, "Well, I guess we all look alike," and then all the black bishops walked out. Paul Moore, bishop of New York, went after them to try to bring them back, without success. At the time, members of the House of Bishops were seated in rows by rank, that is, by the date of their episcopal ordination. So Browning saw all that was happening from the perspective of the back row, along with the other new bishops, Bill Frey of Guatemala, Lani Hanchett of Hawaii, and Bob Appleyard of Pittsburgh. "We were wondering what in the Sam Hill was going on—what had we gotten ourselves into?" Fortunately, Browning said, the meetings of the House of Bishops eventually got better. [69] Facilitating deeper collegiality among bishops would be a major task of his administration as presiding bishop.

By 1971 movements in the political realm to return Okinawa to Japan were accelerating, and Ed and Patti Browning felt it was important for the church to complete the process before the federal government did. A delegation of church leaders from Japan first came with a proposal that the Okinawan church become part of the NSKK, with the proviso that Ed Browning remain as bishop, rather than an elected Okinawan. "No way," was his response. "This was not to be a colonial church, whose own leadership does not lead it, or a church that embodied the second-class citizenship of the Okinawan people in the eyes of the Japanese," he wrote. "The time when the church baptized cultural and ethnic prejudices was coming painfully to an end back here at home—this was the mid-1960s—and I wasn't about to be part of perpetuating that approach in the church overseas." [70] Despite the painful process, the Okinawan church eventually became independent of the United States and elected an Okinawan bishop to succeed Browning; the church in Japan also became enriched by the gifts of the Okinawans. "From a cloud of sinful realities—the fracturing of a society by war, the painful reality of ethnic and cultural prejudice—God brought forth something better. The forces of prejudice and domination did not get the last word," wrote Browning. [71]

Having to leave Okinawa was traumatic for the Brownings. They hoped to live the rest of their lives there. They did not want to leave, even though they were living on the "edge of the Vietnam War" and would "wake up in the middle of the night and hear tanks rolling down Highway 1." [72] "I sincerely believe that God called me to Okinawa," said Browning in his farewell address to the diocese, "he called me to serve as your bishop, he called me to make the decision to resign so as to facilitate the transfer of the church to the Nippon Sei Ko Kai, and now I believe he is calling me to serve in a new endeavor in faith…I look with some anxiety about the unknown of the future, but equally in confidence that God is always the guide and the strengthener." [73] In his closing remarks to the diocese, Browning charged the diocese to work together as a team, to be open to new leadership, to embrace a positive new vision for the future, and to pray without ceasing.

The Browning family's tearful good-bye in the VIP lounge at the Okinawa airport was so wrenching that it took years before they could talk about it. "He was this red-headed Texan who spoke Japanese, and the poor people considered him a hero," said Clyde Jones.[74] Yasuhito Chibana, an Okinawan who was baptized, confirmed, and ordained to the diaconate by Browning, said many of the people were immensely grateful for all he had done for the church there.[75] Patti remembers the night Ed came home after a long day in negotiations with the NSKK. "He came home and lay down on our bed, and said, 'I think we are going to have to leave.'"[76] Both Ed and Patti realized they needed to do what was best for the diocese, and that meant to facilitate the transfer of the Diocese of Okinawa from the Episcopal Church to the NSKK. The diocese needed an Okinawan bishop and to be part of the Japanese church, rather than remain attached to the church in the United States. "We must respect the tradition of people," said Browning, reflecting later on his years in Okinawa. "Part of the church's role is to identify with the hopes and aspirations of [the] people it is called to serve. One key is to be able to listen."[77]

Patti Browning once stated in an interview that Okinawa would always be a special place for the Browning family because "we really grew up there." "You taught us the meaning of family," said Ed Browning to the people on his return to Okinawa as presiding bishop in 1987. "You taught us that the family of God—the family of the church—transcends national barriers, class barriers, racial barriers. You taught us that God indeed calls us to be one." What Ed Browning believes his family discovered in Okinawa was that "it is in community that the love that nurtures and strengthens is found…even though we might be few in numbers, God calls us to be concerned for his creation, to be concerned for the needs of others, for the issues of peace and justice."[78]

Chapter Two Notes

1   Edmond L. Browning (hereafter cited as ELB), "Our World Mission," in *Realities and Visions: The Church's Mission Today*, ed. Furman C. Stough and Urban T. Holmes III (New York: Seabury Press, 1976), 8-9.

2   ELB, "In the Midst of Death the Power of Life," Episcopal News Service, October 26, 1989.

3   ELB, *A Year of Days with the Book of Common Prayer* (New York: Ballantine Books, 1997), June 1.

4   ELB, "Address to Convention," Episcopal News Service, August 6, 1997.

5   ELB, *A Year of Days*, June 1.

6   Patricia Sparks Browning (hereafter cited as PSB), interview by Sheryl Kujawa-Holbrook (hereafter cited as SKH), January 2009.

7   David E. Sumner, *The Episcopal Church's History: 1945-1985* (Wilton, Conn.: Morehouse-Barlow, 1987), 193-195.

8   Philip Browning, interview by SKH, March 2009.

9   ELB, interview by SKH, January 2009.

10   Statistics from www.world-war-2.info. World War 2, "The Battle of Okinawa," http://www.world-war-2.info/battles/bt_15.php.

11   Keyia Aoki's name is often spelled "Keisai" in *Anglicans Online* and other English language sources. "Keyia" is commonly used in the Japanese sources.

12   William Heffner, "Edmond Lee Browning, Presiding Bishop," n.d., Browning Collection.

13   Ibid.

14   ELB, letter, July 27, 1960, Browning Collection.

15   Philip Browning, interview.

16   Newsletter, All Souls' Episcopal Church, June 1961.

17   Heffner, "Edmond Lee Browning, Presiding Bishop."

18   Newsletter, All Souls' Episcopal Church, March 1962.

19   Clyde Jones, interview by SKH, March 2009.

20   PSB, "Diocese of Delaware Clergy and Spouses Conference," n.d., Browning Collection.

21   Janet Surrett, interview by SKH, April 2009.

22   Paraphrased from a testimony to Ed Browning by Bill Heffner, n.d., Browning Collection.

23   "We Talk with the Church's New 'First Lady,'" *Journal of Women's Ministries* 3, no. 2, (Fall 1986): 3.

24   ELB, letter, January 31, 1960, Browning Collection.

25   PSB, interview.

26   Ibid.

27   Anonymous, interview by SKH, March 2009.

28   William Frederick Honaman, interview by SKH, March 2009.

29   R. David Cox, "One Body," Episcopal News Service, July 9, 2000.

30   Stephen F. Bayne, Jr., *Mutual Responsibility and Interdependence in the Body of Christ* (New York: Seabury Press, 1963), 18.

31 Rustin Kimsey, interview by SKH, March 2009.

32 R. David Cox, "One Body."

33 Ibid.

34 Ruth Nicastro, "Patti Browning," *Hawaii Church Chronicle,* September 1985.

35 ELB, interview.

36 PSB, "Diocese of Delaware Clergy and Spouses Conference."

37 Ibid.

38 William Frederick Honaman, interview by SKH, April 2009.

39 *Alumni News Stephens College Bulletin,* n.d., Browning Collection.

40 PSB, letter, September 1959, Browning Collection.

41 Keiko Matsuda, interview by Larry Kirchner, May 2009; translated by Carolyn Francis.

42 Ibid.

43 Yoshiko Miyagi, interview by Larry Kirchner, May 2009; translated by Carolyn Francis.

44 ELB, *A Year of Days,* January 31.

45 ELB, letter, August 10, 1959, Browning Collection.

46 PSB, letter, September 1959, Browning Collection.

47 ELB, letter, September 30, 1959, Browning Collection.

48 ELB, letter, November 14, 1959, Browning Collection.

49 ELB, letter, December 11, 1959, Browning Collection.

50 ELB, letter, June 6, 1960, Browning Collection.

51 ELB, *A Year of Days,* July 25.

52 Ibid.

53 ELB, *A Year of Days,* January 14.

54 ELB, *A Year of Days,* August 7.

55 Samuel Van Culin, interview by SKH, March 2009.

56 PSB, "Speech to the Clergy Spouses, Lexington," February 22, 1996.

57 Ibid.

58 Ibid.

59 ELB, *A Year of Days,* July 31.

60 ELB, *A Year of Days,* January 30.

61 Cathleen Gallander, interview by SKH, March 2009.

62 ELB, *A Year of Days,* September 5.

63 ELB, letter, June 27, 1960, Browning Collection.

64 ELB, letter, November 10, 1960, Browning Collection.

65 ELB, *A Year of Days,* June 16.

66 Joyce Saenz Harris, "Edmond Lee Browning: Presiding Bishop Guides a Diverse Episcopal Flock," *The Dallas Morning News,* December 25, 1994, 3.

67 Ibid.

68 ELB, "Remembrances and Reflections," March 1993.

69 Ibid.

70 ELB, *A Year of Days,* July 5.

71 Ibid.

72 Harris, "Edmond Browning: Presiding Bishop Guides a Diverse Episcopal Flock."

73 ELB, "Farewell Address," May 9, 1971, Browning Collection.

74 Clyde Jones, interview.

75 Yasuhito Chibana, letter to SKH, May 30, 2005; translated by Carolyn Francis.

76 PSB, interview.

77 Dick Snyder, "More Balanced Life for Bishop Browning," *The Living Church,* December 24, 2000.

78 "Browning Trip Renews, Strengthens East Asia Ties," Episcopal News Service, May 28, 1987.

One Mission

1971-1976

I'M NOT CERTAIN, but I think we can say that within the last decade there has been valuable learning experienced at most levels within the life of the Church. That learning is that the mission of the Church is never an either/or proposition. It is never either social action or spiritual renewal, but both. It is never either primarily evangelism or a struggle for global justice, but both. It is never either feeding the hungry or human and material development, but both. Mission is as varied as God would have it. Mission is of God, and it is he who calls us and sets the priorities. His mission is never static. There are times in history when he demands and calls more in one direction than another, and in obedience to the oneness in mission, it behooves us both individually and corporately to be sensitive to one another as God makes his mission known to us through the lives of others. [1]

— Edmond Lee Browning,
"Our World Mission,"
1976

During his three years as bishop-in-charge of the Convocation of American Churches in Europe, Ed Browning worked to bring its isolated congregations together with a renewed sense of corporate identity and mission. True to his sense of the need to listen to the people and respond to the cultural context, Browning listened when he arrived in Europe and found one particular group who had not been heard by the church—Vietnam War resisters and military deserters living in Sweden. As part of his response to the plight of these men and their families, Browning crafted a resolution to go to the House of Bishops at the General Convention. This issue was one that many at the time felt passionately about, including those concerned about the rights of veterans of the same Southeast Asian conflict. The occasion was also significant because it was the first time Ed Browning spoke to the House of Bishops. Characteristically, Ed Browning downplayed his important role in bringing the key justice issues of amnesty and the right of Vietnam War veterans to the General Convention. "I was so damned nervous I called veterans veterinarians," he recalled of the experience. [2]

The Convocation of American Churches in Europe

The first congregation of American Episcopalians in Europe dates from a time immediately after the American Revolution, when the members worshiped intermittently at the embassy in Paris. As American interests developed in Europe, other congregations were founded, and in 1859 the congregation in Paris petitioned the General Convention to allow them to become congregations of the Episcopal

Church. By 1870 there were Episcopal congregations in Paris, Rome, Nice, and Florence. American capitalists such as J. P. Morgan contributed to the building of the churches, with the land and real estate held by boards founded by act of the New York state legislature. The constitutions of the congregations put them firmly under the authority of the Episcopal Church, especially the presiding bishop. Although the congregations initially gained a reputation as havens for the wealthy, the current bishop-in-charge, Pierre W. Whalon, is quick to point out that this image "went down with the Titanic." [3]

As Americans fought wars in Europe, congregations were founded, many of which survive today in cities such as Munich and Geneva. Congregations in Waterloo and Wiesbaden began as chaplaincies of the Church of England. During the world wars the congregations suffered heavy losses within their communities, and were later rebuilt by people other than the wealthy expatriates who had founded them. An Episcopal congregation in Frankfurt worshiped in a Quonset hut after its building was destroyed; the church in Wiesbaden was seriously damaged by an air raid and restored by the United States Air Force; after the church property in Munich was confiscated the people worshiped elsewhere. The longest serving bishop-in-charge of the convocation was Stephen F. Bayne, the primary author of "Mutual Responsibility and Interdependence (MRI)," who served from 1960 to 1968. His leadership energized the congregations and helped move them out of the "club" mentality, focusing on attracting skilled clergy. Ed Browning was not only the first full-time bishop-in-charge to live in Europe, but as presiding bishop he is credited with recognizing the convocation's potential and providing financial assistance from his own budget for an expanded European episcopate. [4]

When Browning began his ministry as bishop-in-charge of the Convocation of American Churches in Europe in June 1971, it was a time of tremendous change. In 1970 the Lambeth Conference had drafted a resolution that focused on the parallel Anglican jurisdictions in Europe and in other areas of the world. In the case of Europe, the Episcopal Church and the Church of England maintained separate congregations and diocesan structures, and at times there was tension between the two entities. At the time of Browning's appointment, he was given the mandate to work with his counterpart in the Church of England, in the hope of working out a dual ministry between the churches and establishing a joint Episcopal and Church of England headquarters on the continent. The Convocation of American Churches in Europe consisted of seven parishes in France, West Germany, Italy, and Switzerland. The Church of the Holy Trinity in Paris was designated the pro-cathedral. The dean was Sturgis Lee Riddle, one of the most senior clergy in the convocation, who was said to be anxious that the new bishop-in-charge establish his office at some place other than the cathedral. Each congregation in the convocation had it own culture and character. The parishes were largely composed of international business people, educators, military, and foreign service people, although there was also a growing diversity in the membership from local communities. Overall, members of the convocation churches were influential, learned, and prosperous. [5]

The move from Okinawa to Europe was in itself an adventure for Ed and Patti Browning and their family. Yoshiko Miyagi had agreed to accompany the fam-

ily and stay with them for a year in Europe to help ease
the transition. The group left for Europe via a Russian
freighter, then traveled across Russia by the Transibe-
rian Railroad and by plane. Arriving in Stockholm, the
Browning entourage stopped for some rest and attended
church. The preacher was none other than John Richard
Satterthwaite, the newly appointed Church of England
bishop of Fulham (Northern and Central Europe) and
Gibraltar (Southern Europe)—and Ed Browning's new
colleague. Satterthwaite, who lived in the bishop of Gibraltar's residence in West Sussex, was a cordial colleague to
Ed Browning, although not firmly committed to shared
governance between the two churches. When plans for a
joint Episcopal and Church of England headquarters in
Brussels fell through, Browning established his office at
Christ the King parish in Frankfurt and continued to
work for greater cooperation between the two Anglican
bodies wherever possible.

Browning's installation as bishop-in-charge not only
included Satterthwaite as a concelebrant, but also included
a commissioning ceremony. Browning was commissioned
by the archbishop of Canterbury and the bishop of
London to officiate in the Church of England parishes
in Europe, and Satterthwaite concurrently received a
commission from the presiding bishop to officiate in the
Episcopal churches on the continent. The installation was
attended by officials of the American embassy in Paris and
the British embassy, as well as ecumenical representatives
from the Anglican, Old Catholic, Orthodox, Protestant,
and Roman Catholic churches. [6]

In looking for a place to live in Europe with a central
location to facilitate travel among the American churches,
the Brownings were first captivated by Nice, France.

There was a large rectory there built by the Vanderbilt family, and both thought it would be a wonderful place to raise the family. However, the presiding bishop, John Hines, was less than enamored with the idea. Embroiled in various controversies, the last thing Bishop Hines wanted was criticism involving one of his suffragans taking up residence on the French Riviera. There was a dearth of rental properties available for a family the size of the Brownings, but after several months the Brownings found a five-bedroom house to rent in the village of Nordenstadt outside of Wiesbaden, West Germany. The house was in the country between two pig farms, but large enough to accommodate the family and the constant stream of visitors they attracted. For instance, when John Tederstrom was called as rector of St. Augustine of Canterbury Church in Wiesbaden, his whole family, including the couple and their four children, moved in with the Brownings for three weeks. German families tended to be much smaller than the Browning clan, and most landlords were reluctant to take on such a large group. The house the Brownings rented came with an imperious landlord who liked to inspect his property regularly and unannounced. Ed eventually had to step in and tell the man not to talk to Patti unless he was at home. There was also a daunting neighbor, Frau Schmidt, who called the police whenever Mark Browning played his music too loudly.

While the Browning family lived in Europe, Ed traveled most of the time and was usually home only three to four days every two weeks. Once when Patti dropped Ed off at the airport for another trip, their youngest son John said, "Well, back to normal." [7] Out of necessity, Patti became more involved with the children and their needs. She also became acquainted with the intricacies of driving on the Autobahn. The Browning children were getting older and needed to be driven from place to place for school activities. They also depended on their mother's moral support in the new environment. The move from Japanese culture to European culture was difficult for the entire family and required adjustments all around. "All seven of us grew together through this in a mutual ministry," said Patti of their years in Europe. [8]

At the time the American churches in Europe were geographically isolated from each other with little holding them together as a community. They reminded Browning of "island congregations." The Brownings hoped their ministry would help the churches become more unified. "I changed a lot of sheets for people coming east and west," said Patti. As was the case with their previous ministries, Patti did not move to Europe with a particular personal agenda in mind. "Long range planning has not been one of my priorities," said Patti. "Ministry arises and becomes apparent as we move into situations, and the needs change quickly." [9]

As in Okinawa, the whole Browning family was an integral part of the ministry and witness in Europe. In Okinawa and Japan the Browning children were actually the first ones to form relationships in the wider community; they had learned Japanese and local dialects quickly, and before long they were playing with local children in sugarcane fields and eating dragonflies. The Browning children had introduced much of Asian culture to their parents, and their friendships helped to grow the church. This same dynamic proved true in Europe, although the people in West Germany where the family lived were more reserved and private than the Okinawans, and thus the transition less spontaneous. While in Europe, Patti shifted gears and cut back on church activities in order to give the children more of her time and energy. "We both realized that we were asking the children to make sacrifices they should not have to be making. In the midst of a heavy schedule, Ed shared my ministry to the children. We felt that each of them was special, with different gifts, and it became a high priority to help them discover their own uniqueness." [10]

The move to Europe also meant challenges in terms of the children's education. Private schools for Americans were established throughout Europe but were very costly. The older Browning children went to high school on the military base, although they never completely felt part of that community. John Browning was enrolled in a German kindergarten, with mixed results. The staff at the school were perplexed by the trilingual, Japanese-English-German-speaking toddler and wanted to hold the boy back a year. By this time Patti had been through many years of negotiation with school officials around the world and would hear none of it. She insisted on a meeting with John's teacher and other school officials to prove that not only did her son understand what was asked of him—but he understood it in three languages! [11]

Although the plan for a shared ministry between the Episcopal Church and the Church of England did not materialize during the Browning years in Europe, and all attempts to move forward on this agenda were scuttled soon after Browning left to join the Episcopal Church Center staff in New York, other innovative ministries developed. Within three years, the convocation formed deeper ecumenical relationships, most notably with the Old Catholic churches. Browning also worked to forge relationships between the Episcopal Church and the

Roman Catholic Church during the papacy of Paul VI and with the Orthodox churches. It was quite a change for Ed Browning to move from the new Christianity of Okinawa to the centuries-old Christianity of Europe. Yet his personable and welcoming pastoral style built solid relationships there which endured for many years.

In April 1974, presiding bishop-elect John Allin visited Europe to meet with officials at Lambeth Palace and the Anglican Consultative Council, as well as the Anglican Center in Rome and the World Council of Churches in Geneva. Allin combined his visit with a stop in Rome to attend the annual convention of the Convocation of American Churches in Europe and to meet the event's honored guest, Cardinal Willebrands, head of the Vatican Secretariat for Promoting Christian Unity. A photo shows Ed Browning, John Allin, and Cardinal Willebrands outfitted with aprons inscribed "They also serve." At the dinner all three men put the aprons to use by going from table to table helping to serve the guests. [12] Browning also joined several tours during his years in Europe, including a trip to Bulgaria with the archbishop of Canterbury and a trip to Istanbul. During the latter, Browning's passport was accidently stamped while he was on his way out of Istanbul. He was eventually smuggled back into the country in a truck covered with a tarpaulin. [13]

At the time of his resignation as bishop-in-charge of the Convocation of American Churches in Europe, Browning was honored for his "personal mission of reconciliation among all men; marking the ecumenical style and content of his teaching that has given a new sense of unity to [the convocation's] parochial diversities and a spiritual renewal to the cause of American unity in Europe." [14] "Part of Ed's genius as a person of the gospel," said John Tederstrom, who was a member of Browning's Council of Advice, "was that almost overnight he created a sense of community and unity. He helped us see the convocation as something larger than our woes, and he made people feel like they were part of the evolution of the gospel." Tederstrom was also the Brownings' rector in Wiesbaden and admitted that under different circumstances it might have been daunting to take on a church where the bishop was a member of the congregation. "But with Ed, what you see is what you get," said Tederstrom. "We were very disappointed to see them go." [15]

As bishop-in-charge of the Convocation of American Churches in Europe, Browning also cooperated with the military chaplaincies and Clarence Hobgood, the Episcopal Bishop for the Armed Forces. In April 1973, three hundred military and civilian Episcopalians gathered in Berchtesgaden, West Germany, for a conference entitled, "Signs of God's Presence in the World," led by William A. Johnson, professor of Christian Thought at Brandeis University and canon theologian at the Cathedral of Saint John the Divine in New York City. Every Episcopal military chaplain in Europe attended the Berchtesgaden Conference, as did many laity and clergy in Germany and about forty children. The conference was designed to be a time of spiritual renewal for military personnel and their families who, because of duty in widely scattered locations, were often isolated from the regular life of the Episcopal Church. It was also a time for civilian and military Episcopalians in Europe to get to know each other. Both Hobgood and Browning gave meditations at the conference. Hobgood's talk focused on the difficulty of being a follower of Christ, particularly when it means trying to understand the actions of some young people, such as those who left the United States to avoid military service or those in militant minority groups. Browning's talk focused on the need for reconciliation and wholeness. On the final evening of the conference, both bishops administered confirmation to children and adults. [16]

The Amnesty Issue

One of Ed Browning's impassioned causes while bishop-in-charge of the Convocation of American Churches in Europe was amnesty for the many young American war resisters living in exile during the Vietnam War. To learn more about their plight he visited exiles living in Stockholm to collect data and to hear first-hand the stories of the men and their families. His visits were meant to raise their spirits and to assure them their country had not forgotten them. Browning announced his intention to visit Stockholm to the convocation's convention in May 1973. The three-day visit occurred in August of the same year. Browning visited Stockholm with two other members of the convocation's leadership, Edward L. Lee, rector of St. James Church, Florence, Italy, and James H. W. Jacks, junior warden of the same parish. Lee had a contact among the war resisters in Stockholm who helped set up the visit, as well as connections with the Episcopal Peace Fellowship (EPF). Tom Hayes, the first full-time executive director of EPF, had gone to Sweden in the late 1960s to work with war resisters, and Browning connected with his work while in Europe. Following the visit to Stockholm, Browning released a pastoral letter in September 1973 to the entire convocation, a month in advance of the upcoming General Convention. "We got some flak for going there [to Stockholm] and giving aid and comfort, but Ed's concern was to find ways the church could minister to them," said Lee, now the retired bishop of Western Michigan. [17]

Between 1967 and 1973 approximately seven hundred men sought asylum in Sweden. When Ed Browning visited in 1973, approximately 450 exiles were living in the country, primarily in the cities of Stockholm, Malmo, and Gothenburg. Along with their wives and children, the community numbered approximately 1,200 persons. Ed Browning and his colleagues met with three different groups of exiles, including war resisters, military deserters, and members of the American Exile Project, a program funded through the department of immigration of the Swedish government and the Swedish YMCA to address the social needs of the war resisters. Browning was moved by the articulate arguments of the men, as well as the sincere desire of many to return home. Browning was convinced the men spoke out of conviction and chose their witness because they could not in good conscience participate in the war. "Across this spectrum of feelings and beliefs, from the very wistful expression to return home to family and friends, to the expression of a very strong international political agenda, there was at the same time an almost unanimous conviction that even more important than the issue of amnesty is the issue of our nation coming to grips with the reasons which involved it in Southeast Asia in the first place, so it never happens again." [18] Browning's commitment to reconciliation comes through strongly in the pastoral letter. "For our own souls' sake, as well as for these men, we must all participate in a process of reconciliation so badly needed in our country," he urged members of the convocation. [19]

In the pastoral letter to the Convocation of American Churches in Europe, Browning promised to take the issue of unconditional amnesty to the General Convention, interdenominational American churches in Europe, and other ecumenical forums. He also pledged to set up a special fund to assist exiles in their pastoral needs. "It is reconciliation that we need at this time," says the pastoral letter, "a reconciliation of those alienated from one another for the purpose of healing the larger human family in America and abroad. We cannot forget that the exiles in Sweden are our fellow countrymen—and there are others like them in Denmark, Holland, France, England, Mexico, as well as Canada—and all of them are in these 'far-off places' because they had to make particular decisions about the war in Southeast Asia which most of us did not have to make. Nevertheless, the issues of that war are no less our issues, and the men in exile represent that fact in a very dramatic way." [20]

The House of Bishops at the General Convention, after an emotional discussion, issued a statement of conscience calling for the "appropriate authorities" of the United States government to grant a general amnesty to all who refused participation in the Vietnam War. Browning worked with Mary Miller of EPF on drafting the statement, and the two remained in touch thereafter. Miller believes that Browning was particularly in tune with peace and reconciliation issues "because of his deep involvement in the Pacific." [21] The conscience statement had been initially submitted as a resoluton for consideration by both houses of the General Convention. It failed in the lay order of the House of Deputies. An alternative resolution, allowing a non-violent resister to serve a period of alternative service, also failed after four amendments were attempted. "Ed and I fell into each other's arms when the resolution failed," said Mary Miller. "Ed was different from some of the other people we worked with. He was a friend. We worked really, really hard on that resolution," she said. [22]

Following the resolution's defeat, the House of Bishops issued it as a statement of conscience. It called for healing the wounds at home and abroad caused by the war. It urged Christians to work for reconciliation and the government to grant Vietnam veterans the same benefits as those veterans of past wars, and called for general amnesty for all who refused to participate in the war. Lastly, the House of Bishops called upon all dioceses and parishes to consider amnesty and the needs of returning veterans in their education and social concerns programs. [23]

A year later in 1974, the White House called Browning personally to inform him that President Gerald Ford had granted amnesty. A resolution on amnesty passed the General Convention three years later, in 1976, without serious opposition.

The Episcopal Church Center

In February 1974, after Ed Browning had served for three years as bishop-in-charge of the Convocation of American Churches in Europe, John Allin, presiding bishop-elect, asked him to return to the United States to serve in his new administration. A. Ervine Swift, former bishop of Puerto Rico and a former missionary, was appointed bishop-in-charge of the Convocation of the American Churches in Europe to succeed Browning. [24] In New York, Browning was appointed to the post of deputy for jurisdictions, with responsibility for both domestic and overseas dioceses of the Episcopal Church, coordinating and administering programs and relationships linking the national church with its 114 jurisdictions. The rather vague title of "deputy for jurisdictions" was revised within the year to "executive for national and world mission of the Executive Council." [25]

Browning was one of John Allin's first three senior appointments after his election in October 1973 (Allin was installed as presiding bishop in June 1974.) Allin's strategy was to make a minimum number of changes early in his term to ensure a smooth transition. At the same time, he made a few significant appointments "so that he would not be the only new person at the top management level. If no changes were made," he said, "he would possibly be only a learner and not a leader." [26]

Each day Ed Browning commuted into Manhattan from Connecticut, stopping just before he entered the Episcopal Church Center to read the dedication, "Whose service is perfect freedom." The text served as his prayer upon entering and leaving the building. "I do that because it is true. We are truly free, fully and radically free only in community defined not by power and competition but by love." [27]

Ed Browning's work at the Episcopal Church Center differed from his previous ministries. He found a large corporate staff structure with plenty of politics and underlying tensions. Presiding Bishop Allin had brought in Browning to replace Carman St. John Hunter, a former missionary to Brazil and radical educator who had supported—and translated—the works of Paulo Freire, a spokesperson for liberation theology in Latin America. Allin was uncomfortable with Hunter's leadership of the mission program, a job she had held since 1972. Although Allin differed from Hunter theologically and philosophically, many also believed that her strong association with John Hines motivated the new presiding bishop to replace her, along with other staff strongly linked to his predecessor. Carman St. John Hunter remained a powerful force among the staff and throughout the church, particularly in religious education. [28] Browning had no clue that he was replacing Hunter in national and world mission until after he arrived on the scene. Although most of the national staff who remained in the new administration were solidly behind John Allin's leadership, there were some highly vocal exceptions. Also, the "irregular" ordination of eleven women to the priesthood in July of 1974 caused division among the staff, as did liturgical reform and the Prayer Book revision process.

The Hunger Crisis

During the 1960s, under the leadership of John Hines, the Episcopal Church had begun to rethink its mission and to reach out to victims of injustice and oppression. The election of John Allin as presiding bishop signaled an apparent change in direction with a focus on the spiritual renewal in the church and a renewed emphasis on evangelism. Throughout his work as executive for national and world mission, Ed Browning resisted attempts to separate out different responses to the mission of the church. He emphasized that there was *one* mission and that it emanated from the one triune God who desires the reconciliation of all humankind. "God is at work in creation," he wrote, "calling his people to join him in the mission he identifies as being imperative for the day. Our obedience comes in our response and commitment to the oneness in mission in all its diversified challenges." [29]

In 1974 John Allin acknowledged the hunger crisis in the United States and throughout the world as "a challenge before all people greater than anything previously experienced in history." [30] Ed Browning was the deputy charged with coordinating the Episcopal Church's response to world hunger. "We see God speaking to us through the starving people of the world. Though we have heard this," he said, "we must reaffirm it to the people of God. There is a mission this church has to the starving. There must be a living, acting, sacramental response to this problem." [31]

In the same year the Executive Council adopted a statement committed to "the short term imperative" of seeking "to interrupt the process of certain starvation for as many as possible of the hundreds of thousands of human beings who will die in the coming months." The council requested that every parish in the Episcopal Church form a task force on hunger to raise awareness of the crisis and to implement strategies for change. In addition, the council approved the convening of two regional conferences to train facilitators for each diocese in the United States and to respond to a similar request from the bishops of overseas dioceses. For individual Episcopalians, the council adopted an "immediate response commitment" of daily prayer "for those who do not have food...and for grace and power to take appropriate action." [32]

Bishop Allin appointed an ad hoc inter-provincial team of church leaders to plan, conduct, and evaluate regional, diocesan, and parish programs to combat the national and world hunger crises. Browning provided leadership as staff person and Norman J. Faramelli of the

Boston Industrial Mission was elected chair of the Inter-Provincial Team of World Hunger. Faramelli believed that changing attitudes was one of the goals of the project and that relief work must be more than assistance with pity and compassion. "It must be seen in terms of justice," he said. [33] Faramelli was impressed with Browning's work with the team and was pleasantly surprised to work with a bishop who contributed so directly and was so involved with the campaign against hunger. "He had a capacity to calm the waters in tense situations," said Faramelli about Browning. "He was also good at mediating between the team and the presiding bishop. Those of us on the team and the presiding bishop had totally different worldviews, but Ed really knew how to get Jack Allin moving." Faramelli said that Browning also knew how to get things done within the larger system. "When we needed to get funds for Province IX people to participate, Ed made sure they were available. He also helped us move the Presiding Bishop's Fund into development work and sustainable agriculture. He wanted to see the church involved with the issues of economic justice," said Faramelli. "It was a breath of fresh air." [34]

Overseas Mission

As executive for national and world mission, Ed Browning's ministry focused on a wide range of human problems throughout the world. Steeped in the theology of the document "Mutual Responsibility and Interdependence" (MRI) from his days in Okinawa and mainland Japan, Browning transferred its spirit to the mission of the Episcopal Church throughout the world. He also drew on the 1973 Dublin report of the second meeting of the Anglican Consultative Council when he emphasized, "There is but one mission and this one mission is shared by the worldwide Christian community." [35]

Browning's own experience profoundly shaped his perspectives on overseas mission, and he challenged practices of control and domination as well as the traditional role of the missionary. He believed that within Anglicanism all are interdependent within the body of Christ, all churches having much to receive as well as much to give. Browning was troubled that the spirit of interdependence within the Anglican Communion seemed unappreciated within the American church and sought to redefine the mission strategy of the church. At the basic level, according to Browning, this meant that the church must become involved with people and their problems, rather than with geographical areas. "This leads me to say that in our overseas relationships we should be concerned about how we as a church might help ourselves, as well as the people and the church in that place, to face and deal with the issues of poverty, hunger, population, justice, and human rights." [36] Browning did not believe that the "missionary era" was a thing of the past. "It is my vision that we are embarking on a new era of mission more exciting and more fulfilling than any we have ever known." [37]

Soon after he came to the Episcopal Church Center, Browning spent several days in the Diocese of El Salvador to learn of the church's work among the poor in that country. There he encountered Luis Serrano, a priest who had developed a program named CREDHO designed to empower the poor and to enhance their quality of life through community health, education, and agricultural training. Browning witnessed a training session where Serrano and human rights attorney Rosa Cisneros worked with 250 campesinos to help them form an association to defend their small land holdings against a large landowner. Cisneros was later executed by the Salvadoran government in 1981. "For four days I watched a priest, a lawyer, a doctor, a young Peace Corps worker, and a community of the faithful exercising a ministry, not *to* the poor but *with* the poor," wrote Browning. "It is a ministry which has heard God speaking out of poverty and injustices being experienced by a part of his creation. It is a ministry that, having forced on it conditions of poverty, hunger, and social injustice, has sought to respond faithfully in helping to change these conditions by enabling the poor themselves to act." [38]

Browning believed that all missionary strategies and overseas relationships should include a basic commitment to the liberation of all humankind. He encouraged the Presiding Bishop's Fund for World Relief to consider as one of its primary tasks the support of development programs that would enable people to deal creatively with their problems. Likewise, he urged the United Thank Offering through its granting process to support training programs that furthered human development and global justice. "It is my conviction that this church is being called by Christ himself to use our leadership and our human and financial resources in every conceivable way to enter into this range of problems—into the lives of the poor and the oppressed." [39]

In addition to overseas development, Browning's experience also taught him about the need for churches to develop indigenous leadership with local cultures rather than transplant American traditions to other cultures.

Browning urged the Episcopal Church to face its paternalistic history in dealing with overseas jurisdictions. "The national church has had to face the question of whether it was seeking to *enable* these jurisdictions in their process of developing a mature life, or was it indeed, through various ways, treating them as adolescents—or even worse acting as a parent not willing to trust or let go."[40] Under the guise of the Overseas Review Committee and the Joint Commission on World Mission, Browning supported policy changes that moved overseas jurisdictions toward self-government, self-support, and self-propagation. Some of these policy changes included the right of overseas dioceses to elect their own bishops, the transfer of property held by the national church to the overseas dioceses, and the formation of a coalition of overseas bishops to foster interdependence and group decision-making.

At the time there was a growing desire among overseas jurisdictions of the Episcopal Church to seek autonomy. Some of the dioceses wished to leave the American church not to be "independent" but "interdependent," to meet with the Episcopal Church as equal partners rather than as children coming to a parent. For instance, in 1965 the Province of Brazil was formed from dioceses that had been part of the American church. In 1971 Ed Browning's former diocese, Okinawa, became the eleventh diocese of the Nippon Sei Ko Kai. While Browning was at the Episcopal Church Center as the executive for national and world mission, the Diocese of Liberia petitioned the General Convention to become an associated diocese of the Province of West Africa. The Diocese of Costa Rica was making similar plans. It was Browning's belief that the capital funding and logistical support needed by these churches proceeding toward autonomy was integral to the mission strategy of the Episcopal Church.

Also integral to Browning's work as executive for national and world mission was the implementation of the Partners-in-Mission Consultation process developed at the second meeting of the Anglican Consultative Council in Dublin in 1973, known as "MRI-Phase II." This process called for every province or council within the Anglican Communion to host a consultation to which they invited other parts of the communion as partners in mission. Within the process of the consultation, the host province and individual dioceses therein were asked to state their mission goals. The partners then shared something of their own mission and questioned, challenged, and affirmed the host province. Lastly, the group determined collectively how they as partners could support the mission of the host province.

During Browning's tenure as executive for national and world mission, the Episcopal Church participated as a partner in over fourteen consultations. Not only did the consultations give the Episcopal Church a broader picture of mission possibilities within global Anglicanism, but the emphasis on cooperation served to share resources more widely than in the past. The consultative process not only allowed both the host and partners to give and receive from each other with integrity, but the sharing of resources that had been kept very parochial in the past was more widely recognized. "The consultation process enabled the invited partner to see very quickly that he is in relationship with a mature church, filled with great vitality and having gifts that could strengthen his own church," reflected Browning.[41] Browning also believed that the Partners-in-Mission process could directly enrich the mission of the Episcopal Church. "We shall discover resources available to us from our partner churches, giving us the opportunity to experience what it means to receive. We shall, by acknowledging our overall goals interdependently, be able to unify this church in its one mission." [42]

Family Transitions

Upon moving to the United States from Europe, the Browning family lived in suburbia for the first time. Patti burst into tears when she first saw their new split-level home in Riverside, Connecticut, but the family eventually settled in and found a nearby parish where they all were happy. "A home is where we hang our pictures," said Patti. "We've moved around a lot, but we always hang up the paintings and bring out the familiar things." [43] Their new home in Riverside was down the street from the home of President Nixon's aide H. R. Haldeman. It was predominately a neighborhood of Christian Scientists, although close to the Episcopal Church's Seabury House in Greenwich.

After fifteen years overseas, with only two furloughs, the Browning family was in deep culture shock. Shortly before the move Patti had undergone major surgery, which made the trip more arduous. "Coming back to the States when our kids were young teenagers after raising them abroad thus far was an eye-opener," wrote Ed Browning. "My kids felt as if they were from Mars. Many, many things here were new and strange to them, and their peers weren't always kind." [44] Accustomed to living in the midst of diverse cultures, the family had little experience of the homogeneity they would find in Connecticut. They also had little experience with electric garage doors, electric toothbrushes, and other technologies uncommon in Okinawa and even in West Germany.

The younger children experienced some negative treatment from their new peers in school. John, the youngest, spoke mostly in German while his siblings were still comfortable speaking Japanese. Neither John nor Peter Browning had ever lived in the United States. "Peter, they just don't like us because we're Japanese," was John's explanation to his brother on a particularly trying day. Ed and Patti were astounded that it had never occurred to John that he was an American. [45] Philip made some friends, but always felt "different" in Connecticut. [46] Mark and Paige Browning, the two oldest children, were on their way to college at the University of the South in Sewanee, Tennessee, their father's alma mater. "For the first time in our married life I felt separated from Ed's ministry," said Patti. "We were not connected to any diocese, and he was on the road 80 percent of the time, and mostly overseas." [47] Patti believes that by the time Connecticut felt like home, the family was leaving again for Hawaii. "The hardest move we ever made was to Connecticut," said Peter Browning. "The move to Hawaii and going back to Asian culture saved our lives." [48]

Despite the stress on the family due to the moves to West Germany and then to Connecticut, the Browning children recognize the advantages of their upbringing, and in adulthood all are staunch supporters of their parents. "My parents are two of the most compassionate people I have ever known," says Peter Browning, a priest in Irvine, California. "My parents love the church and they have given their lives to it." [49] "We always had people living with us," said Mark Browning, a judge in Honolulu. "While growing up we met some amazing people, and politics were always discussed at the dinner table. They [Ed and Patti] taught us to be empathetic, socially responsible, and to give back." [50] Paige Browning, a teacher in Hood River, Oregon, is grateful to her parents for the way they saw the uniqueness of each of their children. "They did not judge us," she said. "They let us be ourselves and develop into who we are today. They are our rock." [51] "We were definitely strongly influenced by Japanese and Okinawan culture in terms of loyalty and the way our family shows concern for each other," said Philip Browning, a physician in Honolulu. "We would not be the people we are if we were not exposed to different cultures and different ideas when we were young. Diversity feels much more *normal*." [52]

All of Patti Browning's children recognize her role in holding the family together during their transitions and when Ed was on the road for long periods. "Mom was our anchor, our port in the storm," said John Browning, a tennis coach in Atlanta. "When we were growing up Mom was an endless well of love. She would do anything for us, and her confidence in Dad made him who he is. They are soulmates." John Browning said his upbringing informs the way he coaches his students. "My parents gave me a model on how to do my job. I believe that we can always talk things through and figure it out through communication." [53]

All the Browning children also agreed that despite their father's busy schedule, Ed Browning was always there when they needed him. "He would drop anything to be there for us," said Mark Browning. "He has always been that way." [54]

Browning remained at the Episcopal Church Center for two years. Though his colleagues appreciated his work immensely, the most he will say is that he did "an okay job." [55] The extensive travel required for the position fueled his thoughts about where the family might serve next. "The spirit never leaves you in one place, in a place of comfort. Spirit moves you all the time. I think it is imperative that [one called to be a bishop] be concerned for his own spiritual development," he said. [56] While several dioceses in the midst of search processes called him, Browning told them he wasn't interested. He had only been in New York for two years, and he felt some loyalty to the presiding bishop who had so recently hired him. Then the Diocese of Hawaii called, several times. After considering the other nominees, Browning felt that he would not be elected in Hawaii, but maybe the "dog and pony show" for the candidates might be a good chance for him and Patti to take a little vacation? As it turned out, Ed Browning was wrong about the "little vacation," as the visit was exhausting. More importantly, his prediction about the outcome of the Hawaii election proved wrong as well.

Chapter Three Notes

1   Edmond L. Browning (hereafter cited as ELB), "Our World Mission," in *Realities and Visions: The Church's Mission Today,* ed. Furman C. Stough and Urban T. Holmes III (New York: Seabury Press, 1976), 9.

2   ELB, interview by Sheryl Kujawa-Holbrook (hereafter cited as SKH), January 2009.

3   Pierre W. Whalon, "The History of the Convocation," The Convocation of Episcopal Churches in Europe, http://www.tec-europe.org/about/convo_history/convo-history.html (accessed May 24, 2010).

4   Ibid.

5   "Bishop Named," *The Living Church,* March 14, 1971.

6   "Installation of Bishop Browning in Paris," Diocesan Press Service, October 22, 1971.

7   Patricia Sparks Browning (herafter cited as PSB), interview by SKH, January 2009.

8   "We Talk with the Church's New 'First Lady,'" *Journal of Women's Ministries* 3, no. 2 (Fall 1986): 4.

9   Ibid.

10   Ibid.

11   PSB, interview.

12   "Presiding Bishop-elect Allin Visits Europe," Diocesan Press Service, April 26, 1974; photo, May 30, 1974.

13   ELB, interview.

14   Certificate from the Convocation of American Churches in Europe, Rome, Italy, April 20, 1974, Browning Collection.

15   John Tederstrom, interview by SKH, April 2009.

16   "Signs of God's Presence in the World," Diocesan Press Service, April 24, 1973.

17   Edward Lee, interview by SKH, March 2009.

18   ELB, "A Pastoral to the American Convocation," September 6, 1973.

19   Ibid.

20   Ibid.

21   Mary Miller, interview by SKH, March 2009.

22   Ibid.

23   "The Amnesty Issue," *The Episcopalian,* March 1973.

24   "Bishop Swift Appointed to Europe Post," Diocesan Press Service, March 22, 1974.

25   For example, see "New Missionaries to Tanzania," Diocesan Press Service, June 11, 1975.

26   "Presiding Bishop-elect Previews His Administration," Diocesan Press Service, February 5, 1974.

27   ELB, *A Year of Days with the Book of Common Prayer* (New York: Ballantine Books, 1997), February 28.

28   Analysis on the late Carman St. John Hunter's situation from John Ratti, November 2009; Ratti was a longtime friend and colleague.

29   ELB, "Our World Mission," 10.

30 "Executive Council Adopts World Hunger Recommendations," Diocesan Press Service, December 12, 1974.

31 Ibid.

32 Ibid.

33 Steve Brehe, "Ad Hoc Inter-Provincial Team on World Hunger Meets in St. Louis," Diocesan Press Service, January 10, 1975.

34 Norman J. Faramelli, interview by SKH, October 2009.

35 ELB, "Our World Mission," 10.

36 Ibid., 11.

37 Ibid., 15.

38 Ibid.

39 Ibid., 12.

40 Ibid.

41 Ibid., 14.

42 Ibid., 15.

43 PSB, interview.

44 ELB, *A Year of Days,* September 28.

45 PSB, interview.

46 Philip Browning, interview by SKH, March 2009.

47 PSB, "Diocese of Delaware Clergy and Spouses Retreat," n.d., Browning Collection.

48 Peter Browning, interview by SKH, March 2009.

49 Ibid.

50 Mark Browning, interview by SKH, March 2009.

51 Paige Browning, interview by SKH, March 2009.

52 Philip Browning, interview.

53 John Browning, interview by SKH, March 2009.

54 Mark Browning, interview.

55 ELB, interview.

56 "Deputies and Bishops Confidently Endorse Hawaii's Browning as Presiding Bishop," *The Voice,* Diocese of Newark, October 1985.

Aloha
1976-1985

I WANT TO AFFIRM that it is the place of this Church to be in solidarity with our Hawaiian sisters and brothers, within and without the Church, and to acknowledge their right to seek justice and dignity of personhood, which is a trust the monarchy gave us in establishing this Church in these Islands. [1]

> — Edmond Lee Browning,
> 100th Anniversary of the
> Overthrow of the Hawaiian Monarchy
> by the United States Government

I HAVE COME TO BELIEVE that nuclear, biological, and chemical weapons are incompatible with the gospel of Jesus Christ. [2]

> — Edmond Lee Browning,
> Monument to the Bombing
> of Hiroshima, 1980

Ed Browning likes to tell stories on himself and his years in the Diocese of Hawaii are no exception. Once, when he visited Holy Innocents' Church on Maui, Charley Burger, the popular and often humorous rector, announced at church that the children could process out at the sermon hymn so that they didn't have to listen to a boring sermon by the bishop. As the children filed out Browning followed them, and Burger called out, "Where are you going, Bishop?" Browning turned and replied, "I don't want to hear a boring sermon, either." The house came down. [3]

A Decade of Change and Healing

Ed Browning was bishop of Hawaii during a decade of change and controversy in the Episcopal Church. A year before the Brownings moved to Hawaii, Integrity, the national organization for lesbian, gay, bisexual, and transgender Episcopalians, held its first national meeting in Chicago. In 1976 the General Convention in Minneapolis approved the ordination of women to the priesthood and the revised draft of *The Book of Common Prayer*. In the same year, the massive Venture in Mission campaign was launched and Charles R. Lawrence, the first African American president of the House of Deputies, was elected. Three years later the General Convention in Denver gave its final approval to *The [1979] Book of Common Prayer* and established a Joint Commission on Peace. The new commission was established on the fortieth anniversary of the Episcopal Peace Fellowship (EPF) and charged to implement the recommendations of the 1962 House of Bishops pastoral letter on peace and war. During these years the Lutheran-Episcopal dialogues began, as did the SWEEP program for congregations to evaluate their mission and ministry through Service, Worship, Evangelism, Education, and Pastoral care. Although many of these changes caused division in the Episcopal Church, Ed Browning welcomed them as signs that the church was moving ahead. Concerned for those who met change with less enthusiasm than he did, he continued to exert a style of pastoral leadership that would hold the church together in the midst of change and controversy.

By the time Ed Browning was elected bishop of Hawaii in 1976 he had already honed his skills as both a pastor and a prophet. His ability to charm and to challenge was perhaps what led to his meteoric rise in the Episcopal Church. He was at first meeting unimposing but very comfortable. He warmed his contemporaries with his low-key affability, and then with great humility issued challenges and spoke prophetically. As former United States Senator Alan Simpson of Wyoming would later say to Browning at an Episcopal reception on Capitol Hill, shortly after his election as presiding bishop, "You know how to tell a person to go to hell so politely that they actually enjoy the ride." [4] His tenure in Hawaii was a period of remarkable harmony in the diocese, a lull before the storms that would increasingly encircle him as presiding bishop.

It was during the "dog and pony show"—the week of pre-election interviews with the candidates for bishop—that Ed and Patti Browning met a number of the people who would become close friends during their days in Hawaii and who remained confidants during Browning's years as presiding bishop and even into retirement. The interviews began in 1976 in Kauai with Jan and Paula Rudinoff as hosts, and then the Brownings were handed over to Dick and Dee Chang. Whatever reservations the Brownings had about the possibility of a move to Hawaii melted away in the warmth of their initial visit to the diocese. [5]

The Diocese of Hawaii was in anything but harmony when Browning first arrived. On May 6, 1976, shortly after his election, the religion news writer for the *Honolulu Star-Bulletin,* Nadine Scott, sent a note to Browning saying, "Since your election, Episcopalians in Hawaii seem to be smiling a lot more. Never have we seen such unanimity in this diocese." [6] Indeed, his election brought together those who had been alienated from one another during the tenure of the former diocesan bishop, E. Lani Hanchett, who had been first elected suffragan bishop by the House of Bishops at the General Convention in 1967—at the same time Browning was elected bishop of Okinawa. Hanchett's election as suffragan had been quietly engineered by Harry S. Kennedy, then bishop of the Missionary District of Hawaii, which also set Hanchett up as front-runner for the diocesan election in 1969. This rankled a number of senior clergy in the diocese, among others, making the 1969 election acrimonious. Nonetheless, Hanchett's election was historic because he was both the first bishop of the new Diocese of Hawaii and the first Native Hawaiian elected to the episcopate. A gentle pastor, Hanchett struggled with divisions among clergy and laity, most notably in the bruising departure of the dean of Honolulu's St. Andrew's Cathedral, John Morrett, in 1970. As a Native Hawaiian, Hanchett struggled with racism and, some believe, issues raised by the fact that the diocese was not prepared for independence. Tragically, Hanchett was diagnosed with colon cancer in 1974 and died from the disease on August 11, 1975.

Following Hanchett's death, those who had supported him and those who had opposed him sought an outside candidate to be a healer and bridge-builder in the diocese. Browning twice declined to be considered, having been at his post in New York less than two years. But Herbert Conley, dean of St. Andrew's Cathedral, reached out to him in a persuasive letter which Browning received after a "bad" day at the office. His deputy, Samuel Van Culin, himself a product of the Islands and part Native Hawaiian, also encouraged Browning to run. So it was that Ed Browning, with support from Patti, decided to see whether God was calling him to the Diocese of Hawaii.

Browning reported that Presiding Bishop John Maury Allin responded very graciously to him after his election in Hawaii. Immediately after his election, Browning also received warm applause from David Kennedy, his closest rival in the election and son of Bishop Kennedy, who along with Ben Benitez, priest and later bishop of Texas, drew enough votes on the first two ballots to force a third ballot, in which Browning emerged with a clear majority among both clergy and laity. Benitez would later become an antagonist during the Browning administration in the House of Bishops over the place of gay and lesbian persons in the church. Kennedy wrote a congratulatory letter to Browning on May 5. In it he recalled, "sometime back when the election process committee came up with its list of 41 names, I told Anna Marie [Kennedy's wife] that you were going to be our next bishop... I never believed that I, or any local candidate, was going to be able to resolve some of the division in the diocese. We were too much a part of it.... And of all the other candidates you were the one we believed had the qualities, personality, and experience around which all of us can rally."[7] Bishop Kennedy, now retired, also sent a note referring to Browning's election as a cause "to jump with joy." He noted that "the only sad part is the mean, underhanded things" a few clergy had said about his son David and his wife Anna Marie during the election process.[8] Herb Conley, who had forcefully resisted any effort to nominate him for bishop, wrote in his weekly letter to the cathedral congregation: "When the final election was announced the joy and applause that burst forth was spontaneous and in depth. It wasn't simply from segments saying 'we won.' It was from everyone...There was unrestrained joy and happiness all over town, and in fact all over the state on Sunday morning."[9] Although Ed Browning had already served as bishop in Okinawa and in the Convocation of American Churches in Europe, Hawaii was the first diocese where the laity and clergy gathered in convention had elected him bishop.

Browning was installed as the second bishop of Hawaii in a service that the local newspapers said "combined medieval pageantry with Hawaiian elegance."[10] Presiding Bishop John Maury Allin preached the sermon, calling for the people of Hawaii, who reportedly had spent a lot of money on the election, "to protect their investment."[11] At the end of the service the new bishop of Hawaii pronounced a blessing on the city of Honolulu and the state from the great porch of the cathedral.

For Ed and Patti Browning, moving to Hawaii was coming full circle from their beloved days in Okinawa. The Brownings were back in the Pacific, in a tropical diocese, a place Robert Louis Stevenson called the "loveliest fleet of Islands anchored in any ocean." Noting Browning's short tenures as bishop in Okinawa, Europe, and at the Episcopal Church Center in New York, Loren Mead, a longtime friend, remarked to him, "I hope you can hold on to this job." In fact, he held on to the "job" for nine years. The joy of his election by both rival camps grew steadily as he ushered in an era of shared leadership and removed from the diocese the last vestiges of autocratic and tight-fisted decision making. From the onset of his ministry in Hawaii, Browning strove to move the church in a more democratic direction and to include laity in decision making and planning.

In his first address to the diocese in October 1976, Browning said, "We have a shared ministry—a shared accountability for one another which hopefully will develop into a love and trust wherein we can challenge, support, and enable one another with the strength for greater service....This does not mean an abdication of leadership, but a sharing of the greater whole." [12]

Immediately after his installation as bishop, Browning and Hawaii's deputation to the 1976 General Convention departed for Minneapolis where Browning joined the majority in supporting the ordination of women. In the first address to his diocesan convention back home, he applauded the decision made in Minneapolis, noting that the decision should "bring a new strength and vitality to the ordained ministry." [13] But he was aware that deployment problems would await many women ordained to the priesthood in the early years. [14] Browning ordained Lynette Schaefer to the priesthood in 1978. She was one of the first women in the Episcopal Church to lead a congregation. Browning—who admitted that his personal acceptance of the ordination of women had not been automatic— acknowledged "that for some, this is a difficult decision to accept and I both recognize and sympathize with this distress....You have my deep concern and desire to stand with you even though we may disagree. To all of you, may I say that I am confident that in God's time it will be a decision bringing blessings to many by His calling certain women to the [ordained] ministry." [15] In the same address Browning advocated active recruitment of persons for the ordained ministry, as well as a particular concern to recruit persons from ethnic communities for ministry. [16]

Much of Ed Browning's thinking about the issues of human sexuality developed during his days as bishop of Hawaii. The 1976 General Convention, while remembered primarily for its approval of the ordination of women to all orders of ministry, also affirmed that homosexual persons are "children of God." Browning supported this relatively mild but significant resolution, which called for equal rights for gay and lesbian persons. While bishop of Hawaii, Browning supported the establishment of a chapter of Integrity, the national Episcopal lesbian, gay, bisexual, and transgender organization founded by Louie Crew. He gave his permission for the chapter to hold liturgical rites on a monthly basis at the cathedral and appointed a priest on his staff as chaplain to the group. At the 1979 General Convention, Browning joined a minority statement of conscience by bishops who objected to the convention's adoption of a resolution declaring it inappropriate to ordain a "practicing homosexual." He also joined an Integrity eucharist as a concelebrant at that convention. His acceptance of gay and lesbian people, including gay and lesbian clergy, was formed in his early days when he knew gay men among his parishioners in Okinawa and responded with compassion to the struggles of a gay military man. His sense of fairness and opposition to all forms of discrimination eventually grew into the position he espoused as presiding bishop that gay men and lesbians could be "a wholesome example to all people," which the 1979 resolution had implied was not possible.

Browning's first diocesan convention in Hawaii was another opportunity for him to exercise leadership. The convention was debating a resolution on the death penalty, an issue the state legislature was reviewing. The debate was contentious and at one point Browning leaned over to his chancellor, John A. "Jack" Lockwood, and said he wanted to speak to the issue. He was reminded that because he was chairing the discussion, he could not speak. Finally, a vote was taken that ended in a rare tie vote. Lockwood leaned over to Browning and said, "Now you can speak." He was also allowed to cast the deciding vote, and Browning didn't hesitate to cast his ballot against the death penalty. The prophet enjoyed the moment, but as always maintained his pastoral sensitivity for those just defeated.

In reflection on the Browning years in Hawaii, Jack Lockwood said that he had an "instant connection" with Ed Browning when they first met and that they developed a solid working partnership as bishop and chancellor. "Ed was phenomenal in the chair," said Lockwood, commenting on Browning's skill in presiding over diocesan conventions. "You could very much see John Coburn's influence there." Yet traveling with the popular bishop brought special challenges. "He was always greeted by everyone," said Lockwood. "Some would genuflect, and some would say, 'Hey, Big Red!' It took *forever*."[17]

The first years of Browning's tenure in Hawaii were spent healing the divisions of the diocese. For most of his ministry there he kept a hectic travel schedule, typically visiting parishes on the various islands for two to three days at a time. "I felt that trying to build community in the diocese and get people to help one another was really the role of the episcopacy,"

Browning said. "And if you try listening, that usually works." [18]

Richard "Dick" S. O. Chang, longtime canon to the ordinary for Browning, both in Hawaii and New York, before becoming bishop of Hawaii himself, spoke of Browning as an "introvert who worked hard to be open for people. He was able to build strong personal relationships and build a sense of trust." Chang said that Ed Browning was always careful to keep clear boundaries between pastoral confidentiality and administrative matters, a practice he later took with him to New York. He noted that Browning's experiences in Okinawa and Europe prepared him to address the divisions of the diocese he inherited. "He set standards and was fair but tough." For his part, Browning was deeply grateful for Chang's support and had tremendous respect for his tact and his gifts. "A very humble guy, with a deep love for his church, serving at All Saints," said Browning at the time of Chang's own election as bishop of Hawaii. "We had a genuine partnership. He was my right hand—not a 'yes' man but always truthful and very loyal," said Browning. [19]

Partners in Ministry

When Ed and Patti Browning moved to Hawaii, their five children ranged in age from eight to twenty, and Patti was still very much engaged with their needs as a parent. Through their children's schools and activities, the Brownings were quickly integrated into the wider community. (Son Peter Browning's basketball team played against the team from rival Punahou School on the island, which included a young Barack Obama.) Ed Browning called the clergy and spouses together in retreat at Hawaii Loa

College that first year in office and asked a clergy team to organize a relationally based program. When asked to make himself vulnerable to his clergy, he shared much of his relationship with Patti, including challenges they had faced as a couple, noting how the relationship required many compromises over the years in order for there to be mutual growth and support. The clergy warmed to this humble and self-deprecating pastor with a sometimes fiery edge, who was willing to reveal his humanity and his struggles. A diocesan spouses group formed in which Patti was active and which she also found personally helpful. "The danger is not finding enough time to evaluate your situation," said Patti Browning. "Couples can lose touch with one another under these circumstances, so there is constant need to dialogue as much as possible and stay in communication with one another." [20]

Jan and Paula Rudinoff both testify to the importance of Ed and Patti Browning's ministry with clergy families in the Diocese of Hawaii. "They made every effort to be inclusive of clergy spouses and kids," said Paula. "They are very authentic people," said Jan. "Very compassionate, fun-loving, true believers." [21] Hollinshead "Lin" T. Knight, one of the cathedral deans in Hawaii while Browning was bishop, said that Ed Browning was not only terrific to work for, but also had a way of inspiring others to become better people. "Seeing Christ in him made it easier to see Christ in myself," Knight said. [22]

One of the hallmarks of the Browning era in Hawaii was the genuine love and hospitality emanating from Ed and Patti's home that allowed various factions to feel accepted and affirmed. They tried to open their home as much as possible, often hosting different groups from the diocese as a way for the people from different islands to get to know each other. Given their large family, the diocese helped the Brownings purchase a spacious home, perfect for entertaining, on a ridge near the cathedral. There they hosted an annual open house each December, which was one of the social events of the year. Patti also hosted events with the diocesan Episcopal Church Women and clergy spouses there. Ed and Patti were also attentive to members of the Kennedy and Hanchett families, who had preceded them. The Browning family felt truly at home in Hawaii and thrived there. Although Ed, like all diocesan bishops, had many demands on his time, during the Hawaii years the family spent a great deal of time together, and the bonds between them continued to grow. When the youngest, John Browning, played tennis in high school, Browning relished leaving the office to be his son's "ball boy" at practice. "I am the highest paid ball boy in Hawaii," he would delight in saying.

Social Outreach

During Browning's tenure new programs were initiated in the diocese, such as a diaconal program and a program to treat alcohol addiction. Given the hardships Browning had experienced as his own father struggled with alcoholism, he was always supportive of Alcoholics Anonymous as a parish priest and now wanted to address the issue as a "health problem rather than a moral one" in the diocese.[23] "Browning consistently reaches out to transcend parochial and insular concerns in Hawaii," wrote one of the Honolulu newspapers when he was elected presiding bishop in 1985.[24] He challenged the church in Hawaii to become more deeply involved in ministries with the homeless, including a "peanut butter ministry" at the Institute for Human Services founded by iconic Episcopal priest Claude Du Teil. He funded the Kalihi-Palama Service Center for immigrants and new programs for seniors in the community. During the years Browning was bishop, the diocese also developed a companion relationship with the Diocese of Polynesia. At the same time he traveled to South African-occupied Namibia and raised about $80,000 (10 percent of Hawaii's diocesan budget that year) to help there.

While in Hawaii Ed and Patti Browning attended Marriage Encounter and Cursillo to show their support to a couple of congregations that embraced the charismatic movement and that needed to be brought into the scope of the larger diocese. At the time there were differences within the diocese about the direction of the charismatic movement, and Browning hoped they could be resolved. [25] While at Marriage Encounter Ed and Patti learned a communication tool called "ten and ten," where one partner takes a subject and writes on it for ten minutes and then shares it with the other partner and they talk about it. Even now Ed will go into the bathroom in the morning to shave and there will be a ten and ten from Patti taped to the mirror. Sometimes it will be a critique and sometimes a letter of support. "But each morning," says Ed Browning, "I move slowly into the bathroom to see if there is anything on the mirror!" [26]

Throughout his years as bishop of Hawaii, Ed Browning attempted to bring together the world of inner spirituality and social outreach. He believed both needed to be broadened and deepened as "ministry to the world's condition." "The spiritual cannot exist without the outreach of love," he said, "and any encounter with society must be enriched by our spiritual pilgrimage." [27]

As when he was presiding bishop, Browning assiduously navigated what to some was a chasm between spirituality and activism and found ways to explain how the two were linked. He entered his ministry in Hawaii with a profound commitment to raising up local leaders, supporting the ministry of the baptized, and addressing the many issues facing both church and society, such as hunger, poverty, unemployment, sexuality, peace and war, economics, and evangelism. "We are, after all, commanded to go into *all* the world," he said. [28] Ed Browning believed that societal violence, the arms race, and the appalling poverty rate were linked. "At this particular moment in history, the church everywhere faces a crisis," he said. "It needs to be the agent of a humane, caring society." [29]

In a diocese with several Episcopal schools and a diocesan camp, Browning led several major fund-raising campaigns. He placed a high priority on the schools and the camp, seeing them as integral to the mission of the church and important ways to nurture the Christian faith. [30] Browning recalled during an interview at his home in Hood River, Oregon, after his retirement, that in the middle of a campaign drive for the Priory School for Girls, his secretary told him Patti was on the phone. Patti Browning always got through to Ed. He mistakenly picked up the wrong line and said "There's only one person allowed to interrupt me during a meeting." The response came from a woman considering a major gift to the Priory who apologized profusely for interrupting him but she wanted him to know she had decided to pledge the full amount for which he had asked. Browning was utterly undone and responded, "except for you, dear lady, of course." On another occasion while raising money for the diocesan camp, he called a wealthy donor to ask for an additional $100,000 and stumbled his way through the conversation saying how much he hated asking for money, especially a gift of that size. The woman later gave the money and remarked to the camp director, "I couldn't say no, he was so cute on the phone." [31]

Native Hawaiians

Hawaii became a territory of the United States in 1900, seven years after the 1893 coup against the reigning monarch, Queen Liliuokalani. The queen was kept under house arrest in her home next door to St. Andrew's Cathedral and the Priory School for Girls. King Kamehameha IV and Queen Emma had founded these institutions and invited the Anglican Church to Hawaii in 1860. The imprisoned queen used to sneak through a gate between the properties to visit and have afternoon tea with the nuns who ran the school. After the overthrow of the monarchy and transfer of Hawaii to the United States, the Episcopal Church took over jurisdiction from the Church of England. The cathedral remains in the heart of downtown Honolulu, near the properties converted to government use. The wound caused by the seizure of a sovereign country remains a source of contention to this day in Hawaii. Although European Americans are a minority of the population, the companies they ran in the new territory, both before and after the overthrow, controlled the economy and increasingly the land. And as with colonization elsewhere, Christian missionaries were soon to follow. With them came smallpox, which decimated the Hawaiian community as it had earlier done to Native Americans. As noted, Anglicans did not come until invited by the monarchy. Each ethnic group that migrated to the

Islands has its own tale of exploitation to tell as wealthy landowners from the mainland set up plantations that housed the workers in enclaves according to their ethnic identity. The Episcopal churches to this day cope with vestiges of this colonial period, with congregations having primary identities with one ethnic group or another, the wealthiest being largely of European American descent.

While Browning returned the diocese to a functioning, healthy whole, with the divisions mostly healed, he also turned a prophetic eye to the wider community of the fiftieth state. His years in Okinawa had prepared him to respond to local and cultural needs in colonized and military contexts. Hawaii was and is a community of diverse peoples and cultures. No ethnic group can claim a majority. Even the haole (white) population makes up only one-third of the people. While the Islands are sometimes seen as exemplary for the way people work together across this diversity, life there is not without its struggles and challenges. Ed Browning's natural instincts for justice made him sensitive to the dynamics that lay just below the surface of what outsiders see as a harmonious community.

The United States military is another major factor in Hawaiian life. It is second only to tourism in the economy and controls vast parcels of prime land throughout the state. At least four congregations on Oahu have large military memberships and some military personnel are found in most other congregations. Browning's past ministry with Episcopalians in the military in other parts of the world had given him an appreciation and respect for their dedication to the church and a deep compassion for the sacrifices the military and their families are called to make. Pragmatically, Browning believed that given the imperfect nature of the world, the military is a fact of life, and the church needs to be pastorally supportive of those called to the armed forces.

Agriculture, which used to dominate the economy in Hawaii, has lapsed in the new global economy, with the land now devoted to housing, further changing the landscape and the shape of Hawaii's lifestyle. Tensions are never far below the surface in Hawaii and Browning discovered he was often treading in deep waters as he exercised his episcopate. [32]

Browning once led a group of clergy to visit the Waiahole Valley, which was privately owned land and a source of conflict with many Native Hawaiians. The group was to receive an orientation on water rights, but found the gate locked and their host for the day absent. After some discussion, they climbed over the gate in clear sight of a "Kapu" or "No Trespassing" sign. When they returned from their hike some time later, the police were waiting, and a potentially embarrassing incident was avoided when the police issued a caution. Browning later appointed a Hawaiian Commission to advise the diocese on indigenous issues and also appointed Charles Hopkins, a Native Hawaiian, as canon missioner at the cathedral for its Hawaiian constituency. At his first diocesan convention Browning mentioned the Hawaiian Commission and asked what the church should do to help homesteaders. "I *would* have this diocese concerned with where people live," he said. [33]

The high profile Ed Browning gave to land issues, called *aloha aina*—love of the land—rankled church members who were leaders of the major corporations and large landowners. He was "summoned" on a number of occasions to their corporate offices to hear their pique, but showed dexterity by maintaining respectful relationships while standing by his principles. He spoke softly, but his passion for justice fueled him and made him a leader whom others wanted to follow. Since seminary Browning had started every day with the phrase-prayer, "Into your hands I commend my spirit." It was during his years as bishop of Hawaii that he began to add a second prayer, "Lord, make me an instrument of your peace." [34]

Thomas Van Culin, a prominent lay leader during Browning's tenure in Hawaii, said that the bishop enabled others to exercise ministry and leadership "which risked people failing. He formed the Hawaiian Commission and allowed it to function independently." Because the Hawaiian community has never been of one mind about how to respond to the 1893 overthrow of the monarchy, Hawaii, including the Episcopal diocese, still struggles with the pain inflicted by that unresolved event. The Hawaiian Commission was one strategy to raise the profile of Native Hawaiians in the community. Browning also provided for Hawaiian liturgies using the traditional conch shell for the call to worship, singing Hawaiian hymns, reading the gospel in Hawaiian, and occasionally inviting groups of hula dancers to participate in the 8:00 a.m. Sunday service at the cathedral. When Browning visited the diocese in 1993, one hundred years after the overthrow, he chose to address this injustice once again and said:

> I want to affirm that it is the place of this Church
> to be in solidarity with our Hawaiian sisters and
> brothers, within and without the Church, and to
> acknowledge their right to seek justice and dignity
> of personhood, which is a trust the monarchy gave
> us in establishing this Church in these Islands.

It is a trust we must honor...We recall the memories of the past to see God's justice for the future, justice that embraces the social, political, and economic needs of the original peoples of these Islands. While supporting equality through civil laws, the church seeks also understanding and reconciliation through love so that justice may be done. So simple and yet so hard. In the hundred and more years of the church's witness in these islands, grace has intertwined with sin more than once. [35]

The Nuclear Arms Race

Another hallmark of Ed Browning's tenure as bishop of Hawaii was his response to the rapid spread of nuclear armaments. In 1980 he visited Hiroshima at the invitation of the Anglican Church in Japan. Browning was taken by a Japanese priest to the monument related to the bombing of Hiroshima on the island of Kyushu. The priest left Browning alone to wander throughout the four-story building looking at the photographs and fragments. The "call to remembrance" was a powerful spiritual experience for Browning. "I want to say I was almost sick," he said a few years later. "I had a conversion experience. My wall of apathy was broken. I came to the conclusion that there was no way I could no longer not say anything." [36]

Ronald Reagan, president at the time, was spending vast sums on armaments and referring to the Soviet Union as an "evil empire." Browning was deeply sobered by his visit to Hiroshima, seeing the effects of one relatively small nuclear bomb on that community which still bears the wounds of that event every day. "The focus of Hiroshima

Day is a call for Americans to affirm creation rather than deny it," he said. [37] Browning believed that the nuclear issue raised serious questions about the church's positions on past wars. "I believe the biblical imperative for peace-making serves as a mirror and challenges us to see who we might be and who we really are." [38] Having a president engaged in an arms race and building a new generation of nuclear weapons and ever more sophisticated delivery systems disturbed Browning to the point that he decided to devote an entire diocesan convention address to the subject, knowing that the reaction would be swift in Hawaii's military community.

In late 1981 the House of Bishops issued a call to peacemaking through a pastoral letter that condemned the nuclear arms race and pledged a year of prayer and fasting for peace. Ed Browning was at the forefront of the discussion and, in an impassioned sermon, reflected on his own visit to Hiroshima, the power of a single Trident submarine to create 2,000 "Hiroshimas," the powerlessness of the medical profession to respond to nuclear holocaust, and the shift from diplomacy to the quest for nuclear superiority. He said:

> Prophetic leadership never comes particularly easy within the life of the church—certainly not from me—partly because of our own fears related to a false sense of security and purpose—partly because the devil would have us convinced that the church has no place in questioning outside of its own realm of expertise. Recently, in reviewing the catechism of our new Prayer Book—the rendering of the ninth commandment was relevant for me—you remember, of course, that is the commandment regarding lying—bearing

false witness. In the new catechism it reads, "To speak the truth, and not to mislead others by our silence." My friends, the nuclear arms race—the use of chemical, biological, and nuclear warfare is a moral, ethical, and theological matter—faith in the Incarnation does not allow us to either escape this truth or to mislead others by our silence. [39]

Within three months of the release of the House of Bishops' pastoral letter many of the dioceses of the church committed the document to prayer and study at local conventions. In Hawaii, Browning gave his address on the subject on the island of Kauai, which hosted Hawaii's diocesan convention. He asserted, "I have come to believe that nuclear, biological, and chemical weapons are incompatible with the Gospel of Jesus Christ." This statement echoed the voice of the Lambeth Conference in 1930, which declared "war to be incompatible with the Gospel of Jesus Christ." Browning would repeat his words again upon his election as presiding bishop in 1985 during his acceptance speech, and the applause on that occasion was electric. On Kauai, the reception was more muted, and while many were grateful to hear such a clear declaration, the military community and some veterans were not. He was again summoned to meet with a Navy leader at Camp Smith to be told of his misdeeds. One Good Friday, Browning participated in a prayer vigil outside Camp Smith, asking that the military take down a cross which a camp commander, an Episcopalian, had put up in full view of thousands of commuters. The objection was that the display of the cross implied a Christian blessing on the arms race. Eventually, the courts did order the cross to be removed as a violation of the constitutional prohibition of any establishment of religion.

Ed Browning embraced his role as peace activist and was often seen marching in Waikiki or near the Capitol on a Palm Sunday with Roman Catholic Bishop Joseph Ferrario, Buddhist leader Yoshiaki Fujitani, and other religious leaders. Just prior to leaving Hawaii, the Buddhists would anoint him as a "living treasure." After he was nominated for presiding bishop Browning spoke out against anti-Semitism "as an issue for Christians to face more fully" and credited Buddhism with teaching him "about the nature of the Other and the calling which we have collectively as part of the human family." One Honolulu journalist claimed that Browning "deepened the ties between the Episcopal, Roman Catholic, and other Protestant churches and developed a closer relationship with the Rabbinate and the Jewish community than any of Hawaii's previous bishops." [40]

Ed Browning had supported amnesty for draft resisters living in exile in Europe when he was bishop-in-charge of the Convocation of American Churches in Europe and had eventually received a call in New York from the White House when President Ford signed an amnesty bill. But he had never met a sitting president, and while he would meet and engage both George H. W. Bush and Bill Clinton while he was presiding bishop, he got a chance to hone his presidential forays when Ronald Reagan made a rest stop in Hawaii on his way to Asia in April 1984. Reagan's intentions may have been to use his stopover as jet lag therapy and to take a dip in the ocean off Kahala Beach, but it was a clarion call for activists to protest his assaults on domestic social programs while diverting huge sums of money to the arms race and driving up the federal deficit. His visit also coincided with Easter Sunday, and the aides managing his schedule determined that St. Andrew's Cathedral would be the best venue for the President and Nancy Reagan to attend services. Although the Reagans were not regular Sunday churchgoers during their years in the White House, a special presidential service was scheduled for the afternoon of Easter Day at the cathedral in Honolulu. The event became the hottest ticket in town and the cathedral was packed for the occasion.

But preceding the liturgy were many negotiations between Reagan's handlers and the bishop's office. The point person for Reagan was a man who was also an Episcopalian and knew something about Ed Browning's reputation. Browning's earlier statements on the arms race had been noted by the White House, and a call to Browning suggested ever so politely that perhaps, since the service would be at St. Andrew's, the cathedral dean would be the logical preacher. In a response that was direct and also very polite, Browning said that the choice of preacher for the liturgy was nonnegotiable. The diocesan bishop would be the preacher. There were many other details to be ironed out as the Secret Service swarmed the cathedral with metal detectors and dogs sniffing for weapons. One oddity was White House insistence that there be a separate chalice for the Reagans to receive Holy Communion. Browning suggested this would not be appropriate and said instead that the Reagans could be the first to receive Holy Communion from the cup, alleviating the concern that someone else might drop poison in the chalice.

As the hordes arrived to take their seats as much as two hours ahead of the service, with Easter hats adding a festive touch, further drama was unfolding a block away in front of the State Capitol. The chair of the diocesan peace commission was leading a protest against the president's policies. The wider activist community had asked for an Episcopal priest to do so because they did not want to be seen as insulting the church on its most holy and festive day. Browning had agreed to let the priest serve this role, but urged him to finish the protest before the service and be inside the cathedral for the liturgy. The Reagans' motorcade route avoided the demonstration as they arrived at the cathedral. Moments after they took their seats the great pipe organ blared forth under the accomplished hands of organist and choir director John McCreary who, as most musicians will do on such occasions, used every opportunity for the choir to perform. A long liturgy ensued.

Ed Browning had agonized over his sermon that Easter Day, wary of using the occasion to challenge a sitting president who had come to worship and celebrate the resurrection of Jesus Christ. Yet he was also mindful of preaching good news to the poor and the oppressed, and he somehow wanted to name the perceived injustices of the Reagan administration. Browning began the sermon with an effusive and warm welcome of the President and predicted it would be a blessing for the whole community. He went on to preach about Christ's resurrection, and there was no hint of criticism as he extolled the hope of all humankind's promise in the risen Christ. But then he uttered one line, a sentence that would be flashed around the world within minutes. "We see a greater share of resources switched from the compassionate face of government to expenditure of arms, while we learn to think the unthinkable in the language of acceptable mega-death and limited nuclear warfare."[41] The media were all over it. Headlines referred to

Browning as Tip O'Neill "in a cope." O'Neill was then Democratic Speaker of the House of Representatives. But no mention of this was made by anyone immediately following the service. Ronald and Nancy Reagan, Ed and Patti Browning, and the dean and his wife all met immediately after the liturgy on the steps of the cathedral. President Reagan remarked to Patti, "The music was lovely."

Then Ronald and Nancy Reagan departed for tea with Governor George Ariyoshi in the house next door to the cathedral, a house formerly used by the Hawaiian monarchy. A deluge of mail to Browning began immediately after the cathedral service. He received some praise but mostly criticism, and he undertook personally to respond to every letter received. Browning talked about one letter that called him "a horse's ass." He even answered that one. (As presiding bishop he continued the practice of responding to his detractors personally.)

The event with President Reagan contributed to Ed Browning's growing notoriety in the Episcopal Church. In 1977 he was selected as the presiding bishop's representative to the Japanese Americans Centenary celebration, and the celebrant for the main eucharist for that event at Grace Cathedral, San Francisco. In 1980 he was singled out for his comments at a House of Bishops meeting on the formation of religious power blocs. Two years later he was again singled out among his brother bishops for an impassioned sermon he gave at a House of Bishops meeting decrying the nuclear arms race. Ed Browning was elected to the Executive Council in 1982, and was appointed to a group of church leaders to plan a synod of Province VIII (to which Hawaii belonged) in Honolulu, focusing on diversity and the Episcopal Church in the Pacific.

He advocated for and received from the Presiding Bishop's Fund for World Relief money to assist victims of a 1982 cyclone in Tonga and a hurricane in his own Diocese of Hawaii the following year. As bishop of Hawaii, Browning also hosted a successful weeklong visit of the Archbishop of Canterbury, Robert Runcie, which highlighted the health and vitality of the Diocese of Hawaii. Runcie soon after appointed Browning to an Anglican delegation to Namibia that included the primate of Japan and Terry Waite (aide to Runcie and later a hostage in Beirut). In Namibia he experienced the dangers of land-mined roads to visit the faithful who were enduring a brutal occupation by the apartheid regime of South Africa. [42]

Namibia

In September 1983 Ed Browning and Charles Cesaretti, staff officer for public issues at the Episcopal Church Center in New York, were asked to join an Anglican delegation commissioned by the Archbishop of Canterbury for a two-week pastoral visit to Namibia. The visit was the most extensive international church visit to Namibia to date. Browning was a member of the Executive Council designated for the visit, and Cesaretti was working closely with Terry Waite, Archbishop Runcie, and Presiding Bishop John Allin to monitor human rights and corporate involvement in Southern Africa. The team visited all the parishes in the Diocese of Namibia, toured the war zone on the Angolan border, visited hospitals and schools, met with Roman Catholic, Lutheran, and African Methodist leaders in the area, and held conversations with authorities from the South African Defense Forces and the administrator general's office. Namibia, formerly known as South West Africa, had been placed under the administration of South Africa by the League of Nations in 1920. Since 1946 attempts to place the country under United Nations trusteeship had failed. [43]

At the diocesan convention in Hawaii in November 1983, after Browning's visit to Namibia, a resolution was introduced calling on the diocese to oppose the apartheid government that controlled Namibia. Debate was intense and Bettye Jo Harris, delegate from St. Christopher's parish, stood up to chastise opponents saying, "Our bishop has risked his life to bring us the story of this evil of apartheid." The resolution passed but barely. The Diocese of Hawaii granted $79,000—10 percent of its budget—to the Presiding Bishop's Fund for World Relief, designated for the cause of rebuilding the church in Namibia, although Browning acknowledged that was not enough to ease the suffering of the Namibian people. [44] In his report to Executive Council on the pastoral visit to Namibia, Browning reported that most of the people wanted the churches to support United Nations action to seek free and open elections and an end to the occupation of that country by the Republic of South Africa. The war between South African forces and the guerillas of the South West Africa People's Organization struck hard at Anglican churches, schools, and clinics in the north; a seminary was destroyed. Both forces admitted terror against the people. [45] In 1984, a year before Ed Browning was elected presiding bishop, the world received news that Bishop Desmond Tutu of South Africa had been awarded the Nobel Peace Prize while teaching at the General Theological Seminary in New York City. [46] Tutu's struggle to end apartheid and the Episcopal Church's contribution to that effort became a major focus of the early years of Browning's term as presiding bishop.

Ed Browning's profile in the Episcopal Church rose yet again, and as the twelve years of John Allin's term as presiding bishop were coming to an end, many U.S. Episcopalians cast their eyes toward Honolulu, where an unpretentious but by now much revered bishop was exercising leadership that offered the change many sought. As members of the nominating committee for presiding bishop came to the diocese to interview Ed and Patti and the people there, Tom Van Culin remembers Browning asking him, "Tom do you have any suggestions for me and my time with the committee members?" Van Culin answered: "During the service you conduct for them, don't sing!" Ed Browning's head "snapped" to the right and he looked somewhat perplexed. "After that conversation, I do not recall hearing him 'sing' the service again," says Van Culin. [47]

At his final diocesan convention in Hawaii, Browning urged those assembled to listen to one another, to pledge the best, to work and give "for the well-being of the whole diocese for the glory of God and for the benefit of this community." Their mandate from Ed Browning was "to love." [48] He also pleaded with the diocese to continue the work they had begun together, especially the renewal of the diaconate, ministry of the laity, and the rebuilding of Camp Mokuleia. Paraphrasing another Browning, poet Elizabeth Barrett Browning, Ed Browning said, "With shoes removed be comfortable in the Lord and see every moment, every opportunity, every challenge as a bush afire with God's presence." [49]

At the time of his election as presiding bishop in September 1985, the press in Honolulu lauded Ed

Browning's many accomplishments as bishop there with "a special feel for Hawaii which speaks of his feel for people around the world." "He is an intelligent, diligent, compassionate and a morally courageous person in a nation and in an age when those qualities are especially needed," read one account. After praising Ed Browning's ministry in the Islands on behalf of the poor and marginalized, it was noted that he had led a relatively small (10,000 member) denomination in the state "to a position of high moral influence and consequence." [50]

Jack Shoemaker, a longtime priest in the Diocese of Hawaii and a friend of Ed Browning, said he had ambivalent feelings about Browning's election as presiding bishop. Shoemaker was also a friend of John T. Walker, another nominee, so that was part of it. But Shoemaker "also wondered whether Ed would be able to deal with all the divergent forces and attitudes within the church." Yet Shoemaker's fears were assuaged by Browning's "strong, quiet (usually), and steely attention to business which he saw as his opportunity to provide a leadership of centrality and unity rather than narrow partisanship and divisiveness." [51] Jack Shoemaker believes that the effectiveness of Browning's ministry was that he was "a most unbishopy bishop." Never one to nurse grievances, Shoemaker feels that Ed Browning's strength lies in his capacity to "never lose his center." "I wish we had more time together," said Shoemaker, as did many in the Diocese of Hawaii on Ed and Patti Browning's departure. [52]

Once again they had believed they would live out their lives and ministries in one place, only to discover that God had other plans for them. "So again, a call, an interim, a ministry, a stability, just as it has been in the past." [53]

Chapter Four Notes

1   Edmond Lee Browning, "Sermon to Hawaii's Diocesan Convention at St. Michael and All Angels," Lihue, Kauai, October 22, 1993, in *No Outcasts: The Public Witness of Edmond L. Browning, XXIVth Presiding Bishop of The Episcopal Church,* ed. Brian J. Grieves (Cincinnati: Forward Movement, 1997), 212.

2   Quoted from "Minister Sees Apathy on Nuclear Arms Buildup," n.d. [ca. 1980], Browning Collection.

3   The core of this chapter was written by Brian J. Grieves and is the result of his own travel and interviews in the Diocese of Hawaii, as well as his examination of the sources related to the Brownings that remain at the diocesan offices (hereafter cited as Grieves Interviews).

4   Grieves Interviews.

5   Edmond Lee Browning (hereafter cited as ELB), recounted these meetings on the occasion of the election of Richard S. O. Chang as bishop of Hawaii. See Browning's, "Hawaii Diocesan Convention and Election Homily," October 20, 2006, Browning Collection.

6   Nadine W. Scott, letter to ELB, May 6, 1976, Browning Collection.

7   David Kennedy, letter to ELB, May 5, 1976, Browning Collection.

8   Harry S. Kennedy, letter to ELB, May 1976, Browning Collection.

9   Herb Conley, letter to cathedral congregation, n.d. [ca. May 1976], Browning Collection.

10   Pat Hunter, "Aloha, Medieval Tradition Mark Induction of Bishop," *The Honolulu Advertiser,* August 2, 1976.

11   Nadine W. Scott, "Browning Enthroned as Bishop," *Honolulu Star-Bulletin,* August 2, 1976.

12   David Tong, "Browning Asks Laity to Get Involved," *The Honolulu Advertiser,* November 6, 1976.

13   "Bishop Opens Episcopal Convention," *Honolulu Star-Bulletin,"* November 6, 1976.

14   Janice Wolf, "Bishop-to-be a Pastor Type and a Thinker," *Honolulu Star Advertiser,* July 28, 1976.

15   *Honolulu Star-Bulletin,* "Bishop Opens Episcopal Convention."

16   Ibid.

17   John Lockwood, interview by Sheryl Kujawa-Holbrook (hereafter cited as SKH), April 2009.

18   ELB, interview by SKH, January 2009.

19   ELB, "Hawaii Diocesan Convention and Election Homily."

20   "We Talk with the Church's New 'First Lady,'" *Journal of Women's Ministries* 3, no. 2 (Fall 1986): 3.

21   Jan and Paula Rudinoff, interview by SKH, March 2009.

22   Hollinshead T. Knight, interview by SKH, September 2009.

23   Pat Hunter, "Episcopal Bishop Calls for Policy on Alcoholism," *Honolulu Advertiser,* March 26, 1977.

24   Nadine W. Scott, "Browning Brings Challenge to Hawaii Diocese," *Honolulu Star-Bulletin,* September 7, 1985.

25 David Tong, "Browning Asks Laity to Get Involved."

26 ELB, *A Year of Days with the Book of Common Prayer* (New York: Ballantine Books, 1997), July 21.

27 John Paul Engelcke, "Interview with Edmond Lee Browning," *The Living Church,* June 2, 1985.

28 Ibid.

29 Sarah T. Moore, "Bishop Presses Church on Social Issues," *The Observer,* La Grande, Oregon, August 3, 1985.

30 Biographies of the Nominees for Bishop, Diocese of Hawaii, collected files.

31 Grieves Interviews.

32 For a discussion of Browning's view on the military see, "Interview with Bishop Edmond Lee Browning, *The Living Church,* June 2, 1985.

33 *Honolulu Star-Bulletin,* "Bishop Opens Episcopal Convention."

34 Moore, "Bishop Presses Church on Social Issues."

35 ELB, "Sermon to Hawaii's Diocesan Convention at St. Michael and All Angels," in *No Outcasts,* 212.

36 Moore, "Bishop Presses Church on Social Issues."

37 Ibid.

38 Ibid.

39 "Bishops' Letter Evokes Wide Response," Episcopal News Service (hereafter cited as ENS), January 14, 1982.

40 Engelcke, "Interview with Edmond Lee Browning;" Scott, "Browning Brings Challenge to Hawaii Diocese."

41 An account of the service can be found at David Nyhan, "Even in Honolulu: No Ducking Fairness Issue," *The Boston Globe,* n.d. [ca 1984], Browning Collection.

42 See reports of the ENS for the period, including December 7, 1977; October 16, 1980; January 14, 1982; April 1, 1982; July 8, 1982; January 13, 1983.

43 "Team Ends Tour, Will Report to Runcie," ENS, November 3, 1983.

44 "Budget, Church Abroad Claim Council Time," ENS, November 23, 1983; "Belize, Namibia Draw Sympathy of Council," ENS, November 23, 1983.

45 Nadine W. Scott, "Browning Evokes Browning in Final Address to Convention," *Honolulu Star-Bulletin,* n.d. [ca. November 1985], Browning Collection.

46 David Sumner, *The Episcopal Church's History, 1945-1985* (Wilton, Conn.: Morehouse-Barlow, 1987), 196-197.

47 Tom Van Culin, letter to SKH, February 3, 2009.

48 Ibid.

49 Ibid.

50 "Browning: Top Choice," *The Honolulu Advertiser,"* September 11, 1985.

51 Jack Shoemaker, letter to SKH, January 25, 2009.

52 Jack Shoemaker, interview by SKH, March 2009.

53 Scott, "Browning Evokes Browning."

Chapter 5

No Outcasts
1985-1986

I HAVE TODAY INVITED YOU, all of you, to share
the diversity of views, of hopes, of expectations
for the mission of this Church. I want to be very
clear—this Church of ours is open to all—there
will be no outcasts—the convictions and hopes of
all will be honored. [1]

> — Edmond Lee Browning,
> Acceptance Speech,
> Anaheim, California,
> September 12, 1985

THERE IS PAIN beyond these cathedral walls
which most of us can barely comprehend. [2]

> — Edmond Lee Browning,
> Installation Address,
> Washington, D.C.,
> January 11, 1986

Shortly before his election as the twenty-fourth presiding
bishop of the Episcopal Church at the age of 56, Ed
Browning had a dream, a vision really, where his father
appeared to him. "I dreamed of my father, a troubled man

who died of alcoholism. Full of light he came to me and said: 'I am well. I am healed. I am okay. Tell your mother I will be with you and her at the cathedral.' " The dream had an enormous impact on Ed Browning and assured him that the father who had missed many of the major events of his life, like his wedding and ordination, was not only healed, but was still with him in spirit. Browning repeated the story during significant events throughout his ministry as presiding bishop. To him the dream was an experience of transfiguration, of transformation—a sign of God's presence amid struggle, an affirmation of the hope of the resurrection.

Yet as significant as the experience was, Browning did not immediately assume that he was going to be elected presiding bishop at the General Convention in Anaheim, California. In fact, when the time came to leave Hawaii for California and the convention, he left his file folder on the presiding bishop nominating committee at the diocesan office in Honolulu. "I actually thought one of the other candidates was going to be elected," he said. "My ego needs were met when I was nominated. Actually being elected was not what I anticipated." During the election in Anaheim, Browning voted for one of the other nominees, expecting another man would assume the office of presiding bishop. [3] Yet in August 1985, two weeks before the election, a member of the deputation from the Diocese of Hawaii was quoted in a local newspaper saying that the national office considered Browning a front-runner. [4] The newspaper of the Diocese of Rochester also listed Browning as a favorite: "Edmond Browning of Hawaii, a middle-of-the-road alternative without much political or geographical baggage, will probably be the pre-convention favorite," the account read. [5] However, Dick Chang, then

Browning's canon to the ordinary in Hawaii, confirmed that the candidate himself believed he would return to the islands. "There was a ten-year planning process in place, and we were in the process of launching new programs," he said.[6]

A More Diverse
Joint Nominating Committee

The nominating committee chosen to select candidates for presiding bishop was a unique one. Unlike previous election committees confined to the House of Bishops, the Joint Nominating Committee that put together the slate for the 1985 election consisted of nine bishops, nine presbyters, and nine lay persons, and thus was widely representative of the church. Two-thirds of the committee was from the House of Deputies, and these members included for the first time two women. John Coburn, bishop of Massachusetts and former president of the House of Deputies, served as chair. (In his early days in the House of Bishops, Browning had actually nominated Coburn, still a priest, for the office of presiding bishop and was promptly ruled out of order.) The search committee claimed that never before in the history of the Episcopal Church had candidates for presiding bishop been so thoroughly screened. After a process of several years, the slate of nominees was announced to the church in the spring of 1985, shortly before the General Convention in Anaheim.

As early as 1983 *The Witness* published an article entitled "Our Ideal New Presiding Bishop." In it was asked the following question: What characteristics would you like to see in the new presiding bishop of the Episcopal Church? The question was answered by leaders of seven of the constituencies served by the magazine: women, blacks, Hispanics, Asian Americans, the gay and lesbian community, the Episcopal Peace Fellowship, and the Episcopal Urban Caucus. Responses were forwarded to the secretary of the Joint Nominating Committee, Charles M. Crump, of Memphis. Overall, the constituencies responded that they hoped the new presiding bishop would have a global vision. They also sought "an effectual advocate of peace; a leader rooted in the gospel; a person of the spirit; a prophetic reconciler; one familiar with the theology of liberation."[7] Byron Rushing of Boston, acting executive director of the Episcopal Urban Caucus, proposed the need for a structural change. He argued that the House of Bishops was far too restrictive a group to propose a representative slate of nominees. Instead, Rushing proposed separating the office of the presiding bishop of the House of Bishops from the office of president of the Episcopal Church. "Let the House of Bishops elect their leader; in 1997 let us all elect a president of the Episcopal Church," wrote Rushing.[8] Another respondent, Marsha J. Langford of Pasadena, the president of Integrity, argued that the new presiding bishop needed to respond to the realities of the 1980s, including gay and lesbian people, women in changing roles, upwardly mobile blacks and Hispanics, and families in transition, regardless of the risks involved. "As 'Chief Shepherd,' the presiding bishop must be sensitive to these needs through listening and praying with his people so that he can articulate what the Spirit is calling us to become in the 1980s."[9]

Browning considered his inclusion in the list of nominees not only an honor for Patti and himself, but for the Diocese of Hawaii that they had been privileged to serve for almost ten years. In addition to Ed Browning, the nominees included bishops John T. Walker of Washington, William C. Frey of Colorado, and Furman C. Stough of Alabama. Walker was strongly identified with urban ministry, his contacts in Washington, D.C., and his fund-raising expertise on major projects, such as Washington National Cathedral. Frey was identified with the charismatic movement and known for his work on the church's peace committee. Stough, also recognized for his fund-raising abilities, was active in the civil rights movement in the early 1960s and was an outspoken critic of capital punishment. For the first time all the nominees had overseas missionary experience. All the nominees were born in the South and all were considered more "liberal" than Presiding Bishop John Maury Allin. Walker was the first African American nominee and, if elected, would have been the first African American presiding bishop of the Episcopal Church. [10]

Browning had personal ties to each of the other three nominees. Bill Stough was an old friend from seminary. He and his wife Margaret were godparents to Ed and Patti's son John and had presided at many family weddings. Browning and Bill Frey had been elected bishops at the same General Convention in 1967 when the House of Bishops chose all overseas bishops. Walker and Browning had been allies in social activism for many years in the House of Bishops. Thus there was a sense of camaraderie among the nominees during the six months leading up to convention, built from long years of friendship, although each man had his own pressures during the process.

Browning reported moments of "fantasy" and "terror" about the possibility of his election. By the time of the election itself his feelings had somewhat shifted, as he had grown more confident of God's grace throughout the process. "I'm scared," Browning said in the first live interview after his election, "but I know I have the prayers of the church and that means a tremendous lot to me." [11] He said it was ultimately Patti's love and support that helped him through the process. While it has been suggested that some of the other nominees were deeply affected by not being elected, such feelings were not shared publicly and the official sentiments were upbeat and supportive. "The church is in good hands. We have elected a super presiding bishop," said Bill Frey after the election. "I haven't lost anything. I get to go back to the place and job I love best—being bishop of Colorado." [12]

Feelings of disappointment ran high among some of John Walker's supporters, particularly in the black community. Some took the defeat as proof that despite all the rhetoric to the contrary, the racism long present in the Episcopal Church was such that the House of Bishops was simply unable to elect the man many considered the leading candidate. At the time African Americans were highly visible throughout the leadership of the Episcopal Church. Soon after his election as presiding bishop, John Allin had conceded to all the requests of the Union of Black Episcopalians, including the establishment of the Office of Black Ministries. Over twenty African Americans were on the staff at the Episcopal Church Center in New York. Charles R. Lawrence's tenure as the first African American president of the House of Deputies assured that black Episcopalians were members of all the committees and commissions of the church. John Walker was instrumental in introducing the new presiding bishop to the black caucus after the election, and Browning later appointed him vice-president of the House of Bishops. [13]

Anaheim 1985

Ed Browning was elected presiding bishop on September 10, 1985, on the fourth day of the convention, on the fourth ballot in a closed session of the House of Bishops, meeting near the Anaheim Convention Center at St. Michael's Episcopal Church. Two hundred bishops, a record number, participated in the election. Browning received concurrence in the House of Deputies almost immediately. No deputies stepped forward to debate his election and only one deputy cast a dissenting vote.

When the names of all the candidates had been placed in nomination on September 9 before the joint houses, no nominations were made from the floor. The actual election in the House of Bishops was conducted in closed session, but the drama of the first election of a presiding bishop since 1973 was later recounted by the bishops present and by Browning himself. At the guarded election site, the House of Bishops began at 7:30 a.m. with a eucharist celebrated by Bishop Allin, who preached on the text of David and Goliath, remembering how David "came to play" in the battle against the giant, and the Son of David in whose name the church gathers. After the first two ballots did not yield a clear majority, the bishops broke for breakfast at the church. Allin was aware that the House of Deputies was not scheduled to convene until 10:00 a.m., and thus thought it important to stretch the election process out. Although Allin himself had been elected on the second ballot, there was a sense in the House of Bishops that the 1985 election was going to take longer, yet the mood in the room was also described as "warm, unified, and relaxed." Bishops were instructed by the presiding bishop not to give details of the actual ballots, although it was reported that John Walker was "a strong candidate until the very end. All four bishops had strong support."

By his own admission and by the observation of those seated near him, Ed Browning grew teary after the third ballot. After the fourth ballot, the election of Edmond Lee Browning was announced and the House of Bishops broke into spontaneous applause. [14] "Ed was sitting right behind me," said Alden Hathaway, retired bishop of Pittsburgh. "When the results were announced his eyes filled with tears and he gasped. I saw the weight of the mantle land on him at the moment." [15] Shortly after his election in the House of Bishops, Browning was briefly left alone outside St. Michael's in a daze, soon to be joined by an executive from the Episcopal Church Center with a large loose-leaf notebook set for his first briefing. His new public ministry had begun. [16]

After the election in the House of Bishops, the action moved to the House of Deputies for concurrence. At 10:45 a.m., two deputies carrying a purple helium-filled balloon appeared on the podium. Charles Lawrence was in the chair and referred the results of the election to the Committee on the Consecration of Bishops, who then convened to consider their recommendation. In the meantime, George Shields, chair of Dispatch of Business, removed the purple balloon from the podium, saying, "I believe I'll retire this until we take our action." Nine minutes later the committee returned and announced the "unanimous recommendation for concurrence with the election of *Edward* Lee Browning," unintentionally citing an incorrect first name. There was no debate. Thirty minutes later Ed and Patti Browning appeared in the House of Deputies wearing Hawaiian leis in the company of the delegations of the Diocese of Hawaii to the convention and to Triennial. Browning acknowledged the standing ovation with the Hawaiian hand gesture meaning "hang loose." "We hope you will accept this office," Lawrence said. After some brief remarks praising the other candidates, Browning replied, "I do believe I am here because of the will of God. I offer you a ministry of servanthood for the whole church." [17]

September 10, 1985 was also Ed and Patti Browning's thirty-second wedding anniversary. During the election, Patti was sequestered at the hotel with the other candidates' wives and family members. The first sign that the election was over was a knock on the door from another candidate's daughter, who said that *her* father had been elected. Imagine Patti's surprise then, when she got the call that the presiding bishop-elect was her husband! Still in shock, and dazed for several days after the election, both Ed and Patti accepted the election with their characteristic deep faith and cautious optimism. "I can't quite believe it's happened," Patti said after the election. [18] Ed himself held it together emotionally until they were ushered into a back room where the delegations from Hawaii had gathered to greet them. "Then I broke down," he said. While both the Brownings were aware of the awesome responsibility that the office of presiding bishop would hold for them for the next twelve years, they were also saddened at having to leave their life and ministry in Hawaii. "It will be hard—so very hard—to leave the wonderful people of Hawaii," said Patti Browning, "even though we are all excited and proud at this new turn in our lives." [19]

The election initiated another long move for the Brownings, this time back to the East Coast, and brought with it the realization that the family would no longer be living in close proximity to one another. "One thing I know is going to be hard," said Patti, "is that none of the family will be with us. We are a very close family." [20]At the time of the election most of the Browning children lived in Hawaii and all lived in the West: Mark was a deputy prosecutor in the Hawaii attorney general's office, Paige had just completed architecture school, Philip was in his third year of medical school, Peter worked as a counselor in a home for abused children in California and was considering seminary, and John was a senior at the Iolani School and the number two ranked doubles player in Hawaiian tennis. Until John started college in California, Patti would remain in the family home in Hawaii. Among Patti's hopes at the time of the election was to have some time to pursue new directions of her own, such as painting, going back to school, or exploring ministries in which she had interest but no time for in the past. "My ministry has been as a wife and mother," she said, "to maintain the stability of the home because he had to be away so much." [21] Well prepared for a life of travel, Patti looked forward to traveling with Ed, something she was not free to do during their previous ministries.

Not all the Browning adult children met the news of the election with undiluted pleasure. Mark, the oldest, was against his father's participation in the election from the beginning. Sensing the stress of the job and the likelihood of negative media attention, Mark was concerned that the enormous pressure would shorten his father's life by a decade. He was also concerned about the move to New York "and how it would break up the family." [22] Browning's call to Mark with the news of the election was not a happy one. When Ed and Patti returned to Hawaii after the convention, Mark was not among the throng of excited greeters. The other Browning siblings—Paige, Philip, Peter and John—felt more positive about the election and accepted it with less reservation, although all were aware that the event would have an impact on family life and at times bring added stress to their parents. "I've just come from talking with most of them," said Browning in reference to his children during the first interview after his election, "and they are happy, but they also have mixed feelings about it. We are very close and I think they're concerned about how that closeness is going to be lived out now." [23] "I think the kids felt that with the move to Hawaii the family finally had a stable home, and now that was gone," said Dick Chang in his reflections of the family during election time. [24] Peter Browning said that of course he was proud of his father, "but I didn't need this to be proud of my father. I have always been proud of him." [25] Early in their term in office Ed and Patti Browning made a commitment to invite each of their five children along on an official visit to share something of the ministry of the presiding bishop; four of the siblings did accompany their parents on an official visit.

Cora Mae Browning, Ed's mother, took the news of her son's election in stride. "I was delighted, but not surprised," she said. "I have always felt that he would do great things." But Ed's youngest brother, Ben Browning, was amazed. "My wife, Sally, and I had gone to the convention not thinking Ed had a chance of being elected," he said. "When I heard the news, I started crying; I just couldn't believe it."[26] At home in Taft, Texas, Patti's parents, Walter and Lyra Sparks, took some time to absorb the news. "I always thought that he would get it; he has so much going for him," said Lyra Sparks. "But I am still trying to absorb the realization," she said. "We have another daughter in New York, and this will make visits a lot easier, as New York is awfully far away."[27]

Church press accounts of the election were overwhelmingly positive and laudatory. It was clear that the church was optimistic about its new presiding bishop and that many were anxious to move forward with him in a spirit of unity and mutual cooperation. The chair of the nominating committee, John Coburn, said, "There emerged a sense of complete unity when the decision was announced." "It was a very happy event," said Paul Moore, Jr., bishop of New York. Browning was seen as a "unifying figure" by many bishops. "He'll have the vision of John Hines and the collegial style of John Allin," said one bishop. "He won't be a daring charismatic figure who will lead the charge into the dusty trails." Bishops tended to downplay the political significance of the election, instead praising Ed Browning's international experience and awareness of diversity, although later in his term some of those same bishops became opponents. "Now that we have covered many of the controversial issues, we are ready to go about the mission of the church, said Donald M. Hultstrand, bishop of Springfield. "There was a time when we felt there were parties in the church. Not now. We aren't thinking in terms of factions or parties." "This wasn't a political election," said William C. Wantland, bishop of Eau Claire. "What we have done is choose a new spiritual leader for the church."[28] Joseph T. Heistand, bishop of Arizona, objected to the label of "liberal" used by the media to describe the new presiding bishop-elect. "Bishop Browning is a Christian," he wrote to his diocese shortly after the election, "a disciple who is completely committed to our Lord and who has demonstrated in his life and actions that he has taken up the Cross of Christ and is willing to give his life completely to the Cause of Jesus." [29]

At the time of his election, at least some were aware of Ed Browning's commitment to the roles of pastor *and* prophet and knew his track record well enough to predict that he would exercise both roles. "He was the first choice of many of the House of Bishops and the second choice of almost everyone, a fact that resulted in his election on an early ballot," said Gerald McAllister, bishop of Oklahoma. McAllister, a friend of Browning from the days they both had served on the staff at Camp Capers, referred to the new presiding bishop-elect as "the little red caboose," after a favorite camp song. Announcing his joy at witnessing the election, McAllister gave this appraisal of Browning's ministry: "Ed Browning is a man of compassion who seeks inclusion rather than exclusion for all sorts and conditions. He will take some unpopular stands in obedience to his prophetic role." [30] Another longtime friend, who ministered with both Ed and Patti Browning in Okinawa, Bill Heffner, said, "God was shaping Edmond Browning in the crucible of the mission field. The basic ingredients were there: a deep and abiding faith expressed in a buoyant love for God and fellow man, a true sense of what Jesus was talking about when he spoke of servanthood, and the courage to witness and to be a prophet when the occasion called for it." [31]

David Rose, retired bishop of Southern Virginia and a mentor to Ed Browning since 1948, was one of the few commentators who ventured to suggest that perhaps during his twelve-year term as presiding bishop, Ed Browning would not be deeply spiritual or personally cheery every day. Confident that his former acolyte at The Church of the Good Shepherd, Corpus Christi, was "on solid ground," Rose spoke from his own experience of the man behind the role. "It would be a mistake in this personal review to paint our new presiding bishop as a plastic saint. His impatience will show; his disappoints, hurts, and his temper will surface; his fatigue will show in stooped shoulders—but not often." [32]

Maury Maverick, a columnist for the *San Antonio Express-News*, in an article entitled "Cheers for 'Red' Browning," was pleased that among the first people Browning called after his election was his mentor and friend, the retired bishop of West Texas, Everett Jones. "That a younger man in the high flush of victory would remember an older man who gave him a helping hand along the road of life says something," wrote Maverick. [33] Bishop Jones said that he believed Ed Browning was going to be "above all else" a good pastor as presiding bishop. "This has been his strength wherever he has served," he said. Jones also took exception to press reports that labeled Browning "a liberal." "This is true if we go back to the first definition in the dictionary: 'one who is favorable to progress and reform.' It is not true if we expect him to promote a fixed political agenda." [34]

John Shelby Spong wrote extensively about Ed Browning's election in an article entitled "A World Citizen Presiding Bishop," and there commented on his pastoral style and prophetic vision:

He is not a powerful orator, a brilliant scholar, or a facile politician. Until his election as the twenty-fourth Presiding Bishop of the Episcopal Church, he was generally regarded as a moderate or centrist who tilted toward the liberal side of the aisle. That was more a commentary on his style than his substance....On Central America, South Africa, the ordination of women to the priesthood and episcopacy, and gay rights, this man is a liberal who is consistent, courageous, and willing to risk controversy and disaffection in order to bear witness to the citadels of power. His liberalism does not erupt in waves of passion polarizing the opposition. It is rather transmitted through the sensitivity of one who is first and foremost a pastor, and it is grounded in a personal security that makes others comfortable in his presence. [35]

Spong suggested that the election of Browning as presiding bishop was "a daring choice. Bishop Browning is a citizen of the world in a way no previous presiding bishop has ever been." [36]

Members of the House of Deputies interviewed shortly after the Browning election articulated a variety of opinions on the candidate's suitability for the office. Many appreciated his warmth and approachability, his keen listening skills, and his prophetic vision. "The church now has a person who combines openness, sensitivity to people, and prophetic vision—a powerful combination," said F. Sanford Cutler of the Diocese of Newark. "His will be a servant ministry which will articulate a vision for the church and for the global village which is our world," said Marjorie Christie, also of Newark. Charles Lawrence, the first African American president of the House of Deputies, expressed his "delight" in the results of the election. Other deputies and bishops yearned for a presiding bishop who would have a calming influence: "Bishop Browning will bring an era of stability—something greatly needed after years of upheaval." [37]

National media were quick to pick up on Browning's election as a move to the left of the current Episcopal Church leadership, at times offering sharp contrasts between the views of the presiding-bishop elect and his predecessor John Allin. Allin's election in 1973 was seen as the result of backlash against then presiding bishop John Hines and the General Convention Special Program of 1967, a controversial initiative designed to increase the economic and political power of marginalized groups, specifically people of color. Allin's administration, in contrast, was described as focused on two ecclesiastical events: the adoption of the new *Book of Common Prayer*, which he supported, and the ordination of women to the priesthood, which he opposed. A *Time* magazine article, "Opting for the Browning Version," dated within two weeks of the election, cited the presiding-bishop elect's support of women's ordination and inclusive language. The article also highlighted Browning's role in 1979 as one of the twenty bishops who filed a fervent dissent against the position that it is inappropriate for the church to ordain practicing homosexuals. "I would hope," Browning told *Time* at the time of his election, "we are not frozen in any kind of set belief about homosexuality." [38] At the same time, *Time* magazine quoted a 1985 Gallup poll of Episcopalians which suggested that among laity, 78 percent did not believe it was the role of the church "to be an agent of political change in the United States," and 76 percent stated that the church should focus on "worship and spiritual matters" more than on political issues. Undeterred by pollsters, Browning stated that it is the responsibility of the church to exercise moral leadership in society. "Peace and justice concerns will be a high part of my agenda," he said.[39] He indicated he intended to support many groups in the church and hoped that as his term ended "we will have reflected an openness and will have tried to value all persons, will have tried to be loving without being legalistic, and will have been deeply concerned about some of the issues demeaning persons."[40]

Browning held up the church's prophetic role at his first press conference after the election. Despite comments at the time that suggested the controversial issues were past, Browning steered straight into them, affirming his commitment to diversity and inclusivity. One wonders if those who expected Edmond Lee Browning to steer away from politics and controversial issues knew *who* they were electing, his ministerial record, or even just his nine years in Hawaii. For Ed Browning, the church's prophetic role is inextricably linked to its ministry locally and in the world. The signs that he would not shy away from controversy in the name of justice and unconditionally believed that no one was beyond the pastoral ministry of the church were there from his first statements as presiding bishop-elect. "I have a feeling that the church is becoming more sensitive to the needs of the world," he said, as he defended South African Bishop Desmond Tutu from the criticisms of Jerry Falwell. Disappointed in President Reagan's limited sanctions against apartheid, Browning said, "I think he could have done much more." Admittedly nervous at the crowded press conference—"I've never been in this situation before," he said—the new presiding bishop-elect answered questions on a challenging array of church and world issues with alacrity and clarity. He stated his firm commitment to the ministries of women and gays and lesbians at every level of the church and his willingness to support the continued usage of the 1928 *Book of Common Prayer*, all because the church is in need of many gifts and we should "embrace all people and all cultures."

Contrary to church polls at the time, Browning stated that he believed the church was growing and in the midst of a "serious spiritual renewal." Further, he quickly reversed the position of his predecessor that divorced clergy should seek lay ministries. In Hawaii, Browning said, "we have divorced and remarried clergy. They are among the brightest clergy in office." Lastly, as presiding bishop, he pledged to "listen" to the priorities of the church on every level, thus setting the course of his early ministry in the office. While much was made of the scope of Browning's international experience during the nomination process and after the election, few mentioned that he was hardly a stranger at the Episcopal Church Center in New York. Since the time of his appointment as a missionary to Okinawa, Browning had been directly involved with national church structures, both as an appointee or staff member and as a member of the Executive Council. [41] "I have probably had more jobs than most bishops," Browning told *The Washington Post*, adding that "when I've gone into something new I have tried to listen to where the church was and what the job called for." [42]

"No Outcasts"

Two days after his election as presiding bishop, Browning addressed a joint session of both houses of the General Convention, as well as visitors and the media. The address was in essence his acceptance speech and enabled him to share his views on the matters of importance to the church and his interpretation of his role. If there is one address or sermon that is identified with Edmond Lee Browning, it is this "no outcasts" address given two days after his election. Today, almost twenty-five years later, as I interviewed people around the church for this book, many if not most of the interviewees still remember and quote the phrase "no outcasts." At the time, many people felt that the new presiding bishop was speaking personally to them. For some, it was the powerful recognition after years of marginalization that they, too, were part of the church. For others, it captured their hope that this humble, sensitive, thoughtful man would lead the Episcopal Church to a deeper level of pastoral concern and prophetic justice. For still others, the phrase "no outcasts" succinctly summarized their experience of Ed Browning as a pastor and prophetic leader.

As I talked with people about the vision of "no outcasts," few spoke of what a church open to all would look like or require of its members. I often wondered if others first heard the phrase as I did: grateful that I was no longer an outcast, but also fearful of looking at the other side of the equation. A church open to all would require all to live in community with people they might not agree with and whom they might not befriend personally. A church open to all would be less about being right or wrong than about resisting polarization and struggling to be in relationship, even in trying circumstances.

Traditional institutions tend to operate within defined boundaries with clear membership criteria and within the confines of incremental change. But the vision of a church with "no outcasts" defies narrow institutional definitions. Many organizational experts say that survival in today's global environment requires traditional institutions such as churches to undergo deep change by taking significant risks and venturing into unknown territory. Based on years of experience in environments and pastoral situations where change was frequent and where traditional models of ministry were ineffective, Ed Browning believed that the way to renew and energize the Episcopal Church was to envision it in a more expansive way. The genius of Browning's vision of a church with "no outcasts" was firmly rooted in his understanding of the gospel and in the distinctive Anglican tradition, yet organizationally open and expansive, adaptive to the changes of the postmodern world and responsive to human need.

Much of the history of the Browning administration, and to an extent subsequent administrations, can be interpreted through the lens of "no outcasts," both as a reality and as a goal to attain. When is a person or group or issue beyond the boundaries of a church open to all? Are tumultuous times a sign that the church is straying from its mission or a sign of transformation and renewal? Have the message of the gospel and the richness of tradition become too diluted to be recognizable, or are we interpreting them anew for the present age? Ed Browning himself often asked: Where is the "radical center" of the Episcopal Church? Have we become a church of polarities, and if so, how can we reclaim the middle as "the center?"

"No outcasts" was a touchstone and a reccurring theme of the Browning administration. Within a month of his election Browning had already answered 1,400 pieces of mail. "What I am *for* you terrifies me. *For* you I am your Presiding Bishop elect; but *with* you I am a Christian...." In the address, Browning commited to being a listener, "not just to some of you, but to all of you," and invited the church to enter into the listening process to identify the future church's mission. After the first year of intensive listening, the new presiding bishop committed to sharing the resultant priorities and to making staff appointments based on them. From the outset, Browning made clear that he intended to hire a diverse and multicultural staff and to follow the same course with appointments to committees and commissions. He also announced his intention to work collaboratively with the officers of the House of Deputies and the Executive Council. (At the same convention, David B. Collins, dean emeritus of St. Philip's Cathedral in Atlanta, was elected president of the House of Deputies, succeeding Charles Lawrence, who served from 1976 to 1985. Pamela P. Chinnis, from the Diocese of Washington, a former presiding officer of the Women's Triennial, was elected vice president, the first woman to hold this office.) Further, Browning made clear in his "no outcasts" speech that he intended to build collaborative relationships with *all* the bishops of the church, particularly in preparation for the upcoming Lambeth Conference in 1988.

The deliberate pastoral care of bishops and their families (along with many other church leaders) was a hallmark of the Browning administration. In an interview following his election, he said he thought that the spiritual life was the highest priority for his own ministry as a bishop and for other bishops. Without ongoing spiritual development, he reasoned, a bishop can't assist others. "The spirit never leaves you in one place, in a place of comfort. [The] spirit moves you all the time." [43] Browning considered the pastoral care of bishops one of his primary responsibilities, throughout his years as presiding bishop and beyond. "When I became a bishop, people said, 'It's going to be a lonely job.' It hasn't been a lonely job," he said, adding, "I just pray I can keep that same kind of relationship." Presiding bishop-elect Browning credited his family, and specifically Patti, as his insulation from burnout. "We have a good team ministry." [44]

Browning had a deep sense of empathy and personal responsibility for those called to be bishops. "I hope sincerely," he said in his acceptance speech, "that by the time we arrive in Lambeth that I would have had sufficient time to have met in small numbers with all of them [bishops], so as to develop the kind of relationship that I know I will need to be the kind of pastor I want to be to each member of the house." [45]

Although the new presiding bishop-elect committed to a first year of listening to the church, he also made clear in his acceptance speech that he already had "identity with and solidarity for" some specific national and international concerns and that the Browning administration would be involved in global issues. This section of his address was specific and foreshadowed the Browning administration for the next twelve years. But Browning was also concerned about domestic issues. He saw no distinction between suffering and oppression in the United States and abroad. Moreover, having been the bishop of three jurisdictions, none of which was on the mainland, Browning understood from personal experience the impact of the United States and its policies on people and other countries. Not unlike his stance during seminary and the desegregation of the University of the South, Browning chose to work from inside the church to make it and the country more responsive to the needs of people in the United States and abroad.

In his acceptance speech, Browning pledged the full support of the office of presiding bishop to Desmond Tutu of South Africa. Browning invited Tutu to participate in his installation on January 11, 1986, "so that occasion itself might sacramentally express our love and our support for this man and his people—an expression of our solidarity in the heart of the nation's capital." In addition to pledging his full support of the struggle against apartheid, Browning promised to visit Panama and Central America during his first term in office and to seek self-determination for the dioceses and countries there. Browning also invited the primate of Japan to his installation and expressed his interest in furthering the ministry of the Episcopal Church in the Pacific Basin. Within two days of his election, Browning also sent a telegram to Paul Reeves, primate of New Zealand, in support of his witness for a nuclear-free Pacific. Browning's position on the nuclear arms race, strengthened by his earlier visit to the Hiroshima memorial, was well known in Hawaii. "I said then, and I affirm now, that I believe the production, testing, and deployment of nuclear, chemical, and biological weapons to be inconsistent with the Gospel of Jesus Christ," he stated in his acceptance speech.[46] Browning went on to name world hunger and the plight of rural America as concerns and commended the work of the Urban Bishops Coalition and the Episcopal Urban Caucus in the nation's cities.

Perhaps the most theologically important aspect of Browning's first major address to the church as presiding bishop-elect was his statement about the relationship between the pastoral and the prophetic aspects of ministry. Browning said he saw his role primarily as that of a pastor, but that he would continue to speak out about issues of peace and justice. Browning used his acceptance speech to state how he viewed pastoral ministry:

> In the several interviews I've had during the past 48 hours—one of the subjects that has been constant was the relationship between the pastoral and the prophetic—as though they were mutually exclusive. For me there could be nothing further from the truth—there is no question in my mind—however uncomfortable it becomes—the Gospel of Jesus Christ requires a pastoral ministry which leads to prophetic witness and action. And I will pledge to you the exercise of both![47]

The Installation

Edmond Lee Browning was installed as the twenty-fourth presiding bishop of the Episcopal Church on January 11, 1986, at the National Cathedral of St. Peter and St. Paul in Washington, D.C. It was the first time a presiding bishop had been installed within the context of the Holy Eucharist, and with Browning at the altar were the newly retired twenty-third presiding bishop, John Allin; John T. Walker, bishop of Washington; John M. Watanabe, primate of Japan; and Desmond Tutu, bishop of Johannesburg. Joseph Ferrario, Roman Catholic bishop of Hawaii and a longtime friend of Browning, presented him with the Bible. Retired presiding bishop John Hines was also present. Estimates of the attendance for the three-hour service vary; between 3,200 and 4,000 people overflowed the cathedral. Close to 200 family, friends, and church members from Hawaii flew to Washington for the installation. The service began with a chanted Hawaiian prayer; anthurium and ginger decorated the cathedral. Many visitors from Hawaii wore leis. One of the communion hymns was the "Queen's Prayer," written by Queen Liliuokalani. [48]

Browning wanted to make the installation not only his celebration, but also an opportunity for all the baptized to celebrate and affirm the ministry of the church. Celebrating the ministry of all the baptized was to remain an important theme throughout the Browning administration.

Browning received a great deal of mail imploring him to stay out of politics and lead the church back to the way it had been (or was remembered to have been) in the 1950s, or at least avoid controversy. For instance, newspaper columnist Smith Hempstone, from Charleston, South Carolina, a former Sewanee classmate of Browning's, suggested in a "Views and Opinions" column dated the day after the installation that the "trouble" in the Episcopal Church actually began in the 1960s with John Hines, "a good but misguided man," who "set out to make the Episcopal Church trendier than thou." Hempstone argued that despite a church that prided itself on diversity and pluralism, a wave of intolerance against traditionalists had been troubling the church since the Hines administration and needed to be addressed:

> Those of us who do not think the church should become an ecclesiastical version of Common Cause, who are unsure about the ordination of women and have reservations about the ordination of practicing homosexuals, who love the 1928 *Book of Common Prayer,* have been branded racists, sexists and reactionaries.
>
> We are none of these things. We are traditionalists who cherish our heritage, love our traditions

and honor our past. We will accept progress, but
we will oppose change for the sake of change. Give
us back our church, Red, and you will be remembered as a good shepherd of your flock. [49]

Hempstone's analysis positions the origin of the
intense friction between traditionalist and progressive
Episcopalians as having begun between 1967 and 1970,
with the controversial General Convention Special Program. While issues such as Prayer Book revision, the
ordination of women, and the ordination of gay and
lesbian people certainly exacerbated the tension, Hempstone and other traditionalist commentators had not
forgotten that the General Convention Special Program
initiative had aimed to make available nine million
dollars in grant money from the church's budget to non-
church organizations aimed at eradicating poverty and
social injustice. Although Hines was optimistic about the
program as a compromise made in response to the Black
Manifesto's call for reparations, the program was a source
of controversy among members of Executive Council and
other church leaders from the beginning. Council members were opposed out of principle to any grants program
that would send funds into a diocese without the consent of the diocesan bishop. On a deeper level, beyond
the polity concerns, there was genuine fear that the
church was funding black separatist organizations rather
than groups focused on racial reconciliation and cooperation. Hines had tried to steer the church through a
middle way, between conservatives who stressed only the
"vertical dimension" of the faith and radicals who sought
to tear down institutional Christianity. Eventually Hines
and other church leaders were caught between two polarized groups: those who believed the church should be

concerned primarily with spiritual matters and those who saw the church as leading social revolution.[50]

Hempstone made a point to say that he disagreed with Hines about the efficacy of giving money to some of the people who received grants, and that while the bishop appeared unconcerned about the money involved, local church people felt differently. "But it did bother the man in the pew, who closed his wallet and found another church (or none) with more congenial practices."[51] The Allin administration figures interestingly into the discussion. Allin supporters characterize his leadership as that of a reconciler, who kept the church together despite the fact that issues such as Prayer Book revision and the ordination of women continued to cause controversy. Others view John Allin as indecisive, one who avoided making judgments on controversial issues. Hempstone's appraisal of John Allin fell into the latter camp, judging him "a good man but an indecisive one. So the drift toward secular liberalism continued with the adoption of *The 1979 Book of Common Prayer*."[52]

During his term as presiding bishop, Ed Browning did not find that John Allin was always his staunchest supporter. Although his predecessor was not involved on a daily basis and the two were always cordial in public, Browning sometimes got the idea that Allin shared the views of his detractors. Allin once signed an official letter lambasting the presiding bishop. Browning called him on it and Allin admitted he had not even read the letter. Still, the two men shared the experience of the office of presiding bishop, which gave them plenty to talk about. Once, in an airport coffee shop on the way home from John Hines's funeral in 1997, the two commiserated over the difficulties in obtaining a decent official portrait. It was one of several reconciling meetings between the two men. Although John Allin was eventually satisfied with his official portrait, Ed Browning wasn't quite so fortunate. "I used to think you were the vainest man in the church," Browning kidded Allin about his efforts to obtain a suitable portrait. "I'm working on my third," Browning wryly admitted to his predecessor. [53]

At the time of his election in 1985, Ed Browning had inherited not only the controversial issues of his two immediate predecessors, but also the polarizing labels of "conservative" and "liberal" Episcopalians and a large number of folk who did not feel they fit in either camp. Not one to create conflict for the fun of it, Browning was also not one to back off from what he saw as his responsibility or the responsibility of the church. His vision of a church with "no outcasts" was one of standing with those who experienced suffering and injustice in the world. At the same time, he saw those who disagreed with him as part of the church and his vision as well. Navigating cultural diversity, gender differences, theological opinions, and differences in sexual identity defined much of Browning's ministry as presiding bishop. He saw himself as a pastor first, and out of that role came prophetic responsibility. He valued the sacredness of every human being and was thus reluctant to label people or support polarization. "It is because we seek the face of Christ in all humanity that I am called to challenge anything that desecrates the creation and denigrates personhood," was his vocational statement in the installation address. [54]

Ed Browning's pastoral gifts—the ability to listen, his approachability, his self-deprecating sense of humor— allowed him to enter into volatile situations on a different level than more ideological leaders. With the advantage of hindsight, his approach to the role of presiding bishop was a compromise between that of John Hines and John Allin. "He [John Hines] was a source of great inspiration to me, and I am deeply appreciative of his being here today," said Browning at his installation. "It has also been a privilege to serve under Bishop Allin, and I hope my own ministry will reflect the gifts I have received from both." [55] Throughout his term of office, Browning maintained the role he knew best from his years in ministry—that of pastor—and he exercised his authority as presiding bishop with an openness of temperament and clarity of vision.

As events unfolded over the course of the next twelve years, Ed Browning defined his role as presiding bishop with great consistency. During tumultuous times, Browning's efforts to maintain a pastoral presence and to conduct business with openness and clarity were met with appreciation by those who felt secure in his leadership and had a sense that the church is bigger than its controversies. Alternatively, his reluctance to polarize further and to disavow people for their opinions, theological or otherwise, irritated other more ideological leaders. The harmony heard on the occasion of his election at times disintegrated into accusations that Browning was out to please everybody or that one group or another felt outcast because he did not agree with them. This was not his intent. "Let no one be alarmed when I am seen with compromised and dangerous people, on the left and on the right. Let no one bind me to a group. My door, my heart, must be open to everyone, absolutely everyone," quoted Browning in his installation address, from the words of Dom Helder Camara. [56]

Ed Browning's installation address attempted to explain his pastoral role within a prophetic vision of the church. In the address he was clear that as presiding bishop he belonged exclusively to no group and that as a prophet he felt called to respond to the gospel in the context of the world as it is. "The Christian imperative" compels us to "enter into the pain and sufferings of others, and to identify with the brokenness of the world." Throughout the address Browning called the whole church to live into a "compassionate spirituality," rooted in baptism, the basis of all Christian spirituality and mission:

> There is pain beyond these cathedral walls which most of us can barely comprehend. There are tears of despair, which we refuse to see. There are cries for help, which we do not hear. There are those reaching out to be embraced, whom we will not touch. But a compassionate Jesus saw; he heard and he embraced them. I want to say to you this morning that our spiritual lives are bankrupt if our prayers do not call us to see, to hear, and to heal. So I say again that compassion is the basis of our spiritual lives that gives hope to a suffering world. [57]

One journalist pointed out that Browning used the words "compassion" and "compassionate" twenty-four times in his address. [58]

Immediately after the service, Ed and Patti Browning and their family attended a press conference for nearly one hundred journalists. There he said he was very serious about wanting to "find a sense of mission that is ours." A related theme he stressed was the need for the church "to become more in the role of advocate in influencing legislation on behalf of the poor." Browning said, "Resolutions do not always carry the day. Sitting down with people of influence is terribly important. It is necessary for people in those positions to get to know the presiding bishop." [59]

At the press conference Browning also said that he had asked the archbishop of Canterbury, Robert Runcie, to place the ordination of women to the episcopacy on the agenda for the next primates' meeting, although he did not expect the discussion to end there. When asked about evangelism, Browning said that it was integral to the mission of the church, but that he was not about to attract members to the Episcopal Church by making comparisons with rapidly growing conservative Protestant churches. "I think the Episcopal Church has a calling to uphold the value of human dignity," he said, "and if we are obedient to that end, I think God will bless us." [60]

The final question of the press conference asked Browning about the impact on his family since the election. After expressing his gratitude for their continuing support, he said, "I've had a lot of moments of sheer terror. They have increased. But in a real way, people have said all my life, 'You are in my prayers,' but I never thought more about the meaning of that than in the last months." [61] In his final statement Browning shared his thoughts on the years ahead:

> When I left Hawaii I asked them to pray that in seeking to interpret the great issues that face us in the light of the Gospel, I be able to maintain my sense of integrity and, in the process, to maintain the unity of the church. I am not sure just how it is to be done, but I know that it is imperative that we both affirm our diversity and maintain our unity. This is the understanding that has come to me since my election, and it is for this that I ask your prayers. [62]

Chapter Five Notes

1   Edmond Lee Browning (hereafter cited as ELB), "Address to the General Convention, Joint Session," September 12, 1985.

2   ELB, "Installation Address," January 11, 1986, *Washington Diocese*, February/March 1986; also, in *No Outcasts: the Public Witness of Edmond L. Browning, XXIVth Presiding Bishop of the Episcopal Church*, ed. Brian J. Grieves (Cincinnati: Forward Movement, 1997), 21-25.

3   ELB, interview by Sheryl Kujawa-Holbrook (hereafter cited as SKH), January 2009.

4   "Hawaii In Spotlight at Episcopal Convention," *The Garden Island*, August 30, 1985.

5   Ibid.

6   Richard S. O. Chang, interview by SKH, March 2009.

7   "Our Ideal New Presiding Bishop," *The Witness* 66, no. 2 (February 1983): 10.

8   Byron Rushing, "Church Needs a President," *The Witness* 66, no. 2 (February 1983): 12.

9   Marsha J. Langford, "'80s Issues Demand Risk," *The Witness* 66, no. 2 (February 1983): 15.

10   Joseph Berger, "Episcopalians to Choose New Leader," *The New York Times*, September 7, 1985.

11   Leonard Freeman, "Personal Interview with Presiding Bishop-elect," Convention Video News Program, September 10, 1985.

12   Virginia Culver, "Hawaii Bishop Voted Top Episcopal Leader," *The Denver Post*, September 11, 1985.

13   Edward W. Rodman, interview by SKH, February 2009; Harold T. Lewis, *Yet With A Steady Beat: the African American Struggle for Recognition in the Episcopal Church* (Valley Forge: Trinity Press International, 1996), 166-167.

14   "Browning Elected 24th Presiding Bishop," Episcopal News Service (hereafter cited as ENS), September 19, 1985.

15   Alden Hathaway, interview by SKH, March 2009.

16   News clipping, n.d. [ca. 1986], Browning Collection.

17   Ibid.

18   "Patti Browning," *Hawaiian Church Chronicle*, September 1985, 5.

19   "Brownings—A Very Close Family," *Washington Diocese*, February/March 1986.

20   Ibid.

21   Ibid.

22   Mark Browning, interview by SKH, April 2009.

23   Freeman, "Personal Interview with Presiding Bishop-elect."

24   Richard S. O. Chang, interview by SKH, March 2009.

25   *Hawaiian Church Chronicle*, "Patti Browning."

26   J. Michael Parker, "Mom to Pray for Strength for Bishop at Investiture," *Express-News*, San Antonio, January 11, 1986.

27   "Browning Will Lead Episcopalians," *Portland News*, September 12, 1985; Cathleen Gallander, interview by SKH, April 2009.

28 ENS, "Browning Elected 24th Presiding Bishop."

29 "A Message from the Bishop," *Arizona News,* n.d. [ca. Fall 1985], Browning Collection.

30 Gerald McAllister, interview by SKH, March 2009; *The Church News*, Diocese of Oklahoma, December 1985, 3.

31 William Heffner, personal reminiscence, n.d., Browning Collection.

32 David Rose, "Edmond Browning Is a Man Whose Life and Prayers Are Inseparable," n.d., Browning Collection.

33 Maury Maverick, "Cheers for 'Red' Browning," *San Antonio Express-News,* n.d.

34 Ibid.

35 John Shelby Spong, "A World Citizen Presiding Bishop," *The Voice,* Diocese of Newark, October 1985.

36 Ibid.

37 News clipping, n.d. [ca 1985], Browning Collection.

38 Richard N. Ostling, "Opting for the Browning Version," *Time*, September 23, 1985.

39 Ibid.

40 Anne Harpham, "Browning to Lead Episcopalians with 'Ministry of Servanthood,'" *The Honolulu Advertiser,* September 11, 1985.

41 Ian Douglas, interview by SKH, May 2009.

42 Marjorie Hyer, "Hawaii Bishop Chosen to Lead Episcopalians," *The Washington Post,* September 11, 1985.

43 "Deputies and Bishops Confidently Endorse Hawaii's Browning as Presiding Bishop," *The Voice,* Diocese of Newark, October 1985.

44 Marjorie Hyer, "Melding the Prophetic, Pastoral Roles," *The Washington Post,* January 11, 1986.

45 ELB, "Address to the General Convention, Joint Session."

46 Ibid.

47 Ibid.

48 Evelyn Pischel, "Browning Shares Hawaii with the Nation in Installation Ceremony," *Priory Bulletin,* Winter 1986.

49 Smith Hempstone, "An Episcopalian's Plea—Give Me Back My Church!," *The News & Courier/The Evening Post,* Charleston, South Carolina, January 12, 1986, 17-A.

50 Gardiner H. Shattuck, Jr., *Episcopalians and Race: Civil War to Civil Rights* (Lexington: University Press of Kentucky, 2000), Chapter 8.

51 Hempstone, "An Episcopalian's Plea."

52 Ibid.

53 ELB, interview.

54 ELB, "Installation Address." For an interpretation of the address, see Robert McCann, "New Presiding Bishop Installed," *The Episcopal News,* Diocese of Los Angeles, California, January/February 1986.

55 Dorothy Mills Parker, "Affirm Diversity, Maintain Unity," *The Living Church,* February 16, 1986.

56 Ibid.

57 ELB, "Installation Address."

58 Frank P. L. Somerville, *The Sun,* Baltimore, Maryland, January 12, 1986, clipping, Browning Collection.

59 Marjorie Hyer, "Episcopal Leader Installed," *The Washington Post,* January 12, 1986.

60 Dorothy Mills Parker, "Affirm Diversity, Maintain Unity"; John Dart, "Episcopal Convention Maintains Liberal Thrust," *Los Angeles Times,* Part II, Sunday, September 15, 1985.

61 "Browning Holds Press Conference," ENS, January 16, 1986.

62 Dorothy Mills Parker, "Affirm Diversity, Maintain Unity."

A Compassionate Church

1986-1997

How does God call us? I believe that at the heart of it God is calling us to be accountable to our foundational belief that our reason for being is to love and serve the Lord, to live the gospel, and to take seriously our baptismal covenant. That is easy enough to say. The living of it is a work of a lifetime, and makes everything else secondary. Everything. The Christian gospel is radical and demands of us courage we didn't know we had. The baptismal covenant is a radical commitment, and we are challenged every day to live up to its promises...

After nine years, God's call to be a compassionate church is echoing ever louder in my ears. In this Convention we proclaim One God, One Family, One Earth. Injustice against people and injustice against the earth are rotten fruit from the same rotten tree. I pray we will emerge from this Convention knowing that the issues of racism, environmental degradation, and economic injustice must be approached as one, and responded to with compassion, and conviction. [1]

— Edmond Lee Browning,
Address to the
71st General Convention,
Indianapolis, 1994

On the first Ash Wednesday after he became presiding bishop, Ed Browning was visiting Buffalo, New York. Following the eucharist and the imposition of ashes was a question and answer session with the new presiding bishop. Although only in office for a few months, Browning had already answered many questions and felt he had learned what to expect. Members of the press and others in the audience usually asked about some controversial issue before the church. Frequently the questions were about human sexuality. But one question that day was unique, and it stopped him. A young man asked, "What do you think is the greatest sin the church has to face?"

"I didn't think, but in the next moments my heart framed the answer," said Browning. Images came to him of all the human suffering he had witnessed those first months as presiding bishop. "Does anybody care?" he asked himself. At that moment he realized that the human suffering he had witnessed was as real as the room he was sitting in, warm and comfortable, drinking coffee. "All of this probably took place in fifteen seconds, but it seemed like minutes later that I answered the question," he said. "I said to the young man, 'Apathy.'" [2]

The First Years

Browning described his first year as presiding bishop as "a kind of existential, spiritual journey." He recalled the many people he met and the places he visited that were filled with suffering—places where he believed the church needed to be present. Shortly after his installation, Browning flew to South Africa to participate in the enthronement of Desmond Tutu as archbishop of Cape Town. "I don't think I have ever seen as much suffering, inhumane treatment of persons, human waste, absolute filth. Their military troops maintain the blacks in that situation." He also visited Palestinian refugee camps on the West Bank and the Gaza Strip. He visited what was then known as the "AIDS ward" in San Francisco, with Bill Swing, bishop of California. Browning reflected on what he had heard about the racist treatment of the people in Navajoland and unemployment in Oklahoma, Louisiana, and Texas. He was confronted every time he left the front door of the Episcopal Church Center in New York with the tragedy of the homeless in the city. Browning said that after his first year as presiding bishop, his vision had been stretched and he had more questions than when he began. "I said that there were no outcasts. There are more who sense themselves outcasts than I thought, which sensitizes me to a greater need for a ministry of compassion and listening; my listening process will never be over. That is part of what ministry means."[3]

Shortly after his installation, a Honolulu-based editor asked Browning "how many legions he commands." Browning was not willing to answer such a question, but he did inform the journalist that he reviewed the daily news for issues that the church should consider and that the business of taking national positions—which seems to be of great interest to journalists—actually consumed only a small part of his time.[4]

After his first year in office, Browning believed that his role as presiding bishop was to hold up the values of reconciliation and restoration. That meant recognizing the brokenness of life wherever it was found and the human need for the healing power of Christ. "I have found that some people who sense themselves as outcasts feel that the only way they can participate in the life of the church is by making other people outcast. A lot of polarization in life exists because people really do not understand our common humanity." Browning was aware of the polarization in the Episcopal Church, dating to the 1960s and 1970s, between those who saw ministry entirely in terms of social activism and those primarily concerned with spirituality and nurture. He affirmed both polarities, with the additional perspective of traditionalists who are unsure of their place in a church of rapid change, as well as those liberals who would like a more inclusive church. It was Browning's belief throughout his term as presiding bishop that all these perspectives were part of a common mission. Rather than feed polarization, Browning sought to enhance the sense of common mission among diverse perspectives. He believed that the diversity of the Episcopal Church was a positive. If the church could grasp the concept of a "common mission," then "we can bring this diversity into play with one another, and not in competition."[5]

Two gatherings held in 1987 showed Browning's optimism about diversity and how it supports the common mission of the church. The first, the Presiding Bishop's Vision Conference, was held in New Jersey. The second was a larger gathering in St. Louis called

"Under One Roof." Other than at General Convention, seldom had such diverse groups of Episcopalians come together. The guiding concept was to bring together the leadership of as many Episcopal organizations as possible to worship and to contribute their ideas on the future of the church. At "Under One Roof," Browning urged participants to a renewal of the spirit of Pentecost. "I believe you and I have been gathered in this place to receive the gift of the Holy Spirit which will empower and restore us, so that our lives can be renewed and that we can speak with clarity across the barriers that have been created by a sinful world." [6] Through such gatherings, Browning sensed his role was to serve as a "bridge" between diverse cultures and factions within the church and to encourage unity by challenging Episcopalians to become more involved in the mission of the church. Although participants in the gatherings welcomed the opportunity to meet with other leaders and explain the work they were doing, some wondered how genuine the dialogue between groups was, given the deep differences that existed. [7]

Patti Browning's Ministry

Patti Browning also used the first year of her ministry as the spouse of the presiding bishop to listen and to discern what she was called to do during their twelve-year term. "Of course our marriage and love for one another is something we believe is very special, in fact, I don't think either one of us could exist without the other," wrote Ed in response to a letter of support addressed to both of them. "Our marriage has been one that has grown over the years and it has been through some struggles that we have learned to appreciate the gifts of one another." [8] Although the Brownings believed they were entering into the office of presiding bishop as a team, there were many assumptions about Patti's role that did not correlate with her own sense of ministry and calling. Never having succumbed to traditional notions of what a bishop's wife should do, Patti Browning saw no reason to begin doing so as the wife of the presiding bishop. Supporting Ed in his ministry was a given, but there were many ways that support could be shaped. Shortly after the election, a delegation of bishops' spouses met with Patti to outline what they needed, giving Patti a year to get up to speed. Patti's predecessor, Ann Allin, had worked for the bishops' spouses group and given her energies to a variety of projects. Patti saw her role differently, just as she had done in other places where she and Ed had ministered together; she gave her support to the bishops' spouses group, yet made it clear that the group would have to take ownership for what they wanted to have happen. "It is not *my* group," she said, "it is *our* group."[9]

Self-described as "not much of a joiner," Patti Browning nonetheless devoted much energy to the bishops' spouses and other organizations that came to her for support. Patti was still discerning what she was called to do as wife of the presiding bishop, but clear that God was not calling her to sit on a lot of boards or to organize conferences.[10] Patti traveled frequently with the presiding bishop and gave speeches, sermons, and addresses in her own right. When in New York she usually attended daily eucharist in the chapel at the Episcopal Church Center.

In New York the Brownings continued the ministry of gracious hospitality characteristic of their household from the beginning of their marriage. "Those of us in the presiding bishop's office were a tightly knit group, and we worked closely with both Patti and Ed," said Judy Mathews, a former assistant. [11] The Brownings lived "over the store," as it were, in an apartment on the top floor of the Episcopal Church Center that included two adjacent guestrooms. Once Patti made the apartment and guestrooms welcoming, on a meager budget, they opened their home to countless people from across the church. Old friends and sharp critics alike benefitted from the hospitality of the Brownings. John Peterson, then based in London as secretary general of the Anglican Communion, tells the story of how he once decided to book a hotel in New York instead of staying in one of the Brownings' guestrooms. He felt he had imposed on their hospitality too many times in the recent past. When Ed got wind of it he was upset. "What are you doing here," he said to Peterson, as the latter was trying to escape into the elevator. "I thought you were my friend." From then on John Peterson took his responsibility for staying in the Brownings' guestrooms seriously. What might seem to others like a high level of traffic in their home was a deeply felt ministry to Ed and Patti, and it built friendships and community with a diverse network of people across the church.

Personal Life and Family

On a personal level, life was very busy for the Brownings during their first years in New York, with a number of events affecting the family. John, their youngest son, graduated from high school in Hawaii and began college in California. Mark, their oldest son, married around the time of John's graduation. Ben Browning, Ed's youngest brother, died tragically in 1986 of an asthma reaction. Both Ed and Patti negotiated beginning a new position and all these events with an awesome sense of responsibility, giving so much to others at a time of so much change in their own lives. By the end of Ed and Patti Browning's twelve-year term, all the Browning children were married and the immediate family had grown to include twelve (now thirteen) grandchildren. Despite the demands on his time, Ed Browning always tried to be available for his family. Judy Mathews, Browning's assistant, remembers his commitment to family. "When I went for my second interview, I was introduced to his very young grandson, and I believe that was a test for me," she writes. "When I was offered the job as secretary to the presiding bishop and accepted, he told me on the first day to always interrupt him for a call from his wife or one of his children. That, to me, was a sure sign of his strong feelings for his family." [12]

After living at the Episcopal Church Center for several years, the Brownings felt it would be helpful to have a place easily accessible from New York where they could spend some of their very limited free time away from the workplace. They settled on a cabin in Pennsylvania, affectionately known as "Dogpatch," and traveled there for refreshment until their retirement. At home in the mountains and in the woods, Ed and Patti enjoyed the privacy and simplicity of life at the cabin. The peace and quiet allowed them to recharge their batteries and to process some of what was going on in their busy lives. One of their favorite things to do at the cabin was to say their prayers outside in the early morning when the birds were celebrating and the sun was filtering through the leaves. "It is a cathedral," said Browning. "The hand of God is so visible in the woods, and I am so powerfully reconnected as part of the earth God has made. I begin the old prayers, prayers I've said all my life, prayers that have bracketed every day at its beginning and again at its end, and they take on an eternal quality." [13]

Browning tells a story about one night at the cabin when he went out to gather dry wood for the fire. Walking through the meadow toward the house he saw a large buck and a doe grazing, not ten yards away:

> They did not run away when they saw me. They just stood and looked at me. They were the most beautiful sight I had ever seen. For a moment, it was as if only the deer and I were alive in the whole world, and the whole world's aching beauty was concentrated in the look that passed between me and them....The sight of those deer, the perfection of their grace and beauty, the wisdom and peace that I saw in their direct gaze, their harmonious partnering of each other seemed, in one wordless moment, to sum up the care of God for the whole complex universe. [14]

The nearest Episcopal congregation to the Brownings' cabin was St. Mark's in New Milford, Pennsylvania, part of Susquehanna County Episcopal Ministries. Newly ordained deacon-in-charge Carol Horton arrived there in 1995 and had an opportunity to get to know the Brownings when they were in town. "When I arrived in the office that first day there was a message on the answering machine," writes Horton. " 'Hi. This is Ed Browning. I'm one of your parishioners and want to talk to you about a baptism.' Needless to say, it was a somewhat challenging moment for this newly-minted deacon," she said, "but proved to be the beginning of a relationship of mutual respect and a wonderful learning opportunity for me." Horton said the Brownings fit right into the informality of St. Mark's, and the congregation instinctively understood not to intrude into their "down time." Sometimes there was a quiet whisper, "The bishop is here," but that was the extent of the reaction. "Throughout the first months of my ministry there," Horton wrote, "Ed was helpful, but never intrusive. At one point he made a small suggestion in passing, which helped me to smooth out what had been an awkward sequence in the liturgy. His gentleness and generosity of spirit helped me settle in as a deacon and then as a priest, and have been invaluable to me throughout my ministry." [15] The story illustrates Browning's pastoral style not only in his home congregation, but in his visits as presiding bishop to individual parishes and major international locales. Gentleness, generosity, and lack of pretense characterized both Ed and Patti as they moved around the church.

The Episcopal Church Center

The transition in leadership to a new presiding bishop is always tumultuous at the Episcopal Church Center. Many staff members feared the changes Browning might bring. At the time Browning entered the scene, there was a great deal of pain among the members of support staff, many of whom felt they were not seen as an important part of the community. Browning's invitation to *all* staff to attend his installation, regardless of status, sent a positive message about his intention to value the work of all. The morale of the Episcopal Church Center staff remained a concern for Browning throughout his administration, although much of the climate that caused staff anxiety was beyond his control. While the decision was made once again during the Browning administration to keep the Episcopal Church Center in New York, two major downsizings and frequent budget cuts, beginning with a 10 percent cut and fifty lost jobs in 1991, caused intense anxiety for the staff. So did shifting attitudes throughout the church about the value of the Church Center operation to dioceses and local congregations. Some dioceses began to withhold funds from the national church, giving parishes the choice to redirect funds they would normally send as their assessment. "The agenda of local churches and the agenda of the national church staff have been on parallel paths for many years with very little communication between them," said John MacNaughton, bishop of West Texas. Some of the members of his diocese believed that the national church's focus on social controversy issues made it ineffective when it came to Christian ministry.[16] Most dioceses gave sacrificially during years of financial hardship, yet the fact that a few dioceses chose not to meet their financial obligation to the national church signaled a shift in the understanding of Anglican polity.[17]

Other mainline denominations were downsizing their national staff and decentralizing at this time, too, and some made the decision to move out of New York City for economic reasons. The trend of the times was the belief that the large denominational bureaucracies built during the 1950s and 1960s were no longer good investments. Some felt that money sent to fund national (and international) mission might better be spent locally and that local leaders were more in touch with the needs of the person in the pew. Seeking to decentralize, provinces of the Episcopal Church began to offer regionally based

resources to dioceses. Meetings between provincial officers and Episcopal Church Center staff became a feature
of the administrative year.

For Browning, the shift to the role of presiding bishop
brought with it responsibility for a large corporation with
over 250 employees, in contrast to the small and personal
staff he had been accustomed to in his other posts. In
one of the first interviews after his installation, Browning
commented on the discipline needed to do the job: discipline
to take care of his own spiritual life, discipline in managing
the duties of the office, and discipline in taking care of
himself and his family. "Those are areas where discipline
is important because you can be overwhelmed in any one
of them." [18] Ed Browning's first "In-House" meeting of
all the Episcopal Church Center staff was a success in
that the staff appreciated his warmth, approachability,
and informality, although those meetings grew fractious
over time as the staff felt increasing pressure from senior
management and parish and diocesan leaders. Although
Browning met most people with grace and kindness, there
were also tough days. "When he put his foot down, that
was it," said Herb Donovan, bishop of Arkansas. "About
the worst thing he ever said to me was, "Donovan, quit
being a *jerk*. But I knew that was it." [19]

A persistent challenge was how to balance the need to
manage the staff and the business of the Episcopal Church
Center with a travel schedule that kept Ed Browning on
the road two-thirds of the time. As early as 1987, Browning
was referred to in one publication as the "itinerating
primate." "Different gatherings are indeed fortunate to
have the chief pastor appear, and to have the benefit of
his gracious and encouraging words. On the other hand,
incessant travel is not the best way of life—certainly not

for someone whose regular schedule must include prayer, reflection, reading and other activities done in quiet.... We cannot expect the finest leadership year after year from someone who is constantly exhausted." [20]

The tension between the presiding bishop's travel schedule and administrative matters in New York continued. Browning's own desire was to be accessible to the wider church, and as a former missionary and an inveterate traveler, his inclination was to go to the people. Moreover, his administrative style was to have complete confidence in his staff and not micromanage. Seeking to be accessible to staff, Browning often made unpublicized appearances at meetings and conferences, and at personal occasions when invited by the staff. When church leaders were unhappy about a staff member or a program, there were complaints that Browning was unable to supervise his staff properly. Initially, Browning worked with staff to craft collaborative management schemes to coordinate the work of the Episcopal Church Center. But by 1995 complaints from the wider church that some senior staff had their own agendas grew louder, and with the embezzlement scandal centred around treasurer Ellen Cooke in 1995, the reputation of the Episcopal Church Center reached a low point. Browning saw the need for more centralized authority and appointed an executive officer to serve as a consistent episcopal presence at the New York office. Charlie McNutt, recently retired bishop of Central Pennsylvania, was hired as executive officer in 1995 in an effort to stabilize church administration and restore the wider church's confidence in it.

All the programmatic efforts based at the Episcopal Church Center during the Browning administration related to the themes of inclusivity and compassion. Ultimately,

Browning said he learned more about the meaning of baptism during his years as presiding bishop and came to see the baptismal vows as the basis of inclusivity and compassion. It was during the Browning administration that the Episcopal Church began to reflect on the meaning of the Baptismal Covenant as the basis for all ministry in the church and the world. "You cannot take the baptismal vows and not think that the issue of racism, the issue of sexism, the issue of human sexuality aren't important in the life of the church," he said. Ed Browning also knew that his priorities "threatened the hell out of some people," but he had pledged from the beginning of his ministry as presiding bishop that the Episcopal Church would have "no outcasts" and he maintained that stance throughout his term of office.

The Executive Council

Ed Browning's first Executive Council meeting as presiding bishop was held in San Antonio, in his home diocese of West Texas. With a deliberately light legislative agenda, the council invited John Carver, an internationally known management consultant, to help them discern their role and scope for the coming years. "Our concern for all meetings will be to have enough time to do the business at hand, to do theological reflection as well as community building among ourselves, and to share in the mission and ministry of the place in which we are meeting." [21] While members generally appreciated Carver's contributions, opinions differed on what they meant for the council. Some felt the primary role of the Executive Council was to serve as "interpreter," distinguishing their role from that of a nonprofit board and the role of the presiding bishop from that of an executive officer. Others suggested a revamping of the whole structure and hiring a consultant "for a radical look at all our processes." The one item on which clear consensus emerged was the presiding bishop's listening process. "We wanted to join you in your listening process," said Barnum McCarty of Jacksonville, Florida. [22]

After the first six months in office and his listening process, Browning felt ready to announce to the Executive Council a first level of staff changes, although he made clear his intention to provide for continuity and access rather than create a rigid bureaucracy, "I want you to know," he said to Executive Council, "of my deep desire to provide our church with an efficient and responsive staff structure which models servanthood and collegiality. The crucial criterion for me is that our structure be appropriate to mission." [23] Browning acknowledged the difficulty of running the Episcopal Church Center while traveling and announced his intention to name an executive vice president and three new cluster executives reporting to the executive vice president. These people were to coordinate the day-to-day operations of the Episcopal Church Center. Browning also announced plans to merge the financial and administrative operations, separated thirty years previously. He preserved the old unit structure of world mission, national mission, education, stewardship, communication, and finance and administration. In addition, the new presiding bishop envisioned an expansion of the Washington Office and changes in the Presiding Bishop's Fund for World Relief that would include more Executive Council participation in the grants process. [24]

In early 1987, amid a climate of high expectation as the extensive listening process drew to a close, the new Executive Council and the new executive team at the Church Center sought to develop a major program proposal to present to the General Convention in Detroit in 1988. Aware that the "time of transition is over," Browning told the Executive Council that "the journey to mission has begun. It is time to move on to Detroit." [25] In preparation for the Executive Council meeting, Episcopal Church Center staff attempted to cluster nearly one hundred separate programs into a proposed group of "mission imperatives." At the same time Executive Council members attempted to create their own sets of clusters and imperatives as a first step toward developing a budget proposal. The process soon bogged down due to time constraints and the huge amount of information in the proposals themselves. With reluctance, the presiding bishop and 'Executive Council agreed to postpone the final process to the next meeting. Browning praised the effort and attempted to quell the anxiety of those present by putting the experience in context: "Now we all see how difficult a task it is to determine with any clarity our task as a national structure and council within the priorities that the whole church holds up." [26]

The mission imperatives that the Browning administration brought to the General Convention in 1988 developed a "vision" for the church:

I   Inspire others by serving them and leading them to seek, follow, and serve Jesus Christ through membership in his church.

II   Develop and promote educational systems and resources which support the ministry of the people of God.

III Strengthen and affirm the partnership of the Episcopal Church within the Anglican Communion in proclaiming and serving God's Kingdom throughout the world.

IV Communicate in a compelling way the work of the church in response to the gospels.

V Strive for justice and peace among all people and respect the dignity of every human being.

VI Act in faithful stewardship in response to the biblical teaching of the right use of God's creation.

VII Support individuals and families in their struggle for wholeness by knowing and living the values of the gospel.

VIII Commit ourselves to the unity of the church and of all God's people. [27]

Browning believed that the eighth mission imperative was "the faithful expressions of a church focused on the vision of compassion, justice, and service—the vision of a church giving itself in that service which is perfect freedom." [28] The mission imperatives, according to Browning, were to be a "message of hope" and to build "structures of grace" that would allow God to enter into people's lives. [29] The use of the mission imperatives as "major guideposts" faded over time as controversies and decreasing budgets demanded attention. The church overall was not at a point where it could be unified. While few commentators on the mission imperatives were completely happy with the way they were expressed, they did bring together diverse agendas into a coherent program strategy. Devised at a time of immense optimism, the general principles of the mission imperatives guided the church throughout the Browning administration and beyond, albeit under different guises.

The Decade of Evangelism

Browning linked his firm belief in a church of "no outcasts" with his sense of evangelism as the transformation of people's lives. The 1990s were designated the "Decade of Evangelism." Resisting the suggestion that the Decade of Evangelism was about numbers or church growth, Browning believed that its success should be measured "in how faithful we have been in the proclamation and sharing of the good news. I think the only way it can be measured is in the transformation of people's lives," he said. "I think it's measured by the way you see men and women reaching out to the suffering…by the manner in which people are concerned with the injustices in communities and the outcasts who live in them," he added. [30]

In preparation for the Decade of Evangelism, Browning commissioned a Gallup poll of Episcopalians. Like other mainline denominations, the Episcopal Church had seen declining membership since the 1960s. The poll indicated that the decline in membership was more about societal factors that affect all churches than denominational issues such as Prayer Book revision, the ordination of women, inclusive language, and same-sex relationships. George Gallup, Jr., a self-identified evangelical Episcopal layman, wrote in his introduction to the poll that the Episcopal Church was "substantially orthodox" and had "a fairly clear sense of direction and mission." The poll showed that "a substantial majority of members—nationwide and by each province—would like to see the national Episcopal Church more involved in these areas: ecology, matters of justice, and war and peace." One of the major challenges for Episcopalians, the poll suggested, was the gap between belief and practice. Thus, the suggestion was not only to encourage evangelism, but also to provide more opportunities through small groups for people to share their spiritual journeys, study scripture together, and deepen their prayer lives. Browning found much to celebrate in the poll and hoped that church leaders and parishes would use it to promote spiritual health. [31] He also implemented the use of small groups to deepen the spirituality of church life in the House of Bishops, Executive Council meetings, the General Convention, and "In-House" meetings at the Episcopal Church Center in New York.

Pamela P. Chinnis and the House of Deputies

Key to the relationships among the Executive Council, the General Convention, and the presiding bishop in the 1990s was the election of Pamela P. Chinnis as president of the House of Deputies in 1991, the first woman to hold the post. Chinnis was elected twenty-one years after women were first seated in the House of Deputies. She had been elected vice president of the House of Deputies in 1985 at the same convention that elected Ed Browning presiding bishop; she was elected president in 1991 and re-elected without opposition in 1994 and again in 1997.

Born into a political family, Chinnis held leadership positions in her home parish and the Diocese of Washington. "Pam was dedicated to the structures of the church," said Pamela Darling, who worked as a consultant to Chinnis while she was president of the House of

Deputies. "She was an expert at parliamentary procedure and she paid a great deal of attention to detail." [32] Pam Chinnis was elected presiding officer of the 1976 Triennial Meeting of the Episcopal Church Women and later served four times as lay delegate to the Anglican Consultative Council (ACC). She was one of only nine official women participants in the Lambeth Conference in 1998. During her tenure as president of the House of Deputies, Chinnis streamlined the legislative process and enhanced the diversity on committees and commissions related to the General Convention. Her newsletter for all convention deputies and alternates was eventually sent to all bishops at their request. Chinnis and Browning developed an effective partnership. "She was devoted to working with Ed, and was honored by the way he shared leadership," said Pam Darling. [33] They discussed and negotiated appointments to committees and commissions. Browning introduced an address from the president of the House of Deputies to stand alongside his address at Executive Council meetings.

Pam Chinnis's unwavering commitment to the full inclusion of all the baptized in the leadership of the church was a hallmark of her ministry. An early advocate for the ordination of women, Chinnis served as chair of the presiding bishop's committee for the Full Participation of Women in the Church from 1985 until 1998. "My commitment is to the inclusion of all people, regardless of their race or sex or class or sexuality. Sexism is only a symptom of a larger problem, which is injustice and oppression....You can't be against discrimination against women and be for discrimination against anyone else." [34] After her election as president of the House of Deputies, Chinnis and Browning intentionally appointed members of Integrity, the organization of lesbian, gay, bisexual, and transgender Episcopalians, to legislative committees of the General Convention. Members of Integrity commented that earlier, even though legislative committees often discussed gay and lesbian people, few committees had gay or lesbian members. The decision to appoint members of Integrity to legislative committees brought criticism from Episcopalians United, concerned about the pain caused to "orthodox Episcopalians by stacking committees with members who are so clearly biased." [35] Bruce Garner, the first openly gay member on a legislative committee and president of Integrity, remembers the historic significance of Chinnis and Browning's decision. "For the first time in history it meant that gay and lesbian people would be present during conversations that involved us, and we could speak for ourselves, rather than having other people speak for us. The move was appreciated by thousands and thousands of people." [36]

Chinnis was keen to insure that laity and clergy maintain their voice and worked to preserve the bicameral system of government in the church. She opposed the growing tendency to centralize church governance in bishops and national church staff, believing that such practices eroded the integrity of the House of Deputies. Chinnis viewed the practice of separate House of Bishops meetings as characteristic of the tendency to focus on bishops, even though bishops cannot act officially without the concurrence of the House of Deputies. "More and more we see efforts to increase the role and power of the House of Bishops and the national church staff. We have every right to be concerned. Eternal vigilance is the price of freedom from a church dominated by the House of Bishops." [37]

Chinnis often reminded Browning that bishops alone do not know what is best for the church. When the House of Bishops focused inward, she was supportive of the presiding bishop but always clear about the agenda of her own role. At times impatient with what she believed was the House of Bishops' dysfunctional behavior and evasion of controversial issues to avoid schism, she encouraged the use of the legislative process as a means to discern the mind of the church. Chinnis was one of Ed Browning's closest advisors during his term in office and was often one of the first people he called in times of crisis. Bruce Woodcock, a staff member in the overseas development office and the General Convention office, pointed out that it was during the Browning administration that the photo of the president of the House of Deputies began to appear alongside that of the presiding bishop in the *Episcopal Church Annual,* also known as the "Red Book." "It was a time when the two presidents of the two houses worked together as equals," said Woodcock. [38]

The Embezzlement Scandal

The major institutional crisis of the Browning administration was the embezzlement of approximately $2.2 million dollars by the Episcopal Church treasurer, Ellen F. Cooke. Cooke was one of the first appointments made by Browning in 1987, and he was lauded for naming a woman to one of the highest posts in the church. But the enthusiasm soon faded. Recommended for her position by at least two bishops, Cooke was a controversial figure from the beginning of her tenure. By most accounts, Cooke's work style was not collaborative, and she had a reputation for heavy-handed money management. Many unit executives at the Episcopal Church Center believed she selectively sabotaged programs not to her taste. She first commuted to New York from her family home in Virginia, raising eyebrows about her availability and questions about the cost of commuting. When she moved to New Jersey, she further raised eyebrows by using a private car service to transport herself to and from work every day. Browning received many complaints about Cooke and addressed issues of collegiality and work style with her on numerous occasions. She always promised to comply. Although he was aware of the controversy she generated, Browning believed that the complaints were personality disputes, not matters of professional competency. "He was mystified at conflict in the staff, and he could not get over it," said David Beers, the presiding bishop's chancellor. [39]

Few criticized Cooke directly to the presiding bishop for fear they would anger him, or worse yet, anger Cooke and risk retribution. Shortly after her appointment, the most highly trained financial staff at the Church Center, including two certified public accountants, left the Episcopal Church's employ. It appears that Cooke was honest, if unpopular, for her first three years as treasurer. Fiercely loyal to his staff, several of whom were unpopular in an era not sympathetic to Episcopal Church Center staff, Browning did not initially believe that the complaints against Cooke justified action beyond requesting she be more available and work more collaboratively with the rest of the staff. [40] Browning's failure to see Cooke's demoralizing effect on a staff of 300 people became a source of immense frustration to those who had to work with her, and they were appalled at his stubborn refusal to act decisively to address their litany of complaints. The staff had enormous affection and respect for the presiding bishop, but his failure to listen to staff and others tested their deep regard for him.

As the General Convention of 1994 approached, however, the working relationship between Ed Browning and Ellen Cooke began to deteriorate. At that time, one-third of the Episcopal Church Center's staff was laid off and there were further budget cuts. Discussions about the budget were particularly charged at the General Convention. Cooke had not been nominated by the church's nominating committee for the office of convention treasurer, a remarkable rebuke to Browning's intransigent support of his deeply unpopular treasurer, and it was only through his support that she was nominated and elected from the floor.

At the same convention, Ed Browning was told in a hallway by a member of the Program, Budget, and Finance Committee that an additional million dollars had been taken out of the budget, more than he had expected. Yet Cooke would not return his calls about the budget. Browning grew angry at her repeated brush-offs and what he saw as a move to curtail the mission of the church. He revised his convention address at the last minute. Spurred on by an address the previous evening, he recalled how theologian Henri Nouwen had spoken of community as "a quality of the heart" and the challenge to the audience to "take a few risks with your heart." Deeply troubled about the state of the budget and "the absolute extreme" mission cuts, Browning decided to advocate for what he saw as a restoration of essential funding for common mission. "We have gone absolutely as far as we can go in cutting back our mission together. Since Phoenix we have cut the legs off of it," he said. "Some would say our financial planning has been prudent. Some would say it was cautious. I am taking a risk with my heart and saying that we are fearful. We are not challenging one another." [41]

Browning not only implored the convention to take another look at the budget, but also encouraged others to join him as a witnessing community in doing the work of the gospel. "As the bishops of this church and the leaders of the dioceses, are you willing to go back and say to your diocese and your parishes that we are one community called to witness boldly together to the gospel? Are you willing to challenge your parishes and your diocese to move beyond timidity to faithful witness?...What are we saying about ourselves and how we are called as a faith community when, as our total assets increase, and our pledges increase, we make the decision to cut the legs off what we do together?" [42] Not only did Browning attempt to restore program funds for the church, but the surprise budget cuts had also left him with serious doubts about the commitment of the treasurer. "My dear friends, I believe we have seen the bottom line and now it is time to look up," he said at the close of his address. [43] Yet, despite all this, he still did not seek Ellen Cooke's resignation.

A few weeks later, Browning convened about two dozen senior staff in West Cornwall, Connecticut, to do some long range planning. But the agenda changed when an outside consultant with no personal knowledge of the Episcopal Church Center noted to all present that he had never worked with such an unhappy and demoralized staff, and he named Ellen Cooke's effect on the staff and the presiding bishop's enabling of her behavior as the primary problem. This stung Browning; he engaged the consultant for several weeks to work with him and Cooke to try to repair the damage.

A few months later Browning learned for the first time, from a third party at a dinner party in New York, that Ellen Cooke would be leaving Montclair, New Jersey, and moving to McLean, Virginia, where her husband, Nicholas T. Cooke, an Episcopal priest, had been called to a new parish. That Cooke had not shared her plans with the presiding bishop left him "ticked" and convinced that she was not a "team player." [44] When confronted, Cooke said she would commute to New York from Virginia, but Browning had had enough and insisted on her resignation by the end of the year. Browning agreed to let her serve as a consultant for a few months while the audit for 1994 was being completed, so that she could protect her professional reputation. The church's lawyers, however, would report to him.

Ellen Cooke's claim for $86,000 in back vacation pay, for which she said she would provide documentation later, and other benefits not allowed under Episcopal Church Center personnel policy led to her final downfall. [45] On the day that Cooke was to sign her severance agreement, the controller told the acting treasurer, Donald Burchell, about her undocumented back pay and some other apparent irregularities. That led to the discovery of Cooke's embezzlement. On February 7, 1995, the presiding bishop learned of the missing funds. Cooke had used eight different methods to misappropriate money, including transferring funds intended for the presiding bishop's discretionary fund into personal accounts at the same bank. Missing funds were also traced to her corporate credit card and brokerage accounts, Cooke's husband's parish in New Jersey, and as tuition payments to her children's private schools. Eventually Cooke went into therapy. "In the psychiatrist's opinion I experienced a breakdown precipitated by many factors external to me and the workplace," she later said, implying that institutional sexism at the Church Center had caused her stress. [46] Given her unprecedented access to the church's money, most of those who had worked with Cooke did not believe she was a victim of sexism. "When he [Browning] appointed [Cooke]," said Marge Christie, from the Diocese of Newark, "he was enormously proud of bringing a woman into such an enormous leadership role. So he found it very hard to accept the fact that the woman he brought in wasn't a team player. But he never dreamed that not only was she not a team player, but she was ripping him off." Jim Solheim, the director of the Episcopal News Service at the time of the embezzlement, suggested that "if anyone really took the time, they could trace directly back to Ellen Cooke the suspicion and frustration that the dioceses of the church have with 815." [47]

If this crisis was the low point of Edmond Browning's term as presiding bishop, his steps after the discovery of the embezzlement provided some of his finest moments. He acted swiftly after the misappropriation of funds was revealed and agreed to cooperate fully with federal authorities. One of Browning's first steps was to fly to Virginia to personally tell Cooke and her husband that the investigation had uncovered financial irregularities. He did not consider designating someone else to handle this highly charged confrontation. He also wanted to be sure that someone from the Diocese of Virginia, the Cookes' home diocese, was present for the meeting. Since the diocesan bishop could not be reached in time, it was arranged that the diocesan chancellor, Russ Palmore, would be present for the meeting with the Cookes. Wendy White, the church's new attorney retained to undertake an investigation into the apparent embezzlement, was also present. Browning was determined to treat everyone involved with compassion. "He was clear and gentle," said Palmore about Browning's meeting with the Cookes. "He was not expecting anything from them, and directly told them he was simply conveying information. He was real graceful throughout." [48]

Cooke pleaded guilty to charges of embezzlement and tax evasion in February 1996. Browning cooperated with the prosecution but never sought vengeance. At the time of her sentencing, a letter written by seven senior members of the Episcopal Church Center staff was sent to Judge Maryann Trump Barry: "While we have no desire for retribution or the imposition of more guilt on Mrs. Cooke's family," the letter read, "it…is our collective belief that a lenient sentence would add further to the damages we have suffered." [49] Among the signers of the letter were the presiding bishop and Pamela P. Chinnis, president of the House of Deputies. The letter also stated that contributions to the church had declined since the scandal, that "the psychic impact on the staff and organization has been more debilitating," and that former staff members who lost jobs due to economic retrenchment found it hard to believe there was no connection between Cooke's activities and the decline in church income.

Judge Barry referred to the crime as "particularly heinous" because of the church connection and sentenced Ellen Cooke to a five-year prison sentence, followed by three years of supervised release and an additional fine. The sentence was stiffer than guidelines recommended and was upheld on appeal. "We have looked carefully at how it happened and took such steps such as it can never happen again," said Browning after the sentencing. He added that the job of the national staff was "restitution of what has been stolen, restoration of confidence, and the assurance of a financial operation of soundness and integrity. We have faced the equally difficult task of coming again and again to our knowledge of sin, repentance, redemption, and healing. My prayers are with Ellen Cooke and her family." [50] Ellen F. Cooke was released from federal custody on January 1, 2001. [51] During her incarceration, she declined requests from the presiding bishop to visit her. [52]

A civil suit initiated against the Cookes by the church was settled in April of the same year. Browning said: "I personally have faced the difficult fact that this was ultimately my responsibility. We together have faced both the practical and the spiritual implications of such a massive betrayal." [53] The impact of the betrayal hit Browning harder than any of the other controversies of his administration. "I saw everyone coming against me," he said. "I felt terribly abandoned. You begin to look at all the slings and arrows pointed toward you, and your paranoia rises to its highest height. You begin to question your own worth and purpose." [54] Browning was most relieved when the year-long struggle was at its end. "He suffered tremendously," said Martin Smith, then chaplain to the House of Bishops. "He is a deeply sensitive person and very trusting—the complete opposite of detached—and he felt the betrayal to his heart. Yet he did not go into isolation; instead he acted bravely and took responsibility and kept going." [55]

As Ed Browning and the church progressed through the trauma of the embezzlement, the process of restitution, and the resolution of the court cases, he was heard to say on a number of occasions, "It's been the worst year of my ministry. No doubt about it." [56] Before the embezzlement was revealed, Browning had thought that the last three years of his administration would be "a piece of cake." "I just grieve for [Ed]," said Bill Stough, then assistant bishop of Alabama, a former senior executive at the Episcopal Church Center and a longtime friend of the presiding bishop. "Thank God he's got only two more years, for his own sake and for Patti and the children too. Fortunately, he really is trying to take care of himself health-wise. But I don't know what he is going to do about this stress." [57]

Browning was criticized from all sides during the embezzlement scandal. While the initial investigation was underway, he was criticized for not aggressively seeking prosecution; when the letter to the court opposing leniency went out with his signature, he was criticized for a lack of compassion. "This is nothing new for Bishop Browning, or any other presiding bishop for that matter. With nearly every decision, every announcement or lack thereof, the presiding bishop will take a hit from somewhere. ...Unfortunately, it seems to go with the territory," wrote *The Living Church* in 1996. [58]

In the aftermath of the embezzlement, the presiding bishop, his staff, and the Executive Council worked to regain the church's confidence and to find some redemption in the experience. Browning said that despite the strife caused by the embezzlement, he saw "glimpses of God's grace. The wounds dealt to our community have made us stronger. Scar tissue is the strongest tissue there is." [59] Don Burchell, who served as assistant treasurer with

Cooke, rose to the occasion and helped with the investigation and initial recovery of the funds. Steven Duggan was hired as treasurer in early 1996, amid a climate of declining diocesan contributions. Duggan found the issues in the financial area "formidable and pervasive" at the time of his appointment.[60] The calm presence, warm demeanor, good cheer, and collaborative working style of new chief operating officer Charlie McNutt also boosted the morale of the staff over the remaining two years of Browning's tenure.

Almost the entire $2.2 million was eventually recovered. When Wendy White, the church's attorney, walked into Browning's office one day just before Christmas 1995 and handed him a check for one million dollars, he bowed his head and said, "Thank you, Jesus."[61]

As the church's financial resources began to be restored, several initiatives creating opportunities for dialogue and a renewed focus on mission were organized. In October 1995 Browning and Pam Chinnis called the first-ever joint meeting of the church's interim bodies. Chinnis had been stalwart in her support of Browning throughout the embezzlement ordeal. She looked forward to the interim bodies' meeting "as a time for turning the corner, putting the worst of the crises behind us, shedding the gloom and focusing on the future toward which God calls us."[62] In her address to the conference, Chinnis referred to the interim bodies (the term used for all committees, commissions, boards, and agencies that function "in the interim" between conventions) as the "diaspora," meaning groups scattered about the church with little coordination. "So the presiding bishop and I thought it might be time to call the diaspora together, so we can see and experience the interim leadership of the Episcopal Church and together work at improving our institutional structures so they will better support our life as people of God," she said. [63] The joint meeting of interim bodies was not only for the purposes of community building, although many there appreciated the time to meet with other groups, but also an effort to maximize staff time by allowing them to meet with multiple groups and save some of the church's resources.

In 1996 the Executive Council and Episcopal Church Center staff began an additional series of visits to the dioceses. An initial round of visits had been completed in 1993 in all but one of the domestic dioceses of the church under the guise of the Linkage Program. The intention in 1996 was to involve more grassroots participation in the visits. In the second round all but four dioceses agreed to a visit, one of which declined because of disapproval of the direction of national church policy. Data for the visits was used in the development of the triennial budget for the 1997 General Convention. "We really have something to share," said Browning at the time of the visits. "I think the church is going to be blessed by the visitations." [64] Post embezzlement scandal, the church and Ed Browning were moving on.

Chapter Six Notes

1   Edmond Lee Browning (hereafter cited as ELB), "Address to the 71st General Convention," Indianapolis, August 25, 1994.

2   ELB, "The Church's Greatest Sin," *The Witness* 78 (1995):16; also, Terry Mattingly, "Church's Major Sin Is Apathy, Bishop Says," *Rocky Mountain News*, August 31, 1987.

3   Elizabeth Fuetsch, "A Year in the Life of a Presiding Bishop," *Crossings*, Church Divinity School of the Pacific, special issue, No. 3, 1987.

4   A. A. Smyser, "Activist in an Active Church," *Honolulu Star-Bulletin*, n.d. [ca. May 1986], Browning Collection.

5   Ibid.

6   ELB, "Under One Roof," June 11, 1987, notes from Jim Solheim.

7   "Vision for the Future" and "Meeting in Saint Louis," *The Living Church*, July 5, 1987.

8   ELB, letter to Howard Anderson, March 4, 1986, Browning Collection.

9   Patricia Sparks Browning, interview by Sheryl Kujawa-Holbrook (hereafter cited as SKH), April 2009.

10 Ibid.

11 Judy Mathews, interview by SKH, March 2009.

12 Judy Mathews, letter to SKH, March 23, 2009.

13 ELB, *A Year of Days with The Book of Common Prayer* (New York: Ballantine Books, 1997), July 30.

14 ELB, *A Year of Days,* November 12.

15 Carol Horton, letter to SKH, May 5, 2009.

16 J. Michael Parker, "National Staff Draws Frowns from Episcopalians," *San Antonio Express-News*, n.d. [ca. 1991], Browning Collection.

17 "Episcopal Church in 1991: Many Divisions, Budget Cuts Pose Challenges," *The Living Church*, January 5, 1992.

18 ELB, interview by Victor Lipman, Honolulu, 1986.

19 Hebert Donovan, interview by SKH, March 2009.

20 "Itinerating Primate," *The Living Church,* July 5, 1987.

21 "Divestment, Reflection Dominate Council Meeting," Episcopal News Service (hereafter cited as ENS), February 13, 1986.

22 Ibid.

23 "Browning, Council Rings In Changes," ENS, June 26, 1986.

24 Ibid.

25 "P.B., Council Launch 'Journey to Mission,' " ENS, March 19, 1987.

26 Ibid.

27 "Revised Mission Imperatives," *The Living Church,* December 13, 1987, 6.

28 "Browning Calls Bishops to Teaching Ministry," ENS, October 8, 1987; "Browning Further Articulates Church's Mission," ENS, May 26, 1988.

29 "Browning Further Articulates Church's Mission," ENS, May 26, 1988.

30 David Kalvelage, "Defining Our Mission: An Interview with the Presiding Bishop," *The Living Church,* March 29, 1992.

31 "Gallup Poll Says Episcopal Church Has a 'Clear Sense of Direction and Mission' Despite Gaps Between Belief and Practice," ENS, March 14, 1990.

32 Pamela W. Darling, interview by SKH, March 1994.

33 Ibid.

34 Pamela W. Darling, ed., *Decently and In Order: Selected Reflections of Pamela P. Chinnis* (Cincinnati: Forward Movement, 2000), xvii-xix.

35 "Committee Appointments Promised Integrity Members," *The Living Church,* August 15, 1993.

36 Bruce Garner, interview by SKH, October 2009.

37 Pamela P. Chinnis, "Bishops Act Apart from Clergy and Laity," in *Decently and In Order,* 5.

38 Bruce Woodcock, interview by SKH, September 2009.

39 David Booth Beers, interview by SKH, March 2009.

40 ELB, interview by SKH, January 2009.

41 ELB, "Address to the 71st General Convention."

42 Ibid.

43 Ibid.

44 David Booth Beers, interview by SKH, March 2009.

45 Ibid.

46 Andrew Brown, "Disorder of Service," *The Independent,* London, June 24, 1995.

47 Jan Nunley, "Embezzling Power: the Ellen Cooke Affair," *The Witness* 78, no.6 (June 1995).

48 Russell V. Palmore, interview by SKH, October 2009.

49 "Five-Year Prison Sentence for Mrs. Cooke," *The Living Church,* April 4, 1996.

50 "Ellen Cooke Pleads Guilty," *The Witness* 79, no.3 (March 1996): 27; James Thrall, "Former Church Treasurer Sentenced to Five Years for Embezzlement," *The Witness* 79, no. 9 (September 1996): 26.

51 "Five-Year Prison Sentence for Mrs. Cooke"; "Mrs. Cooke's Sentence Upheld," *The Living Church,* April 20, 1997; Ed Stannard, "Former Treasurer Will Be Released Soon," ENS, November 27, 2000.

52 David Booth Beers, interview by Brian J. Grieves, December 2009.

53 "Cooke Can't Remember But Still Pleads Guilty," *Anglican Journal,* March 1, 1996.

54 "Bishop Browning to Staff: 'We're Moving Ahead,'" *The Living Church,* August 6, 1995.

55 Martin Lee Smith, interview by SKH, February 2009.

56 ELB, interview by SKH, January 2009.

57 Jan Nunley, "Embezzling Power," 35.

58 "Pressure On the Presiding Bishop," *The Living Church,* April 18,1996.

59 "Executive Council Deals with Finances, Racism—and Healing," ENS, March 7, 1996.

60 Ibid.

61 David Booth Beers, interview by Brian J. Grieves, December 2009.

62 "Interim Bodies Make New Connections at Joint Meeting in Minneapolis," ENS, October 19, 1995.

63 Pamela P. Chinnis, "Structures—Re-Examining How We Work Together," Joint Meeting of Interim Bodies, Minneapolis, Minnesota, October 12-14, 1995, in *Decently and in Order,* p.11.

64 David Kalvelage, "An Opportunity to Be Heard," *The Living Church,* March 10, 1996.

Young Edmond Browning, at age five, riding the range in Corpus Christi, Texas.

Courtesy of the Browning Family.

Still riding tall in the saddle at Ring Lake, Wyoming, 1999.

Courtesy of the Browning Family.

Patricia Alline Sparks and Edmond Lee Browning married on September 10, 1953, at The Church of the Good Shepherd, Corpus Christi, Texas. *Courtesy of the Browning Family.*

THIS WEEK
ON OKINAWA
Est. 1955 as THIS MONTH ON OKINAWA

Nov. 18, 1966

15¢

Vol. 12 No. 46

Rev. Edmond L. Browning Appointed Archdeacon

The Rev. Edmond L. Browning has been appointed Archdeacon for the work of the Episcopal Church in the Ryukyu Islands. The appointment was effected by the Rt. Harry S. Kennedy, Bishop of Honolulu, upon his recent visit to Okinawa. In the position of Archdeacon, Fr. Browning will work as an assistant to the Rt. Rev. Charles P. Gilson in the Ryukyu Islands.

The new **Archdeacon first came to Okinawa** in 1959 as the Rector of All Souls' Episcopal Church, serving in this capacity until 1963, at which time he went to Kobe, Japan for two years of language study. Since his return from Japan in 1965 he has been the priest-in-charge of St. Matthew's Episcopal Church, Oroku.

Rev. Edmond L. Browning

After graduating from St. Luke's Seminary, Sewanee, Tenn., in 1954, Fr. Browning served several Episcopal Churches in the Diocese of West Texas. He last served in that diocese as the Rector of the Church of the Redeemer, Eagle Pass, Texas.

Fr. Browning married the former Patricia Sparks of Corpus Christi in 1954. There are four children in their family—Mark, Paige, Philip and Peter.

This Week on Okinawa article announces Browning's appointment as Archdeacon for the Ryukyu Islands, 1966.
Courtesy of the Browning Family.

Patti and Ed Browning at the Missionary Retreat Center in Nojiri, Japan, 1968.
Courtesy of the Browning Family.

Browning receives the Bible from Presiding Bishop John E. Hines at his consecration as Bishop of Okinawa. Co-consecrators *(left to right)*: James Wong of Hong Kong, David Rose of Southern Virginia, Michael Yashiro, Primate of the Anglican Church of Japan, and Harry Kennedy of Hawaii, 1968.
Courtesy of the Archives of the Episcopal Church.

Edmond L Browning, appointed Bishop-in-Charge, Convocation of American Churches in Europe, 1971. *Courtesy of the Archives of the Episcopal Church.*

The Brownings at home in Nordenstadt, Germany, in 1973.
Patti, Philip, Peter, Paige, John, Mark, and Edmond, and family pet Floyd.
Courtesy of the Browning Family.

While Executive for World Mission, Browning exercised leadership in the newly formed World Hunger Task Force. New York City, 1974. *Courtesy of the Browning Family.*

The Bishop of Hawaii doffing his miter after the liturgy at St. Andrew's Cathedral, Honolulu, 1977. *Courtesy of the Browning Family.*

Browning signs "I love you" on his acceptance of election as Presiding Bishop. Anaheim General Convention, 1985. *Courtesy of the Archives of the Episcopal Church.*

Edmond Lee Browning, Installation as XXIV Presiding Bishop, Cathedral of Sts. Peter and Paul, Washington, D.C., January 11, 1986.

Courtesy of the Archives of the Episcopal Church.

Installation Eucharist, January, 1986. *(Left to right)*: Browning, Bishop John Walker (Diocese of Washington), Bishop John Watanabe (Primate, Nippon Sei Ko Kai), and Archbishop Desmond Tutu (Archbishop of Cape Town, Primate, Province of Southern Africa).

Courtesy of the Archives of the Episcopal Church.

Browning, surrounded by family members, greets the congregation at his Installation Service.
Courtesy of the Archives of the Episcopal Church.

Browning with his brother primate, Archbishop Michael Peers of the Anglican Church in Canada—world travelers, confidants, and friends, 1987.
Courtesy of the Archives of the Episcopal Church.

Browning, on his first trip to meet with ecumenical leaders, meets Pope John Paul II in Rome to exchange prayers, gifts, and commitment to the unity of the Church, 1987.

Courtesy of the Archives of the Episcopal Church.

Browning ordained Barbara Clementine Harris, Bishop Suffragan for the Diocese of Massachusetts, as the first woman bishop of the Episcopal Church, February 11, 1989.

Courtesy of the Archives of the Episcopal Church.

Members of the Episcopal Church delegation to the Anglican Consultative Council gather around the Archbishop of Canterbury, Robert Runcie. Left to right: James Ottley, Bishop of Panama, Austin Cooper, Pamela P. Chinnis, and Browning. 1990.

Courtesy of the Archives of the Episcopal Church.

Presiding Bishop Browning joins the bipartisan congressional group in support of the proposed Civil Rights Act of 1990. Included among the speakers: Senator Ted Kennedy, Senator Al Gore, Elliot Richardson, and Coretta Scott King.

Courtesy of the Archives of the Episcopal Church.

A time of meeting, prayer, and inspiration with Dom Helder Camara, Roman Catholic Archbishop of Recife, whom Browning called "a living saint."

Courtesy of J. Patrick Mauney.

Browning meets with President George Bush in the Oval Office at the White House, 1991. President Bush signed the photo "To Bishop Browning—Leader of our church, pastor, and respected friend." *Courtesy of the White House.*

Browning met with Alexsy II, Patriarch of Moscow and All Russia and Primate of the Russian Orthodox Church, at the Episcopal Church Center, New York City, 1991. The two shared a deep spirituality and friendship.

Photo taken by James Solheim.

Courtesy of the Episcopal Church Archives.

Celebrating the life of Martin Luther King Jr., Browning gathers with church and civic leaders at Washington National Cathedral, 1992. *Left to right*: Browning; Pamela P. Chinnis, President of the House of Deputies; Senator John Danforth; Dr. Thomas Law, St. Paul's College; Dr. Prezell R. Robinson, St. Augustine's College; and Mayor Sharon Pratt Kelly of Washington, D.C.

Courtesy of the Archives of the Episcopal Church.

Much loved by the youth, "the church, today, not just tomorrow," Browning addresses the national Episcopal Youth Event (EYE) at Amherst, Massachusetts, in 1992.

Courtesy of the Archives of the Episcopal Church.

Retired Presiding Bishop John E. Hines is introduced by Presiding Bishop Browning to the meeting of the Primates of the Anglican Communion and the Anglican Consultative Council at Kanuga Conference Center in North Carolina. Archbishop of Canterbury George Carey joins the applause. A fellow Texan, Hines was a mentor and treasured friend of Browning.

Courtesy of the Browning Family.

Browning lights a candle in memory of assassinated Prime Minister Yitzhak Rabin of Israel at a sidewalk shrine near the Episcopal Church Center in New York City, 1995.

Courtesy of the Archives of the Episcopal Church.

Browning participates in the Sabeel International Conference held at the Muqata'a, Ramallah, 2004. The panel included Browning, Yasser Arafat (President, Palestinian National Authority), Hanan Ashrawi (Palestinian Christian legislator and leader), and Naim Ateek (Director of Sabeel International).
Courtesy of the Browning Family.

Over 200 bishops of the Episcopal Church and the Evangelical Lutheran Church in America met to discuss Full Communion between the two churches. Presiding Bishops Browning and H. George Anderson welcomed Archbishop of Canterbury George Carey and University of Chicago religious scholar Dr. Martin Marty to this historic meeting in 1996.
Courtesy of the Archives of the Episcopal Church.

Browning, Pamela P. Chinnis, and the Rev. Ted Karpf, director of National AIDS Coalition, visit the AIDS Quilt Memorial to view some of the 40,000 panels displayed on the Mall, Washington, D.C., 1996.
Courtesy of the Archives of the Episcopal Church.

Prayers of repentance and reconciliation were offered at the signing of the New Jamestown Covenant at Jamestown, Virginia. Browning is flanked *(left to right)* by Frank Oberly (Osage-Comanche), Dr. Owanah Anderson (Choctaw and Native American Ministries Staff Officer), Pamela P. Chinnis (House of Deputies President), and the Rev. Cn. Brian J. Grieves, (Peace and Justice Officer). 1997.

Courtesy of David W. Perry.

Browning and House of Deputies President Pamela P. Chinnis celebrate the last Executive Council meeting of Browning's term in Honolulu, Hawaii, 1997.

Courtesy of the Archives of the Episcopal Church.

Browning talks with Japanese governmental minister Sadaaki Numata and Provost John Petty in front of the Coventry Cross at Coventry Cathedral. Earlier they recited the Coventry Litany of Reconciliation. 1997.

Courtesy of the Archives of the Episcopal Church.

Patti and Ed Browning were honored at the 1997 Philadelphia General Convention with a special evening celebrating their lives and ministries. *Courtesy of the Archives of the Episcopal Church.*

In a historic moment, three presiding bishops shared in the opening Eucharist of the General Convention held in Anaheim, California, 2009. The Most Reverend Katharine Jefferts Schori welcomed the Right Reverend Edmond Lee Browning and the Right Reverend Frank Tracy Griswold before the liturgy.

Courtesy of David W. Perry.

Generations of Brownings gathered at the Browning home in Hood River in 2008. Missing from the photo is grandson, Freedom.

Photo by JenningsPhotography.com, Hood River, Oregon. Printed with permission.

Chapter 7

God's Image
in All People
1986-1997

THERE IS NOTHING MORE IMPORTANT than our
call to awaken in all people the awareness of their
dignity, the awareness of God's image in all people,
the awareness of God's presence in the community
of those who call upon God's name. [1]

> — Edmond Lee Browning,
> "Christ for a New Century:
> A Sermon to Open the
> Decade of Evangelism," 1990

Ed Browning was one of the first national religious
leaders to show compassion for and give material support
to those affected by HIV/AIDS. Jerry Anderson, a priest
of the Diocese of Los Angeles, shared this story of Ed
Browning's participation as the AIDS Quilt was unfolded
at the General Convention in 1988:

> On the morning that the AIDS Quilt was to be
> unfolded in the exhibition hall on the floor under

the level where the delegates were meeting, Browning presided over a healing service with 600 people in attendance. He blessed panels for the quilt, and then we had a solemn procession down to the quilt and then he was the first person to read names of those who had died, as the quilt was unfolded. Several of us on the committee stood behind him on the platform. I felt we were glimpsing something of what the apostles must have felt with Jesus on the Mount of Transfiguration. It was one of the most sacred and holy experiences of my life. [2]

HIV and AIDS

Acquired immune deficiency syndrome (AIDS) and the human immunodeficiency virus (HIV) first were identified in the United States in 1981 and continue to spread today. AIDS is a progressive, degenerative disease caused when the virus attacks the immune system. Over time it leaves the body defenseless to opportunistic diseases that can be fatal. There is no cure for HIV or AIDS, although in recent years drugs have slowed the progress of the virus in some people. Browning was among the first Christian leaders to advocate for people with AIDS, and he did so as presiding bishop from the time of his election. In 1985, when Ed Browning was elected presiding bishop, cases of AIDS-related illness were rapidly increasing in number and expanding in terms of population and geography. An AIDS diagnosis was a death sentence. By one estimate more than 10,000 people contracted AIDS between 1981 and 1985; over 80 percent of those diagnosed in 1981 were dead by 1985. [3] Although AIDS was originally thought to be confined to gay and bisexual men, it was soon evident that babies were being born with HIV/AIDS, that intravenous drug abusers were the second largest group contracting the disease, that some people contracted the disease through blood transfusions, and that prostitution was contributing to the spread of the disease in the heterosexual population. Some Episcopalians were concerned about the possibility of contracting the disease through the common cup. Some Christians also believed that the disease was a punishment from God. HIV/AIDS was often compared with leprosy and great epidemics in the past. Episcopal AIDS education efforts in the mid-1980s focused on the need for compassion and mercy amid the agony and isolation of the disease.

"It appears that the epidemic is at a minimal level focused largely in the New York and San Francisco areas, and it is on its way to frightening escalation that might touch countless cities and people across this land," wrote William E. Swing, bishop of California, in 1985. "A plague of death stands on our doorstep, and it is vitally important that the church enter the arena with genuine concern."[4] In the same year John Fortunato, president of Integrity, wrote an impassioned plea for shelter, food, clothing, financial support, hospice care, prayer, and spiritual sustenance to the dying. If the church was truly *to be* the church in the midst of such human suffering, it must reach out to the outcast: "God favors the outcast. The *anawin* nestle especially close to God's bosom. This assertion is scripturally unavoidable and true no matter how tightly some in Christ's church hang onto their hypocrisy and comfortable pews."[5]

Concerned that little was being done to ameliorate the suffering of people with AIDS, Browning mentioned in his acceptance address as presiding bishop that caring for those with the disease deserved more national attention. He then began to devote time and resources to a national Episcopal AIDS ministry. HIV/AIDS advocacy and ministry was a major program focus during Browning's term as presiding bishop. At first some in the church claimed not to know any person who was HIV positive or who had full-blown AIDS, but the rapid spread of the disease soon silenced those voices. Within a few years of Browning's election, the Episcopal Church developed an extensive AIDS ministry, much of it due to his indefatigable advocacy. One of his visitations in his first year as presiding bishop was to meet AIDs patients and activists in the San Francisco Bay area. He declared November 9, 1986, as "A Day of Caring," for the Episcopal Church to pray for those with AIDS. "Even parts of the religious community have issued judgments that can only increase the myths and phobia to the point of demeaning," he said. [6] Instead, Browning urged the Episcopal Church to provide for the spiritual and pastoral needs of people with AIDS and those who share their suffering. "We can be a fountain of ever-flowing love and a foundation for a community of grace," he said. [7]

During the 1988 General Convention in Detroit, Browning announced his intention to establish a "pastoral relationship" with a person with AIDS that summer. Although the man's identity was never made public, Browning visited him until his death and challenged other bishops and pastors to do the same. "We are being called anew to trust in God and to be willing to suffer with others," he said. "I call for compassion." [8] Browning helped launch the National Episcopal AIDS Coalition (NEAC) at the same convention, where the NAMES Project AIDS Memorial Quilt was on display. Several times he read the names at a memorial service for those who had died of AIDS, and the poignancy of the experience never eluded him. The duration of the epidemic reminded him of the many people who had been moved to acts of kindness by the tragedy in a way that became a permanent part of their lives. "Every stitch of that quilt speaks of heartbreak," he wrote. "But every stitch also speaks of sweetness. This ongoing tragedy has brought about the largest sustained expression of compassion the world has ever seen." [9]

On October 15, 1989, representatives from a broad spectrum of Christian churches were invited by Ed Browning to participate in an Ecumenical Service of Compassion and Healing for Persons Living with AIDS at the National Cathedral in Washington, D.C. Representatives included leaders from the Presbyterian Church USA, the Roman Catholic Church, the Greek Orthodox Church, the Orthodox Church in America, the United Methodist Church, the Church of the Brethren, the Christian Church-Disciples of Christ, and the Russian Orthodox Churches in the United States. The service included the laying on of hands. Afterwards participants discussed their experiences with persons living with AIDS. The group drafted a "Statement of Concern and Hope," recommitting themselves and their churches to HIV/AIDS ministry and urging governments, the private sector, and all people of the nation to provide moral and financial support to ease the suffering of those affected by the pandemic. The statement also urged churches to designate the second Sunday of October as AIDS Awareness Sunday. [10] Two months later Browning was a participant in a major event sponsored by the Carter Center of Emory University in Atlanta, "AIDS—the Moral Imperative: A Call to National Leadership." The ecumenical and interfaith event is believed to be the single largest gathering of religious leaders focused on HIV/AIDS to date. There Browning reminded the conference of the moral and ethical responsibility of religious leaders: "I believe that we in the religious communities have a unique ministry in that we are the popular, public, and identified repositories of ethical, moral, and prophetic witness. People want to know what we think about this disease and what we see as a faithful response," he said. [11]

Within four years of the birth of NEAC, twenty-four dioceses and many parishes responded to the General Convention's resolution and developed AIDS policies, although there was concern about the ninety dioceses that were unresponsive. For Ed Browning, the suffering of people with AIDS and the impact of their anguish on the broader community went to the heart of his faith and what it means to be the church. "The suffering of each of these persons physically, mentally, and spiritually is incalculable. The personal search for a cure or relief is often frantic and ultimately fruitless and costly. Parents and friends react in varying degrees of horror, panic, fear, and shame," he wrote. And he went on to say, "The physical pain is joined by social ostracism and the politicization of the condition. The agony of the person living with AIDS, family, friends, and loved ones, goes beyond dispassionate telling." [12]

Browning's commitment to HIV/AIDS ministries was not without controversy. The Episcopal edition of a resource published by Advocates for Youth in Washington, D.C., entitled *Teens for AIDS Prevention* (TAP) and commended by the presiding bishop, underscored the church's traditional teaching on sexual behavior but also included information such as a condom demonstration. While the resource continues to be used in the church today, it caused consternation among many who objected to its sexually explicit content. [13]

Ed Browning traveled widely and participated in a variety of public events related to HIV/AIDS ministries. In the later years of his administration, as the life expectancies of those with HIV/AIDS improved through better treatment options, Browning continued to advocate for a cure. Because of his early and lasting support, Browning is often referred to as the "father" of HIV/AIDS ministries in the Episcopal Church. "We Episcopalians must not be content with the notion that it is now possible for people living with HIV/AIDS to live longer. We must pray and work together for the long haul. The call is for ongoing, substantive research that seeks a cure to this scourge, which elicits both the very best and the worst from us." [14]

In 1996 Browning was one of ten national sponsors of the display of the NAMES Project AIDS Memorial Quilt in Washington, D.C. The event included President Clinton and took place on the National Mall where 40,000 panels containing the names of 70,000 persons who had died from AIDS were displayed. Both Browning and Pam Chinnis joined in the public reading of the names of the dead. NEAC held a conference in conjunction with the event where Browning celebrated the eucharist.

The closing years of the Browning administration brought the continuation of the Standing Commission on HIV/AIDS and concern about the impact of the disease among youth and people of color. The General Convention in 1997 committed to continuing the participation of the Episcopal Church in the response to the spread of HIV/ AIDS throughout the nation and the world.

Advocacy and Public Policy

Ed Browning's vision of the Body of Christ led him to affirm the church's prophetic role in the political arena. He worked assiduously as an advocate for public policy issues. "Our vision of being one in Christ makes us whole and forms our spiritual as well as public body," he said. Such a vision "is the grounding of public policy—the actions, the behavior, the programs, the polity we form and advance." [15]

To support these efforts, Browning expanded the Washington Office of the Episcopal Church and through that office developed key relationships with Episcopalians and others who were members of the House of Representatives, the Senate, and the White House staff. The Washington Office was launched in 1979 and operates with a small staff in comparison with other mainline denominations, despite the fact that Episcopalians have the largest representation per capita of any religious denomination in Congress and are well-represented in the Cabinet, senior administration, courts, and other government departments and agencies. [16] Browning believed that all political decisions were essentially moral and reflective of "the dynamic and reforming power of interaction and interdependence of the various sectors of society." [17] It was Browning's hope that with an increased staff presence on Capitol Hill, the Episcopal Church would have more direct contact with lawmakers and more opportunities to enhance the church's contact with constituents there.

In 1987 Browning was the keynote speaker at the fifteenth annual IMPACT briefing in Washington, D.C. IMPACT, a national lobbying effort supported by twenty-three Episcopal, Protestant, Roman Catholic, and Jewish groups and the Washington Interreligious Staff Council (WISC), is run by staff of the various church bodies based in the nation's capital. "If we are to press our opinions on the body politic, they must be balanced opinions, carefully framed, and subjected to debate among ourselves," Browning said to the assembled conference of 125 official delegates, of which Episcopalians comprised the largest group.[18] Delegates to the conference participated in a three-hour training in advocacy skills designed by the Public Policy Network, the Washington Office, and the partner networks.

As members of Congress wrestled with the federal budget and aid to the Nicaraguan Contras, Browning also visited Episcopal senators as a "step in creating partnership between the Washington Office and our leaders in Congress."[19] Browning met with senators Claiborne Pell (R-R.I.), the Senate Foreign Relations Committee chair; Nancy Kassebaum (R-Kan.); Alan Simpson (R-Wyo.); and John C. Danforth (R-Mo.), an Episcopal priest. Browning used the meeting to discuss the results of his "year of listening" and his recent visits with ecumenical leaders in Rome, Jerusalem, and Istanbul. He also met with the ambassador from Turkey to discuss the rights of the Christian minority there. Aid to the Nicaraguan Contras became a major focus of the conference after the cultural attaché of the Nicaraguan embassy told the delegates that support of the Contras was "against the expressed purpose of the U.S. to promote democracy in Nicaragua."[20]

Although Browning criticized the Reagan administration for its exclusion of mainline churches in favor of more conservative religious voices, he developed strong relationships with the George H. W. Bush (1989-1993) and

Bill Clinton (1993-2001) administrations. It was always his hope to have a pastoral rather than an adversarial relationship with U.S. presidents, even when they disagreed. Browning's first meeting in the Oval Office was in May 1989, the day President Bush was coping with the election crisis in Panama. "This is a long way from South Texas," Browning thought as he waited to meet with the president.[21] (The only other head of state to elicit the same reaction from Browning was Pope John Paul II at the Vatican). Diane Porter, Public Ministries Officer, and Robert Brooks, Staff Officer of the Washington Office, were also present, as was Douglas Wead, the president's deputy for public liaison. Browning shared with Bush his insights on Panama from his visit two months earlier with three other Anglican primates. Browning also presented Bush with an inscribed copy of *The Book of Common Prayer*, an Episcopal cap, and a personal letter from the Episcopal Church Center receptionist, a Panamanian named Luis Nazario. He assured the president of his prayers and the prayers of all the primates of the Anglican Communion. In the course of the brief meeting the presiding bishop and the president established a way to keep in touch. This method was used a week later when Browning learned that Bush had declined to meet with Desmond Tutu, archbishop of Cape Town, and other South African religious leaders when they visited Washington, D.C. Browning urged the president to reconsider. Although why Bush changed his mind is not a matter of public record, he did agree to see Tutu later that month.[22]

George H. W. Bush had been an active Episcopalian all his life, and yet it was difficult for him to acknowledge publicly how his Christian faith influenced his decisions.

A man who believed in the power of prayer and was deeply faithful, he was "not too comfortable" in sharing "this heretofore very personal area" of his life in the political arena. He said he was not a man "to wear my faith or my religion on my sleeve." Yet, Bush believed that "we are one nation under God" and his religious values informed his views on government. Browning and Bush, chief pastor and chief executive, did not agree on many matters of public policy, yet each respected the faith and the vocation of the other. "In one conversation [with Bush] we noted that we have some different ideas, some different visions of our responsibilities in this global village," said Browning. "We discussed the fact that this is not likely to change. And we accepted that. Christian life isn't about agreement or disagreement. It is about being faithful, struggling to discern."[23] Browning believed it was his role to serve the president, to pray for him and with him, and to remain in communication whether they agreed on policies or not. Still, Browning was concerned that Bush gave a strong ear to the religious right and tended to use God's name in partisan contexts. Browning was one of twenty-three religious leaders who condemned the president's use of God's name at the Republican National Convention in a way that implied a righteousness unique to the Republican Party. Yet Browning appreciated the openness of the president to personal contact. "Mr. Bush has been a president who has been very open to me and willing for me to bring concerns to him when necessary, much more open than Mr. Reagan was, and I admire him for that," he said.[24]

The Episcopal Church endorsed a major economic justice plan at the 1988 General Convention in Detroit. The so-called Michigan Plan was linked to Browning's call for mission in the world and focused on the needs of the poor throughout the nation. It called for up to $24 million to be raised through grants, ecumenical programs, and other major fund-raising efforts in support of a "National Episcopal Fund for Community Investment and Economic Justice." [25] "It was an extensive plan and the presiding bishop was part of it every step of the way," said Norman J. Faramelli, who worked on the Michigan Plan. [26]

In the same year, Browning visited coal miners in southwestern Virginia, invited by the Bible study group from St. Mark's Church in St. Paul, Wise County, Virginia. The people of the region were torn apart by Appalachia's biggest coal strike in years. The group wanted Browning, seen as a prophetic pastor, to speak for the silent voices in the impoverished area. In his sermon at St. Mark's, to a congregation of mining families, Browning affirmed the community's ministry of presence and compassion. "The church's role is the role of presence, not of answers," he said. "God came into the world in the person of Jesus to bring wholeness and well-being to brokenness and division. The church has a responsibility to be in that brokenness." [27]

In 1990 Browning was asked by Senator Edward M. Kennedy of Massachusetts to represent the religious community at a press conference to announce the new proposed Civil Rights Act. It was an auspicious honor and an indication of Browning's reputation as a moral leader. A powerful bipartisan group from both houses of Congress had drafted the legislation. Their goal was to address recent Supreme Court decisions that had made it more difficult for victims of discrimination to secure justice in the court system. The framers of the legislation and Browning himself believed the Supreme Court had severely undermined the Civil Rights Act of 1964. "And so we return today," Browning said, "to make sure that America does not turn back—that it does not turn away from the goals of equal opportunity and equal justice for all and turn back to the injustice, the divisions, and the turmoil of a shameful past."[28] President George H. W. Bush subsequently vetoed the bill. An attempt to override the veto narrowly failed.[29]

The Bill Clinton administration brought with it a spirit of optimism in the churches about the president's openness to the church's moral agenda. Top religious leaders from fourteen Protestant and five Orthodox bodies met with Clinton for an hour in March 1993 to share their insights and tell the president "what they think is important." Joan Brown Campbell, general secretary of the National Council of Churches (NCC), believed that Clinton considered the churches a resource. Ben Chavez of the United Church of Christ's Commission for Racial Justice believed that church leaders had not had such access to the president since the administration of Lyndon Johnson. It was Clinton's intention to give religious leaders access to every agency of his administration. Each religious leader shared a major issue with Clinton. Browning spoke of the many trips he and Patti had made to the Middle East and stressed the need for peace talks and justice for the Palestinian people. "I told him that violence was hindering the peace process and that the voice of the moderate Palestinians was being lost, the delegation was being marginalized," said Browning. "At this point the Palestinians had nothing to show for their involvement in the peace process."[30] To address the situation Browning proposed the formation of an Eminent Persons Group under the sponsorship of the NCC that could travel to the area and report directly to the president, a suggestion Clinton considered. A year later Browning was invited to a breakfast with Clinton at the White House, where he affirmed the need for universal healthcare coverage. Browning stated then that he considered universal access and comprehensive benefits key to the church's commitment to "the dignity of every human being—which we affirm and serve in our baptismal covenant."[31]

In the summer of 1993 Browning met with another influential Episcopalian in Washington, General Colin Powell, chairman of the Joint Chiefs of Staff and the former senior warden of a parish in Virginia. Browning was accompanied at this meeting by Charles Keyser, suffragan bishop for the Armed Forces. They thanked Powell for his long service to the country and affirmed the Episcopal Church's ongoing pastoral concern for persons in the military. "We emphasized that the church's ministry has always been concerned with pastoral outreach to people in the military," said Keyser, "even at times when our position differed from that of the administration, such as the Persian Gulf War." Browning and Keyser also had a discussion with Powell about gays in the military in which the general explained how he had "agonized" over the situation.

During the same visit to Capitol Hill, Browning spent two days with members of Congress and the new Clinton administration discussing both domestic and international issues. In a visit to the office of the Congressional Black Caucus, Browning assured executive director Amelia Parker that "many of the things you are struggling for are also important to our church." Browning shared details of his visits to south central Los Angeles after the riots there, and the church's plans to fight racism.

He met again with senators Danforth and John Chafee to discuss universal health care. The presiding bishop praised Chafee for supporting handgun control legislation. He met at the State Department with officials engaged with Africa, the Middle East, Latin America, and Asia— regions of particular interest in the Anglican Communion. Asked how advocacy and public policy in Washington connected to his ministry, Browning replied that all his efforts in these areas "are linked in my own personal attempt to put my prayer life into action." [32] Browning drew strength for the challenges of public policy advocacy from the baptismal vow to strive for justice for all human beings. "It is part of our vocation as Christians to build God's reign on earth and that requires us to speak the truth as we see it to those in authority," he said. "Our spiritual life and our public witness are not separate but woven together in our calling to be stewards of all creation." [33]

In 1995 Browning was a key figure in a consultation to structure the Washington Office of the National Council of Churches. At the time, mainline churches were scaling back their efforts at public policy advocacy, and the radical right Christian Coalition was gaining influence. Long a supporter of the National Council of Churches, Browning challenged the mainline churches to reclaim the language of morality and Christian values from the religious right and to highlight the scriptural basis for public policy advocacy. The religious community has "quite an impact when all of the individual voices come together with the same message," he said, such as caring for children, and the poor and sick and needy. [34]

Near the end of the Browning administration, in February 1997, the Episcopal Church's commitment to justice and peace was celebrated at the Justice, Peace, and Integrity of Creation (JPIC) Summit. The event drew more than 500 people to Cincinnati, Ohio, from ninety dioceses, as well as international participants. It affirmed the prophetic leadership of Ed Browning and his commitment to the church's role in public policy advocacy. Pam Chinnis viewed the summit as a time "to take stock, to build connections, to renew our faith and love and commitment, to celebrate the Good News of Jesus Christ in our day as countless hosts have done before us." [35]

At the JPIC Summit a compilation of Ed Browning's statements, addresses, and correspondence related to public policy was introduced. Entitled *No Outcasts: The Public Witness of Edmond L. Browning, XXIVth Presiding Bishop of the Episcopal Church*, it was edited by Brian J. Grieves, peace and justice officer for the Episcopal Church. There was also a video, with the same title. Both resources highlighted Browning's immense contributions to the public policy witness of the Episcopal Church. Characteristically humble in the midst of the crowd and always more comfortable giving praise than receiving it, Browning saw the summit as "a sure sign that the issue of justice for God's earth, God's creatures, and God's human family will remain alive long after I'm gone through the ministries that you carry out in this church." [36] Astounded that some in the church would belittle and isolate peace and justice issues to the sidelines, Browning was convinced that the summit was a sign that "there had been a shift in the life of the church that has moved the issues of peace and justice to center stage. It's just that some folks haven't figured it out yet."

The JPIC Summit had organizational challenges. Given the sheer numbers of participants and the diversity of people and issues, along with the limited time available, it was difficult for small groups to come to a consensus and a strategy for action. Some feared that their passionate concerns would be lost in the final report or so watered down that the report would be irrelevant. Most participants were effective advocates at home, and there was "rebellion and resistance" from those who felt excluded from leadership at the summit. Many were not skilled at talking about issues raised by other people and devising a common vision. Still, the impassioned atmosphere at the JPIC Summit was encouraging to many and a signal that the church could no longer walk away from the tough issues. Many at the JPIC Summit attributed the Episcopal Church's passion for justice to the courageous leadership of Edmond Lee Browning. "Browning's legacy of a Gospel-centered concern for peace and justice is well planted in this church," said Ted Karpf, executive director of the National Episcopal AIDS Coalition. [37]

The first presiding bishop to be a member of the Episcopal Peace Fellowship (EPF), Browning had worked with the organization since the 1970s, starting with his involvement in issues affecting the Pacific. "When Ed was elected a whole lot of people, especially EPF, laid a heavy load on him," said Mary Miller, an executive director of the organization and a close advisor to Browning. "Nothing happened under John Allin, and enough remembered John Hines to want to establish a relationship with the presiding bishop. He attended our national meeting the spring after his election and from that point on either he was personally in conversation with us, or it was one of his staff." Miller said that the way Browning exercised his ministry as presiding bishop by making public statements and by appearing at public events was a new way of doing business. The presiding bishop also worked with EPF to plan events such as the peace vigil the night before the consecration of Charles Keyser as suffragan bishop of the Armed Forces, and a similar event across from the White House on the eve of the Persian Gulf War. "For me, he was always there," said Mary Miller of Browning. "It was hard work, but the road was astonishing." Miller said about the only thing she learned *not* to say to Browning was, "You look tired." The observation drove Browning crazy. "He would always snap back, 'Don't say that—it makes it worse,'" said Miller. [38]

Children and Youth

A pastor, a parent, and a grandparent, Edmond Browning often expressed his concern over the plight of the world's children. Early in 1987 he appeared in a series of Episcopal Church sponsored public service announcements in support of Defense for Children International, a child advocacy organization. In their travels, both Ed and Patti Browning were profoundly moved by the suffering of women and children and thus stood ready to assist organizations advocating for them. Browning invited the internationally known child advocate Marian Wright Edelman to speak to the 1994 General Convention. Two years later during the Stand for Children march in Washington, D.C., the Browning administration organized national Episcopal participation, which included advocacy training. A staunch supporter of Episcopal Schools and of Christian education, Browning was always interested in the catechetical work of dioceses and local congregations. "I believe the ministry of our schools is an incarnational ministry. We should model our work on Christ's work.

We must widen the view of our children—sensitize the affluent to the pain and suffering of the world." [39]

Ed and Patti Browning regularly attended the triennial national Episcopal Youth Events (EYE), which grew steadily in numbers throughout the Browning years. At the EYEs the Brownings greeted hundreds of young people. For their part, the enthusiasm of the young people for the presiding bishop never waned. Despite often cramped conditions and the summer heat, Browning captivated the hearts and spirits of young people with his daily meditations. At times one could hear a pin drop in a room packed with more than 1,000 adolescents. At other times the crowd chanted "Eddie! Eddie! Eddie!"—a sign of affection and respect. Browning's daily reflections at youth conferences focused on his own experience as a young person active in the church and his diocesan camp, the ways he met Jesus in daily life, and on the themes of inclusivity and compassion. "Those two values of inclusiveness and compassion threaten the status quo that often protects the power and comfort that we enjoy. The values of inclusiveness and compassion often threaten our unwillingness to be in relationship with people who are very much unlike us," he said at an EYE in Montana in 1990. [40] The young crowds were usually at the edge of their seats or off them for much of Browning's meditations. His low-key approachability and willingness to go along with ridiculous skits or wear anything for them, along with Patti's gentleness and kindness, made the Brownings favorites among young people across the church. Many who were young during the Browning aministration and who met the Brownings at EYE or another conference say that Edmond Lee Browning will always be "my PB."

Institutional Racism

Ed Browning often spoke out against racism and affirmed the need of the church to live intentionally into its diversity. Committed to the struggle against apartheid in South Africa, Browning also realized that the Episcopal Church could not maintain its integrity if it fought racism elsewhere but not at home. "The whole issue of racism in our country is more serious today than it was during the Civil Rights era" of the 1960s, he said. "Before we talk about bringing down apartheid, we must look at ourselves. Racism in this country is an evil that needs to be addressed." [41] During his first year of listening to the church after his election, Browning noted how often the issue of racism was raised by different communities. He preached at gatherings of the Union of Black Episcopalians (UBE) and visited Native American, Asian, and Hispanic congregations. "The issue of racism keeps coming forward as I travel and I meet with church people in this country and representatives from abroad....often that issue is translated into different means: quality education, medical care, employment, housing, and social services." [42]

Countering institutional racism took on a variety of forms. Beginning in 1987 a series of anti-racism training sessions was designed for the staff at the Episcopal Church Center to look at institutional racism systemically, in response to the General Convention mandate to eliminate racism from the church. Anti-racism sessions were regularly scheduled throughout the Browning years. At the same time consultants were hired to provide anti-racism training to the various committees and commissions of the church. They also assisted with local racial justice programs.

During Easter Week in 1989 the black Episcopal bishops drafted a special pastoral letter to African American Episcopalians, in an effort to address their struggles to live out their faith in a predominantly white denomination. The pastoral letter was designed to provide an opportunity for black Episcopalians to take stock of what had been accomplished and to "shape the vision for the next stages of their journey." [43]

At the time Browning was elected presiding bishop, African American Episcopalians had enjoyed unprecedented access to every level of church governance through the agency of presiding bishop John Allin and Charles Radford Lawrence, the first African American president of the House of Deputies. Although many African Americans in the church had hoped that John T. Walker, bishop of Washington, would be elected presiding bishop, they were hopeful when Browning was elected, particularly with his commitment to "no outcasts." Critics of the Browning administration, however, believe that the gains of the African American community under Allin were lost under Browning. Some note that Browning's early ministry had taken him outside the continental United States with the exception of five years in Texas, and hence he lacked personal experience of the Civil Rights era of the 1960s. Others say that although racism had not been eradicated, the church under Browning shifted its focus to sexism, heterosexism, and clericalism. Thus there were white laywomen on Browning's senior staff but no African American ordained men. "At the time, he [the presiding bishop] did not see the pattern of black male clergy terminations," said Ed Rodman of the Urban Caucus. [44] Some believe that critical issues of black clergy, particularly black men, such as deployment and roles in the administration, were downplayed or ignored. Some black leaders also argue that they were cut off from regular communication with the presiding bishop and that he did not seek their counsel.[45]

Access and representation of the African American community during the Browning administration were complicated by the position of Diane Marie Porter, who joined the staff in 1988 as deputy for public policy after a distinguished career in government. Porter, an African American and an Episcopal laywoman, was appointed unit executive, and then senior executive for program. A controversial and influential figure among staff at the Episcopal Church Center, she was seen as an energetic and dedicated leader disinclined to share responsibility. Some believed that Porter, a brilliant strategist, commanded the presiding bishop's attention to the exclusion of others and that she was primarily responsible for the firing of African American staff. Porter advised the presiding bishop on a host of issues and traveled widely with the Brownings. Staff feared her controlling work style and the possibility of retribution if they crossed her. Some members of the black community perceived that the issues they brought to the presiding bishop were always filtered through her. Although Porter's rise in the church's hierarchy was significant, it came during a time when other black staff decreased in numbers and influence. When Browning received complaints about Porter's work style, he initially viewed them as personality disputes and urged both parties to work toward reconciliation. Porter said that working in a "church as family" situation was difficult and that while Ed Browning's strength was in pastoral situations, he did not always see the systemic implications of an issue. She also believed he was easily triangulated and thus confused decisions already made. [46] As the controversies worsened, however, Browning sought the counsel of members of the African American community and other church leaders. Browning and Porter agreed that she would leave the staff in March 1997, nine months short of the end of his term as presiding bishop. [47]

Judith Conley, former president of the Union of Black Episcopalians (UBE) and a member of Executive Council and the Anglican Consultative Council during the Browning years, saw Browning overall as "open and responsive" to the African American community. He met with UBE leaders when there was an issue to discuss and attended their national conferences when invited. "He was always fair enough to sit with us and hear what we had to say, and there never was a time when he did not open his door to talk with us," said Conley. [48] She said the presiding bishop often addressed questions of racism even when others in the room ignored them. Conley also believes that it was logical for Browning to trust that Diane Porter would act on behalf of black people. "Race and sex and power are always an issue," said Conley, who acknowledged Porter's capacity to steamroll, yet also found her highly skilled and helpful. [49]

Institutional racism in the Episcopal Church was brought sharply into focus when a referendum to establish the Martin Luther King Jr. holiday was defeated in Arizona, the chosen site for the 1991 General Convention. The decision to witness against racism at the 1991 General Convention in Phoenix was a controversial one, despite the presiding bishop's presence at a major march in support of Martin Luther King Jr. Day in Arizona seven months before the event. According to church canons only the presiding bishop, with the advice and consent of the Executive Council, is able to alter the date or site of a General Convention. Browning discussed whether or not to go to Phoenix with a variety of church leaders, particularly those he knew had strong opinions. Despite protests that the church should boycott Phoenix as the site for the 1991 General Convention because Arizona did not observe the holiday, Browning decided, after much prayer, to go to Arizona to witness against racism and launch a major program initiative in the area.

Browning's decision was based partially on his experience of returning to Sewanee while in seminary after the Board of Regents of the University of the South had barred blacks from the school and then later voted to admit them. Browning had chosen then to return to the school and work for reconciliation and to stand with any black students who might be admitted. It was not easy for him to seek reconciliation in such a conflicted situation while in seminary, and it was even harder years later as presiding bishop. He also recalled that Henry Knox Sherrill, the twentieth presiding bishop, had moved the 1955 General Convention from Houston to Honolulu due to Houston's segregation laws. Browning insisted that making the decision to stay in Phoenix was "the most difficult choice," but that "my heart, my gut, my reason, my experience…my whole being says 'go to Phoenix.'" He believed that the Episcopal Church should go to Phoenix as an act of solidarity with the church and the people of Arizona who had worked against racism and "pledge our commitment in the struggle however long it may last." [50] Browning saw the General Convention in Phoenix as an opportunity for the church to claim its ministry of reconciliation. "God has given us Arizona as a gift—as a place to go, to stand, to hope, to confess our own racism, and to witness to justice," he said. "In Arizona God is asking the church in all its pain, suffering, and confusion to come in the spirit of St. Paul to share the sufferings of one another." [51]

The majority of African American church leaders had opposed meeting in Phoenix. For them the convention decision was more about addressing institutional racism than about reconciliation. [52] Browning also discussed the decision with the bishop and members of the Diocese of Arizona. One factor that swayed his decision was the opportunity an Arizona location gave the Diocese of Navajoland to co-host the convention and to maintain a large presence there. The Navajos felt that as Native Americans they were often the most invisible group in the Episcopal Church and that the Arizona location would enable them to participate at an unprecedented level. Some members of the African American community suggested that the convention be held in Navajoland, instead of the convention center in Phoenix, to show the church's solidarity with the people who suffer most from racial discrimination in Arizona.

Many deputies and bishops remained opposed to the decision to meet in Phoenix. Individuals, organizations, and deputations discussed whether to boycott entirely or to limit their own participation. On the first legislative day in Phoenix, lay deputy Antoinette Daniels of New Jersey and Walter Dennis, suffragan bishop of New York, announced during roll call that they and many others were "present under protest." Many wore strips of purple ribbon in solidarity with those who believed holding the convention in Arizona was inappropriate. Some felt that the witness against racism planned by the church was eclipsed at the convention by the vitriolic debates on human sexuality. [53]

Strategies were developed to help the church intentionally combat racism. Offerings collected from daily worship services at the Phoenix convention were designated for the Martin Luther King Jr. Scholarship Fund, established to support students of color. Plans to scale down the funds spent at the convention were put in place, including a request to organizations and exhibitors to cut back on booth space and special dinners. Compliance with these actions was mixed. The entire convention participated in a "racial audit" designed to assess the attitudes of Episcopalians about race. Not surprisingly, results were divided by race and by gender. Judith Conley said the audit was "the first time we have had actual raw data to support the fact that racism does exist in this institution." Still, while Conley felt the discussions about racism at the convention were helpful, she was not optimistic that they would lead to action at home. [54] In responding to the racial audit results, Browning said he would do all in his power to "combat institutional racism at every level" of the church. [55]

The Native American community played a highly visible role in the worship life of the 1991 General Convention. Blending the rituals and prayers of different Native traditions, bags of earth from different tribal lands were mixed on the altar to consecrate it as holy ground. Native American Episcopalians testified to their struggles to maintain their indigenous cultures in the midst of the majority culture. The convention voted to support the religious freedom of Native Americans. "We have survived genocide, manifest destiny, and John Wayne," said Robert Two Bulls, a Lakota Sioux.[56] While many of those at convention were moved by the experience of Native American spiritualities there, some denounced the rituals as examples of "pantheism" and "syncretism."[57]

Although not all the resolutions on racism brought to the 1991 General Convention were acted on, several were passed that had long-term impact. The establishment of the Martin Luther King Jr. Legacy Scholarship Fund was a key accomplishment. In addition, the 1991 General Convention pledged to focus on institutional racism for the next nine years. Another resolution urged dioceses to conduct their own racial audits and another called for the establishment of diocesan committees or commissions on racism. Also mandated was a House of Bishops' pastoral letter on racism to be completed prior to the next General Convention in 1994. Browning believed that the eradication of racism was the largest challenge facing the church and that the sin of racism must be addressed "as the church." "We have to keep asking what we can do and praying for the strength to do it," he said. "The task is enormous, but the power of God is truly unlimited."[58]

Less than a year after the General Convention, the presiding bishop made a pastoral visit to the Diocese of Los Angeles, following the incidents of violence sparked by the acquittal of police officers who had beaten Rodney King, a black man. Outraged and saddened, Browning called for action and pleaded for Episcopalians to recommit to their baptismal vows and seek healing, understanding, and tolerance. Browning also called for all congregations to pray for racial justice on Sunday, May 3, 1992. "The events in Los Angeles—the brutal beating, the acquittal, the equally brutal misplaced response—have given us a chilling reminder that racism is rampant in our midst," said Browning. "We have dismal fresh evidence of our capacity for sin and evil. Though this is not new information, it compels us to confess that in the twenty-five years between the hopeful dream of Martin King and the hopeless nightmare of Rodney King we as a nation have made little moral progress....This church is committed to the eradication of racism." [59]

As part of his visit to Los Angeles, Browning visited the Church of Saint Mary in the Koreatown neighborhood to pray and to grieve. "While smoke still hung over a battered City of the Angels...the service at St. Mary's was a sacramental reminder for me of what Christian community is," wrote Browning in his *Episcopal Life* column. [60] In Koreatown, Browning promised to stand by the people of Los Angeles. "I knew in the deepest recesses of my heart...that I had to come to Los Angeles and stand with you," he said. [61] The presiding bishop also visited Compton, California, a predominately African American community that suffered great devastation during the Los Angeles riots. "It is very clear to me that the church must make a continuing witness of our solidarity with those who struggle to rebuild, to heal the wounds, and to be instruments of transformation....I know sin when I see it....Let us not shrink from naming it for what it is. This is deep sin that was bred in greed and leads to violence, to the death of hope, of dreams, and to tragic waste of human potential." [62] Fred Borsch, then the bishop of Los Angeles, said that the visit of the presiding bishop was significant to the diocese, then in deep pain. "Ed not only visited, he was pastorally involved wherever he visited in the diocese, and he used his office to do whatever he could to help the people most affected by the tragedies." [63]

Browning criticized the Bush administration for an inadequate response to the Los Angeles riots. Angry that government officials attributed the consequences of racism to the absence of "family values," Browning argued that, "with each blow inflicted on Rodney King, three hundred years of slavery, lynching, Jim Crowism, degradation, marginalization, and lack of opportunity for African Americans came vividly and painfully to mind." [64] Before returning to New York, Browning said that he saw congregations moving forward in three areas: dispersal of relief, cross-cultural training to deal with racism, and taking a lead in redeveloping the "community that has been so devastated. If that doesn't happen we will be back to where we were." [65]

Shortly after his visit to Los Angeles, Browning embarked on a four-state tour of black ministries, with stops in Connecticut, South Carolina, Tennessee, and Illinois. While planned before the riots in Los Angeles, the tour took on a special significance and served as "a stark reminder that racism is not dead, but alive and well," said Harold Lewis, staff officer for black ministries who coordinated the tour. [66] While in New Haven, Connecticut, the first stop on the tour, Browning preached at St. Luke's Episcopal Church, the third oldest black Episcopal congregation in the country. "Racism is a sin because it is incompatible with the vow we took at baptism to respect the dignity of every human being," he said. [67] Browning also helped serve meals at the St. Luke's soup kitchen, and, with Patti Browning, met with children and clients of the adult services center. On the next stop, Browning praised the efforts of the Diocese of South Carolina to recruit African American clergy and laity for leadership.

There he visited Camp Baskerville, one of the most holistic community outreach ministries in the Episcopal Church, and two local congregations. "The sin of racism all too often finds a happy home in the bosom of the church— and racism cripples us all," Browning said at St. Cyprian's. In Memphis, Tennessee, the presiding bishop visited Emmanuel Episcopal Center, in the middle of 1,400 public housing units, which runs almost forty programs for the community. While in Memphis he also preached at an ecumenical service and toured the National Civil Rights Museum. In Chicago, Browning visited another exemplary Episcopal institution, St. Edmund's Church, and dedicated the congregation's first venture in rehabilitated housing. He commended the people of the congregation for their "unfeigned loyalty to a church that has not always accorded you the respect you deserve." [68] Other Chicago stops were a neighborhood feeding program at Sts. George and Matthias Episcopal Church and a Head Start program and domestic violence shelter operated by St. Thomas Episcopal Church. Upon his return to New York Browning said he was profoundly moved by a deeper sense of spirituality than at any other time in his ministry. He reminded Episcopal Church Center staff that "we can't do our ministry unless it is undergirded by a spirituality that begins with our own brokenness and how we are met by Christ in that brokenness—healed and transformed so we can be opened to brokenness in others." [69]

The "Pastoral Letter on the Sin of Racism," adopted by the House of Bishops in the spring of 1994, is a lasting contribution of the Browning administration toward the eradication of racism. The first teaching on racism addressed to U.S. Episcopalians, and framed within the context of the Baptismal Covenant, the pastoral letter did not attempt to touch on all aspects of racism, but to stimulate discussion throughout the church.

> Escalating violence in America illustrates the complexity of racism. At the heart of the matter is fear. We fear those who are different from ourselves, and that fear translates into violence, which in turn creates more fear. Institutionalized preference, primarily for white persons, is deeply ingrained in the American way of life in areas such as employment, the availability of insurance and credit ratings, in education, law enforcement, courts of law, and the military. [70]

The pastoral letter sparked dialogue throughout the church. Nearly one hundred dialogue groups participated in the discussion at the General Convention in Indianapolis in 1994. Key to the document was an eight-point covenant developed by the House of Bishops pledging a personal commitment to the eradication of racism and proposing strategies to transform systems which perpetuate injustice throughout the church and the larger society. "We will teach and preach the gospel in ways that sustain a vision of justice and peace among all people," states the pastoral letter. [71] Further, the bishops committed to the creation of a standing committee within the House of Bishops to monitor and implement the covenant.

The fight against racism remained a central issue during the last triennium of the Browning administration. In 1996 the Episcopal Church worked with ecumenical partners to respond to a rash of burning of black churches. The ecumenical involvement in the issue raised its visibility and supported work toward identifying the perpetrators.

The House of Bishops continued its intensive work on racism throughout the triennium. The presiding bishop and the president of the House of Deputies released a joint letter to the whole church announcing a major initiative to dialogue on racism beginning on Martin Luther King Jr. Day in 1997. The dialogue on racism continued and developed further in the next administration. These efforts begun in the Browning years eventually developed into a far-reaching anti-racism network within the Episcopal Church and beyond through ecumenical partnerships.

Native American Ministries

From the time of his installation, Ed Browning gave unprecedented attention to Native American ministry, supporting efforts in self-determination and the creation of governing structures consisting solely of Episcopal American Indians. During his first eighteen months in office Browning visited Navajoland, attended the Oklahoma Consultation on Native American Ministry, participated in the Niobrara (South Dakota) and Minnesota, North Dakota, and Eau Claire convocations, met with the National Committee on Indian Work, and visited Living Waters, the Denver urban Native American congregation. In response to a call for greater inclusion of native voices in church decision-making, Browning appointed a record number of eighteen Native Americans to committees, boards, and commissions. Within weeks of his installation he appointed a Blue Ribbon Task Force on Indian Affairs to advise him on the spiritual, social, and legal concerns of native peoples.

A turning point in the governance of Native American ministry in the Episcopal Church came in 1988 when the Executive Council met in South Dakota and visited the Pine Ridge Reservation and the site of the Wounded Knee massacre. "This week you and I have witnessed how hopelessness ravages the human body, soul, and spirit as we visited the reservation," Browning said. "Wounded Knee is a dramatic monument not only to an historic event of inhumanity, it is constant testimony to injustice that continues to this day.[72]

While attending the Niobrara Convocation, Browning spent an afternoon listening to the concerns of local people. He sat unattended on a wooden plank supported by concrete blocks, beneath a vast brush arbor. He also brought Holy Communion to the sick, visited a domestic violence shelter operated by the White Buffalo Calf Women's Society, and observed a cross-section of reservation life. He was honored during a name-giving ceremony. During this generations-old solemn ritual of the people of the Plains, Browning stood in the center of a great circle of American Indians. Clyde Estes, a Lower Brule Sioux and an Episcopal priest, proclaimed the name of the presiding bishop to be *Inyan Wichasa* (Man of Rock), to the sound of the drum. Browning then joined with others to dance the honoring dance at the end of the ceremony.[73]

An outcome from the Executive Council visit to South Dakota was a charge from Browning to create a Blue Ribbon Task Force on Indian Affairs to develop a comprehensive native ministries model. The resultant model for the Episcopal Council of Indian Ministry (ECIM) combined elements of the National Committee on Indian Work and Coalition 14, which responded to funding needs for Native American ministries. In addition to providing a structure for communication and budgeting, the ECIM designed program activities, including culturally relevant evangelism models and a new educational resource, *In the Spirit of the Circle,* shared throughout the Episcopal Church and with ecumenical partners.

In 1990 ECIM began the first of several visits to the Maori Anglicans of Aotearoa/New Zealand, which led to the development of a new network, the Anglican Indigenous Network (AIN). It included not only the Maori and indigenous people in the continental United States, but native people in Canada, Hawaii, and Australia. Network founders included Paul Reeves, the former primate of New Zealand, himself partially of Maori descent, and the current Anglican Observer to the United Nations. The network expanded into the South America when an international delegation of Anglican Indians participated in the Anglican Encounter in Brazil in 1992. [74]

At the opening session of the World Council of Churches' 1991 General Assembly in Canberra, Australia, the Anglican Church of Australia, after abominable treatment of aboriginal peoples for generations, honored aboriginal Australians smeared with white ash and playing the didgeridoo. However, the message was lost when five minutes later the Prime Minister of Australia greeted the crowd with the statement, "We are a nation of immigrants." "Indigenous people clearly got the message," wrote Owanah Anderson, a Choctaw and staff officer for Native American Ministries in the Browning administration. "Nothing had changed. We were still the invisible inhabitants of *terra nullius,* 'land belonging to no one,' the general principle the British applied when occupying and colonizing Australia in the late eighteenth century." [75]

Indigenous people from all over the world began to find each other at the World Council of Churches Assembly. Later a peace demonstration was planned to march across the city. As Owanah Anderson recalls:

> The Aboriginals had been informed they were to lead the march and invited other indigenous peoples to march with them. We met at the appointed place. As we were lining up, there suddenly appeared a formidable white woman with many small white children, around eight or ten years of age, each carrying a small round globe with "Peace" written thereon. In no uncertain terms she told the Aboriginal people to step aside immediately, she and her swarm of yellow-haired children were leading the march. Grumbling and sounds of discontent became audible, but the white lady tromped right ahead followed by her crash of yellow-haired kids, bobbing their peace globes as they haughtily trod on. Caught off guard and surprised, the people of color stepped aside momentarily. A current of anger crackled across the crowd. Then someone said, "Let's go. Let's show them. We've been invisible far too long." We marched in the middle of the street in the hot February sun of the Southern Hemisphere. The low deep voice of an African American sang out, "We shall overcome." We joined. Suddenly, I was conscious that someone was marching right beside me, step for step, in the hot sun. A few feet further and I glanced over. There, looking seriously committed—and quite validating—was Edmond L. Browning, my boss and the twenty-fourth presiding bishop of the Episcopal Church. [76]

Browning's commitment to validate the history and culture of Native Americans was equally clear at the 1991 General Convention in Arizona. During the second major service, a Navajo holy man stood beside the Navajo bishop as the church witnessed to the pain of native peoples' five-hundred-year encounter with European culture. Following the traditional invocation, which addresses the four directions, fifteen Native Americans reflected on their culture's experience with white people since 1492. The same convention passed a resolution designating an appropriate observance of the 500th anniversary of the voyage of Christopher Columbus on October 12, 1992, at the National Cathedral in Washington, D.C.

Browning was celebrant at this three-hour worship service. "Celebration of Our Survival" was a testimony to the struggles and hopes of Native Americans. It was, as one Native American priest said, "the proudest day in my life as an Indian person." [77] In his statement that day, Browning revealed his "deep disquiet" with the perception that the Americas were first "discovered" by Europeans. "Looking deeply into our past we will see not only the cruel and unjust fate of the Native American, but the consequences on other people of color who came to this land, many against their will. From black people brought in slavery to the gross mistreatment of Asians who migrated to the North American continent, we see a pattern of violence, abuse, and genocide." To those of European descent, he added that the occasion was an opportunity for reflection and repentance. "And from such reflection we may then be moved to celebrate the diversity of our nation among its peoples and cultures." [78]

The "Celebration of our Survival" was hailed as a high point in the history of the Episcopal Church. ECIM continued to grow over the course of the Browning administration. The Martin Luther King Jr. Scholarship Committee, established at the General Convention in Phoenix in 1991, gave scholarships to forty-six native students in a variety of fields, and native communities contributed to the fund for seminarians. Annual Paths Crossing and Winter Talk events and triennial National Native Youth Festivals brought people together, offered training, and developed cross-cultural understanding. ECIM also worked with and endorsed the Vancouver School of Theology's Native Ministries program for seminary students. Though downsized due to budget cuts in 1995, ECIM continued to provide leadership through the triennium. In the same year, the Episcopal Native American community gathered at Winter Talk and issued a "Statement of Self-Determination," pledging to move out of the missionary model and to claim leadership in the Episcopal Church and Anglican Communion. [79]

Twice during his administration, Ed Browning, working through the Washington Office of the Episcopal Church, petitioned the White House and members of Congress to protect the Arctic National Wildlife Refuge from oil exploration. The refuge is home to the Gwich'in Indians of Arctic Village, virtually all of whom are members of the Episcopal Church. Oil exploration would scatter the caribou herds on which the Gwich'in depend. A government source reported to the Washington Office that it was the effective advocacy of the Episcopal Church that persuaded President Clinton to veto any bill that threatened the Arctic National Wildlife Refuge. [80]

On All Saints' Day, 1997, in Jamestown, Virginia, the site of the first permanent English settlement—and during one of the last major events of his administration—

Browning led the Episcopal Church to join in a "new covenant of faith" with the indigenous people of the United States. The Jamestown Covenant commits Episcopalians to strive for justice in reconciling the painful history of colonization, to work with indigenous people in finding solutions to political and social challenges, and to stand together to honor and protect the earth. "[King] James and his advisers would never in a million years have guessed that their descendents would be led by the gospel to pursue the radical equality of the human family," said Browning. [81]

God Without Limits

"God is not limited by our structures," said Edmond Lee Browning in his sermon to mark the opening of the Decade of Evangelism. And so it was throughout his administration. The pastor's heart of the presiding bishop saw no issue or member of the human family as beyond the reach of God and the call of the gospel. Thus when discussing the controversial topic of abortion, Browning affirmed that personal decisions should not be dictated by governments and at the same time pleaded with Christian communities to reach out to pregnant women with the resources needed to continue pregnancies. [82] In the same vein, while not condoning terrible crimes, Browning opposed capital punishment. He stated that those who commit such crimes "remain children of God, brothers and sisters of the One who sought out sinners as his earthly companions, human beings who retain the right to hope as long as they retain breath in their bodies." [83] As Ed and Patti Browning read the newspapers every day they not only reflected on the day's events and added names to already lengthy prayer lists, but always asked, "What can we do?" The answers to that question are detailed in the many initiatives, dialogues, conferences, and programs of Ed Browning's far-reaching administration that stretched throughout the Episcopal Church and challenged its structures to respond more fully to all.

Chapter Seven Notes

1   Edmond Lee Browning (hereafter cited as ELB), "Christ for a New Century: A Sermon to Open the Decade of Evangelism," Episcopal News Service (hereafter cited as ENS), May 10, 1990.

2   Jerry Anderson, letter to Sheryl Kujawa-Holbrook (hereafter cited as SKH), February 3, 2009.

3   John Fortunato, "AIDS: The Plague That Lays Waste at Noon," *The Witness* 68, no. 9 (September 1985).

4   William E. Swing, "AIDS: How Should the Church Respond?" *The Living Church*, 1985.

5   Fortunato, "AIDS," 9.

6   J. Michael Parker, "Bishop: Church Leaders Ignored," *San Antonio Express-News*, September 27, 1986.

7   "Bishop Browning Sets AIDS Day of Prayer," ENS, May 15, 1986.

8   "Bishop Will Befriend an AIDS Patient," n.d. [1988], Browning Collection.

9   ELB, *A Year of Days With the Book of Common Prayer* (New York: Ballantine Books, 1997), July 11.

10   "Browning and Religious Leaders Issue Statement on AIDS," ENS, October 26, 1989.

11   "Growing Ecumenical Concern over AIDS Produces Landmark Document," ENS, December 19, 1989.

12   ELB, "Letter on AIDS," September 10, 1987, in *No Outcasts: the Public Witness of Edmond L. Browning, XXIVth Presiding Bishop of the Episcopal Church,* ed. Brian J. Grieves (Cincinnati: Forward Movement, 1997), 108-109.

13   David Kalvelage, "Read This Before Proceeding," *The Living Church*, May 21, 1995.

14   "Open Letter on HIV/AIDS Ministry from Presiding Bishop Edmond L. Browning to the Episcopal Church," ENS, September 17, 1991.

15   "Presiding Bishop Lays Out His Vision for Moral Leadership During House of Bishops," ENS, September 26, 1990.

16   "Expansion Eyed for D.C. Office," ENS, June 26, 1986.

17   ENS, "Presiding Bishop Lays Out His Vision."

18   Marcy Darin, "Browning Keynotes Impact Briefing," ENS, April 2, 1987.

19   Ibid.

20   Ibid.

21   ELB, interview by SKH, January 2009.

22   "Bush and Browning Meet in Oval Office," ENS, March 25, 1989.

23   George W. Cornell, "Episcopal Bishop Says U.S. in Moral Decline," Associated Press, n.d. [1992], Browning Collection.

24   Don Hunt, "Keep Religion Out of Campaign, Bush's Pastor Tells Convention," *Kalamazoo Gazette*, n.d. [1992], Browning Collection.

25   "Economic Justice Plan Wins Convention Approval," ENS, July 14, 1988.

26   Norman J. Faramelli, interview by SKH, October 2009.

27   Mary Lee Simpson, "Browning Visits Southwestern Virginia, Talks to Miners," ENS, June 8, 1989.

28 "Presiding Bishop Joins Bipartisan Congressional Group in Support of Proposed Civil Rights Act of 1990," ENS, February 8, 1990.

29 "Church Leaders Urge Support for 1991 Civil Rights Act," ENS, May 14, 1991.

30 "Church Leaders Meet with President Clinton, Hail New Openness to Their Concerns," ENS, April 1, 1993.

31 "Presiding Bishop Joins Religion Leaders at White House Breakfast with Clinton," ENS, September 7, 1994.

32 Ibid.

33 Ibid.

34 Thomas Hart, "Presiding Bishop Urges Rethinking of Christian Churches Advocacy," ENS, December 12, 1995.

35 "Peace and Justice Summit Illustrates Church's Continuing Commitment to Issues," ENS, March 7, 1997.

36 Ibid.

37 Ibid.

38 Mary Miller, interview by SKH, March 2009.

39 Ann Ball, "Browning Addresses Episcopal School Leaders," *Churchwork*, Episcopal Diocese of Louisana, December 1987.

40 David Skidmore, "Experience of Inclusive Church at Montana Youth Event May Help Shape the Life of the Episcopal Church," ENS, August 23, 1990.

41 Roxanne Evans, "Episcopal Leader Hails Diversity: Bishop Urges Church to Fight U.S. Racism," *American-Statesman*, Austin, Texas, n.d. [ca 1986], Browning Collection.

42 ELB, "Remarks to Executive Council," November 1986, in *No Outcasts*, 114-115.

43 *But We See Jesus: A Pastoral Letter From the Black Episcopal Bishops to Black Clergy and Laity in the Episcopal Church* (New York: Office of Black Ministries, June 25, 1990).

44 Edward W. Rodman, interview by SKH, February 2009.

45 Harold T. Lewis, *Yet With A Steady Beat: The African American Struggle for Recognition in the Episcopal Church* (Valley Forge: Trinity Press, 1996).

46 Diane M. Porter, interview by SKH, March 2009.

47 Lewis, *Yet With A Steady Beat*, 168-171; "Senior Executive for Program Diane Porter Leaves National Staff," ENS, March 7, 1997.

48 Judith Conley, interview by SKH, September 2009.

49 Ibid.

50 "Executive Council Affirms Phoenix Site; Shape of the General Convention Still in Question," ENS, January 11, 1991.

51 ENS, "Executive Council Affirms Phoenix Site"; Gardiner H. Shattuck, Jr., *Episcopalians and Race: Civil War to Civil Rights* (Lexington: University Press of Kentucky, 2000), 65-66.

52 Shattuck, *Episcopalians and Race*, 216-218.

53 Susan Erdey, "1991 General Convention in Arizona: Lots of Heat, Not Much Life," *The Witness* 74 (July/August 1991): 22-24, 26.

54 Ibid.

55 "Divisive Issues Force Episcopal Church General Convention to Grapple with the Meaning of Community," ENS, July 25, 1991.

56 Ibid.

57 Ibid.

58 "Message on Racism Sets Tone for Council," *The Living Church,* July 5, 1992.

59 "A Message from the Presiding Bishop on the Violence in Los Angeles," ENS, May 1, 1992.

60 ELB, "Of Community and the Contrite Heart," *Episcopal Life,* June 1992, reprinted in *No Outcasts,* 119-120.

61 "Episcopalians Respond with Aid and Prayers in the Wake of Los Angeles Riots," ENS, May 13, 1992.

62 Edmond Lee Browning, "The Sin of Racism," Address to Executive Council, June 16, 1992, in *No Outcasts,* 120-122.

63 Frederick Houk Borsch, interview by SKH, April 2009.

64 "Presiding Bishop Takes Anti-racism Message on Four-state Tour of Black Ministries," ENS, July 30, 1992.

65 ENS, "Episcopalians Respond with Aid and Prayers."

66 Ibid.

67 Ibid.

68 Ibid.

69 Ibid.

70 "The Sin of Racism: A Pastoral Letter from the House of Bishops of the Episcopal Church," March 1994, Browning Collection.

71 Ibid.

72 Owanah Anderson, *400 Years: Anglican/Episcopal Mission Among American Indians* (Cincinnati: Forward Movement, 1997), 122-126, 328-330; Owanah Anderson, interview by SKH, April 2009; Grieves, *No Outcasts,* 123-124.

73 Anderson, *400 Years,* 330-331.

74 Ibid.

75 Ibid.

76 Ibid.

77 Ibid., 333-335.

78 Anderson, *400 Years,* 333-336; Grieves, *No Outcasts,* 128-129.

79 Anderson, *400 Years,* 336-343.

80 Grieves, *No Outcasts,* 112; Anderson, *400 Years,* 338.

81 "Covenant With Indigenous People Signed at All Saints' Day Service," *The Living Church,* November 30, 1997.

82 "Presiding Bishop's Statement on Abortion," *The Living Church,* September 20, 1987; "A Statement by Church Leaders on the Subject of Abortion," December 19, 1989.

83 "Presiding Bishop Attacks Capital Punishment at Conference on Prison Ministry," ENS, May 18, 1995.

Guardians
of the Faith
1986-1997

IT IS NOT AN EASY THING to be a leader in these days...any kind of leader. It is not a comfortable thing. Even so, it is a glorious thing, and awesome thing to be a bishop of the church in these times. I believe that, for the most part, none of us would want to be anywhere else right now.

Our toughest challenge right now, I believe, is simply this: We are challenged to be the church, not a political party, not a corporate entity. We are called back to our roots. In every age our greatest gift has been in being who we are. It has never been more true than in these times of societal upheaval and redefinition.

Though some of us may have a gift for politics, and our service is certainly public service, we are not politicians. What the world needs from us is not politicking but proclamation. Similarly, though we have management and fiduciary responsibilities, we are not a corporate view but a vision of the divine reality. [1]

— Edmond Lee Browning,
House of Bishops,
Portland, Oregon,
September 28, 1995

One of Barbara C. Harris's favorite stories about Edmond Lee Browning occurred the night before her ordination as suffragan bishop of Massachusetts in 1989. Harris was the first woman bishop in the Anglican Communion. Much excitement surrounded the occasion, and a stellar cast of Episcopal dignitaries and Harris's friends and family were gathered for dinner the night before the service. Despite the controversy surrounding the event, the dinner was a joyful occasion. When it came time for the evening's speeches, Browning greeted the crowd, and then he looked down, smiled, and raised both of his hands high. "Barbara is ready," he said, "and you as a diocese are ready—and *these hands are ready*." [2] Years after the applause from that greeting ceased, both Ed Browning and Barbara Harris remember that image of raised hands as symbolic of an historic moment in the Episcopal Church.

Women in Ministry

Ed Browning advocated for the ordination of women to the episcopate. At the time of his election as presiding bishop there were no women bishops in the Episcopal Church, although women had been nominees in several diocesan elections. At the time of his retirement there were eight women bishops and only four dioceses that would not ordain women to the priesthood.

Soon after his election, Browning requested the archbishop of Canterbury to place the ordination of women to the episcopate on the agenda of the 1986 primates' meeting in Toronto. The issue divided the Episcopal Church and the wider Anglican Communion. "We intend not to depart from the traditional catholic doctrine of holy orders," said Browning in 1986, "but to expand and open it to the other half of the human race." [3] The primates' meeting in Toronto was Browning's first as presiding bishop. "Ed received high marks from the other primates for that meeting. He was matter-of-fact and clear; he did not preach, but he did not try to hide anything, either. His handling of the issue was appreciated," said Michael Peers, now retired primate of the Anglican Church of Canada. [4] After telling the primates that he believed ordaining a woman to the episcopacy was "just and appropriate" and that the Episcopal Church had no intention of hurting the Anglican Communion, Browning was cautioned that such action would have serious consequences. [5]

At the 1978 Lambeth Conference the bishops had approved a resolution recognizing that a member church of the Anglican Communion might elect a woman to the episcopate. However, the resolution also stated that no decision to consecrate a woman should be made without consultation with the primates and that there should be a clear mandate for the election, lest the office of bishop become a symbol of disunity. At the 1985 General Convention the House of Bishops voted 112-31 that they would not withhold consent to the election of a bishop on the basis of gender and asked Browning to convey this information to the Anglican primates. Although the Episcopal Church was clear about its desire to consult with the primates to discuss the impact of such an action on the Anglican Communion, it was also clear that it would not be asking for permission; the canonical and theological justifications were already decided when women were ordained to the priesthood. Other churches in the Anglican Communion—Canada, New Zealand, Kenya, Uganda, and Cuba—added their names to a growing list of churches where the ordination of women to the episcopate was not far from a reality.[6]

The chief opposition to women bishops came from the Church of England, which viewed itself as the head of the Anglican Communion and did not ordain women to the priesthood nor recognize the orders of women priests ordained elsewhere. Robert Runcie, then archbishop of Canterbury, was concerned that the election of a woman to the episcopate would create a bishop not in communion with other bishops, thereby causing a serious rift within the worldwide episcopate and yet another obstacle to women in churches where ordination to the priesthood was not yet a reality. The archbishops of Canterbury and York appointed a commission to study the issues pertaining to women and the episcopate. That group was not to report until the Lambeth Conference in 1988, yet within the Episcopal Church, there was a distinct possibility that a woman would be elected before 1988. "Instead," said the *Canadian Churchman,* "the primates should accept the likelihood that such actions will probably happen before Lambeth and devise steps by which they would deal with such an eventuality."[7]

At the General Convention of the Episcopal Church in Detroit in 1988, the House of Bishops overwhelmingly approved a resolution to provide visiting male bishops to congregations unwilling to accept a woman bishop. Browning believed the resolution was essential to preserving the unity of the church. "I believe it is one of the most important decisions we will take here in our time in Detroit," he said.[8] Opponents of the measure felt the resolution was insulting to women, and some bishops objected to what they saw as an attempt to legislate pastoral care by interfering with the diocesan bishop's right to determine how to deal with recalcitrant parishes.

In September 1988, Barbara C. Harris, director of the Episcopal Church Publishing Company and assistant priest at Church of the Advocate in Philadelphia, was elected suffragan bishop of Massachusetts. "I have been elected a bishop of the church, not a symbol or token," she said.[9] In response to this historic event, Browning called all members of the Episcopal Church to prayer and sought to minister pastorally to those on all sides of the issue, while upholding the historic significance of the event: "Our church, in a prophetic manner, has made that witness and continues to do so around the issues of women in the episcopacy—it's a witness I earnestly believe will be a contribution of real significance to other parts of Christendom."[10]

After receiving the required canonical consents, Browning ordained Barbara Harris as the first woman bishop in the Anglican Communion on February 11, 1989. Harris said she was initially "floored by the presiding bishop's enthusiasm for her election. He tried to be pastoral in every way," she said. Aware of the joy of the event for many as well as the anguish it caused others, the presiding bishop said, "This consecration will be both a momentous and solemn occasion, and a time of great joy and celebration...I (have) asked the church to be sensitive to the convictions and feelings of others. I have felt that sensitivity being expressed by the majority of the church...." [11]

In June 1989, Ed Browning, Barbara Harris, and other ordained women from the Episcopal Church met with the archbishop of Canterbury's Commission on Communion and Women in the Episcopate (Eames Commission) on Long Island. It was the first meeting of the commission after Harris's consecration as bishop. Women priests from Canada and the United States and representatives of the Evangelical and Catholic Mission joined Harris at the commission meeting. The Eames Commission was charged by the archbishop of Canterbury to create pastoral guidelines for opponents across the communion to "respect" each other's views on women's ordination. [12] Browning was encouraged by the Eames Report, and believed that its work improved the relationship between the Episcopal Church and the Anglican Communion. Like many of the primates, he was also concerned by "the great divide in consciousness" in the Anglican Communion that surfaced on issues such as the ordination of women, human sexuality, and the nature of authority. Browning explained this divide in consciousness as between those who tend to see tradition as an evolving, dynamic reality with the capacity for continuing revelation and those for whom tradition is a fixed reality. Despite these two perspectives on tradition, or maybe because of them, Browning repeatedly maintained "that we need each other for the integrity of the *whole* church's unity, witness, and mission." [13]

As a pastor, a bishop, and as presiding bishop, Ed Browning's support of ordained women was very public, yet the ordination of women remained a subject of debate in the church. After Barbara Harris, the next two women elected to the episcopacy in the Episcopal Church were Jane Holmes Dixon, as suffragan bishop of Washington in 1992, and Mary Adelia McLeod as bishop of Vermont in 1993, the first woman diocesan bishop in the Episcopal Church. Both bishops stated how Browning went out of his way to provide support and counsel. "He made sure I was welcomed and was extremely generous," said Dixon. "He also put me on the agenda sub-committee of the House of Bishops, and he called on me to represent him on several occasions; it was his way of taking me seriously," she said. Dixon said that Browning also reached out to her husband, the first male bishop's spouse. "Very early on he gave us his phone number and told us to call him anytime...The thing about Ed is," said Dixon, "he did this for everyone—*everyone* is important to Ed. It's the heart of how he sees the gospel." [14]

Mary Adelia McLeod remembers that the first time she spoke with Browning was the day after her election as bishop of Vermont. Not only had he done his homework—Browning called her by her preferred name, "Mary Adelia"—he also said how happy he was to have a woman elected diocesan. Browning showed an interest in her, in her husband's reaction to the election, and in her children and grandchildren. "Ed made me feel our conversation was just a chat between old friends," she writes. On the day of her consecration, "Ed pulled me aside and told me there would be a protest during my consecration and how he would handle it....As always, he was gracious, pastoral, and sensitive. He had a special way about him that made one feel he had nothing else to do except being engaged in the person with whom he found himself." McLeod said that Browning checked in often in the early days of her episcopate, like her first meeting of the House of Bishops. At the General Convention in 1994, after an intense debate in the House of Bishops on women's ordination, he beckoned her to meet with him. Ed was concerned that the session was especially painful for her and for bishops Harris and Dixon. "I do not believe he said the session pained him, but as we spoke, I remember sadness in his eyes and voice," said McLeod. [15] Browning and McLeod shared a lighter moment at a House of Bishops meeting in 1995 when he mistakenly recognized her from the chair by saying, "Yes, sir." "Thank you, ma'am," said McLeod in response. [16]

The intense debate at the General Convention in 1994 focused on the eighteen-year-old canon on women's ordination. The House of Deputies voted to guarantee access to ordination for both women and men. After two days of tense discussion, the General Convention passed a resolution directing supporters and opponents of women's ordination to engage in dialogue and for the first time officially recognized both theological positions. The convention "managed to keep the peace," yet supporters of women's ordination were embittered that the House of Bishops declined to affirm that the three orders of ordained ministry were equally open to women and men. [17] The General Convention in 1997 in Philadelphia, Browning's last as presiding bishop, made women's ordination mandatory in every diocese, while at the same time expressing respect for the theological views of those who oppose it. [18]

Browning also staunchly supported the ministries of lay women. Ginger Paul, a former national president of the Episcopal Church Women (ECW) and member of Executive Council, was impressed with Browning as someone who cared about the ministry of the ECW. Paul recalled the time when the ECW advocated for a panel on sexism that would be heard not only by the Triennial Meeting, but also by the entire General Convention, "in prime time." "Although some staff members 'growled' at the request, Ed Browning encouraged us to go ahead with our plans if it was really what we wanted to do," said Paul. "I remember talking to the presiding bishop on the phone before the Planning and Arrangements meeting and anticipating that the idea would not be well received. 'Are you sure that you really want to do this, Ginger?' asked Browning.'" Paul said she responded, "Yes, but *can* we do it? Will they let us?" Browning replied, "Ginger, it's called *faith.*" "That is what I will always remember about him," said Paul. "It was his faith—his faith was so transparent to us. He tried so hard to give us his heart and soul and body." [19] Eleanor Small of the Council of Women's Ministries echoed Paul's sentiment. "Bishop Browning was always supportive of our work. He was interested and ready to help." [20]

Patti Browning also supported women's ministries. "As you travel around," she said, "you become attuned not only to people's concerns but to where those concerns aren't being dealt with. The Holy Spirit leads you from one thing deeper into another. It's like the windows opening before you." [21] Through years of ministry, some in remote contexts, Ed and Patti Browning had been formed for ministry together. Browning always considered his wife a full and equal partner and weighed her opinions and concerns carefully. "Ours has been a shared ministry from the very outset, and I would find it incomprehensible for it to be otherwise," she said. [22] When the couple grew out of synch and lost touch with their shared ministry and focus, they cleared their calendars and went off for a week of prayer, Bible study, tennis, and conversation. "The ministries to which you and I are called may not seem bold and daring," Patti Browning said to the Episcopal Church Women of the Diocese of Oregon in 1988. "But we are all called to minister within the communities we find ourselves at a particular time in our lives. Mine has been experienced in Okinawa, Europe, Connecticut, Hawaii, and wherever Ed and I are called to serve." [23]

A combination of gentleness, compassion, and relentlessness, Patti Browning preferred to work mostly behind the scenes, to the extent that was possible for the presiding bishop's spouse. Her eldest son, Mark Browning, recounts his mother's courage. He remembers how Patti stood up to military commanders when base hospitals refused to treat her children or to school officials who did not understand them. Mark Browning gave his mother the nickname "Commy Mommy" after Patti's trips to Nicaragua. "My mother is brilliant," he said. "Had she been born at a different time she could have easily been a chief executive herself." [24]

Patti sought to use her institutional access to bring the concerns of the marginalized to the whole church. "It's kind of hard to analyze your own impact," she said. "As you talk with people, sometimes you are able to see yourself better. It's not only my presence, but theirs to me." [25] After many years as a clergy spouse and as a bishop's spouse, Patti Browning knew the challenges and unrealistic expectations that beset such couples. "First, you need to care for your marriage, for that relationship. Everything comes back to that. If you are not solid together, the tough times are even tougher to take," she said to a clergy and spouses retreat in the Diocese of New York. "The second thing is the importance of the spiritual life, of being well-grounded in that, in whatever form it takes you. [26]

Throughout the Browning administration, Patti Browning traveled in her own right, often speaking to agencies and diocesan groups. As she traveled the world she grew more confident in her role and her voice grew clearer and stronger. She continued providing access to the resources of the church, and her sense of her ministry grew deeper theologically as she claimed her own voice and used it in the service of those who had no voice:

> When Ed became presiding bishop I really didn't have an agenda of my own. But, as we traveled throughout the world, I have seen so much suffering, so much oppression. More and more I have felt called to be a voice for the voiceless. I have asked myself what are my responsibilities as a baptized Christian in trying to help make a difference and in using gifts I have been given and the circumstances of my life. One of the best ways I can help is to tell stories and to stand in solidarity with the oppressed in response to the gospel. [27]

Patti Browning often referred to the ministry she shared with her husband as a spiritual journey of transitions: a ministry of moving, adapting, listening, and responding to a local context and its people. Through the many transitions Patti Browning found Christ among the people, and as her ministry has progressed, she feels his presence more strongly. "There is no shortage of Jesus here; he is where we will see him. No matter where we go or what we do, we are called to seek him out," she wrote. "And sometimes we don't even have to do that: sometimes he just sits himself down beside us on the couch and starts talking.

And as we listen, we have the sense of having heard that voice before. Many times. It is the Lord." [28]

Another of Patti Browning's assets is her strong sense of humor. Like her husband, she tells stories on herself. In controversial settings, her children always say, "Don't stand next to mother." Patti's father often referred to her as a hypochondriac. She withstood many painful surgeries during Browning's term as presiding bishop and her accumulation of medical knowledge grew legendary. She got to know their New York physician, Dr. Harvey Goldberg, well and often called him several times a week. Patti referred to him as "Dr. Feelgood" because he always assured her that she was fine. "You know what they will write on my tombstone," said Patti Browning. " 'I told them I was sick!' " [29]

The House of Bishops

The largest number of bishops ever to attend an interim meeting of the House of Bishops, 176, gathered in San Antonio in late September 1986, for Edmond Lee Browning's first meeting as presiding bishop. Browning explained his values in working with the House of Bishops, including collegiality, trust, dialogue, diversity, the integration of the pastoral and the prophetic, the need for church and state engagement, and the importance of "traditional values" as touchstones. He urged the bishops to regard tension and conflict as a "creative catalyst" and a sign that "no part of this diversity holds all the answers to our well-being." [30] He crafted the agenda of the House of Bishops meeting to emphasize the connection between the pastoral and the prophetic, and the church's moral agency in the greater society:

> I believe that it is the role of the Church to place and champion the national agenda. Whether these issues affect foreign or domestic concerns, human rights, justice, employment, accessibility for people with physical handicaps, criminal justice, social security, or medical care, the Church must give moral leadership. This leadership comes with ministry with the persons involved, education of the general population, and advocacy before legislative and judicial bodies. I do not need to rehearse for you the number of concerns affecting the common good which had their genesis and championship within the religious community. The religious community has been effective because it has been the conscience of the nation. [31]

In closing his comments to the House of Bishops, Browning tied his vision of inclusiveness to Anglican spirituality, calling the gifts of tolerance, openness, and inclusiveness "a gift we give to our religious partners....With God's grace, we will accept and exercise this ministry of inclusiveness, holding together the many parts of Christ's Body, bringing meaning to the lives of all God's children out of our deep spirituality." [32]

A year later, while making his second report to the House of Bishops after a year of listening to the needs of the church, Browning set forth the eight mission imperatives that he intended to use as guidelines for his leadership during his term in office that he hoped would be the framework for the mission of the church. "I believe that this church is on the move," he said to the bishops assembled. "The message I got everywhere is let's get the show on the road."[33] As a way forward, Browning urged the bishops to use the teaching role of the episcopate to enable both the pastoral and the prophetic aspects of ministry. He said that his vision of the Episcopal Church was of a "missionary church":

> A church that takes the issues of our time into the center of the life of faith...a vision of the people of God gathered to hear and to do God's will...engaged in compassionate service...gathered around their bishop to reflect and think theologically about their active service in the world... a vision of a people of God working for justice, peace, and equality...a vision of a church gathered to share and be nourished by the good news of its Lord and Savior."[34]

A high priority for Browning was his role as pastor to other bishops. He spent many hours at his desk, on airplanes, and at the cabin making phone calls and writing notes to offer support to bishops and their families. (Many other family members, friends, staff, and people around the church were included in this ministry as well.) Browning's faithfulness as pastor was also a source of criticism. Some questioned the wisdom of trying to get personally involved with so many people and suggested that no one presiding bishop could possibly be everyone's pastor. Others felt that it was not helpful to exercise the ministry of the presiding bishop from the perspective of a "family" model. What happens when the family model fails? Does that mean that some are left outside the family? Browning's pastoral style was more traditional than systemic and when he had to delegate, he delegated almost everything *but* pastoral care. Browning knew no other way to be the presiding bishop but to carry his office through his own body. "I believe the role of the church is to try to be pastoral and compassionate and those are not soft words," he said. "Those are hard words....Part of the problem of trying to be a pastor is that you don't come down hard on one side because you polarize people out of the church." [35] Aware that it was not his role to dictate what people believe in and loathe to resort to legalism, Browning felt his power as presiding bishop was linked to his ability to be present and authentic.

Browning believed that a presiding bishop needed the skill of "moral persuasiveness" and that "the church has a real need to listen to other sides of the issues and to try to have a fair hearing of those." [36] By midway through his twelve-year term, he admitted that getting people to listen to all sides of the issues was more difficult than he had originally imagined. As in his years as a missionary, much of Browning's ministry as presiding bishop was conveyed through his presence and his ability to make all sorts and conditions of people feel valued and recognized. It was also through these brief but intimate encounters, Browning said, that he most often felt God's presence: "I realized that I am called to this life in order that I may find God in it. So wherever I have gone, I listen for the presence of God. I watch for the signs—not just for the obvious signs, the ones you find in churches, but for the unexpected signs of God's presence. And, in forty years, there has never been a time when I did not find them." [37]

Stories abound of Ed Browning's care and concern for bishops and their families. "He was *my* pastor," is the statement this author often heard from retired and active bishops. "When I was ill, he not only called to see how I was, he stayed in touch with my wife, and then with both of us after the initial illness. I was surprised that with all the things he had to do that he was able to keep track of what was going on with people to such an extent. It would have been easy for him to get away with not doing it," said Hays H. Rockwell, retired bishop of Missouri. "He is a man of consummate kindness, with a tough streak. He got things done against tremendous odds. Yet he never closed the door on a person, he always kept the door open." Rockwell said that Browning has "zero tolerance for behavior that crosses the bounds of civility," such as it did in the House of Bishops on occasion. "He is a Southern gentleman, after all. He was not going to let the House of Bishops erupt into a donnybrook." Rockwell said that on his travels with the presiding bishop that Browning was always considerate of his hosts and would wear or eat anything he was given, even if the custom was new to him. Rockwell reminisced about a time they both were on a visit to Kansas and invited to participate in Native American dancing. Rockwell felt odd about participating; not only was he wearing rochet and chimere, but he did not know what to do. "I don't think I am doing this," said Rockwell within earshot of Browning. "Oh *yes* you are," replied the presiding bishop. [38]

"We had a solid friendship and would have lunch maybe once a month. I felt like he was genuinely interested about what was going on with myself and the diocese," said Alden M. Hathaway, retired bishop of Pittsburgh. Although the two men were not in the same camp theologically, they became good friends. "Ed has a missionary's heart and saw the gospel in a world context," said Hathaway. "I appreciated that." Hathaway went to Africa for the first time in January of 1997. "I traveled to Uganda and stayed at the guest house on Namirembe Hill just below the cathedral....That trip was the beginning of a missionary outreach to East Africa carrying solar equipment to rural church facilities. It was a grant of $11,000 [from Program, Budget, and Finance], which Ed endorsed, that launched Solar Light for Africa. I shall always be grateful to him for that." [39]

Robert Hodges Johnson, retired bishop of Western North Carolina, had a similar story to tell. "Ed invited me to stay at their apartment when I came to New York for 'Baby Bishops' School,' " said Johnson. "He made me feel comfortable, and despite the fact that I was not a bishop for very long, he asked me to do things and share leadership in areas like Total Ministry, the Committee for the Status of Women, Church Deployment, and the House of Bishops' Office for Pastoral Development. I learned from Ed that there are many things that it is important not to try to do legislatively, but should be handled pastorally. I miss him terribly." [40]

"I have always considered Ed a role model," said J. Jon Bruno, bishop of Los Angeles. "He is not willing to cast out anybody; not willing to throw any person away. When I feel I want to throw the church out with the bathwater, I think about what Ed Browning would do," he said. "I feel like a big tanker ship and Ed is my pilot." Bruno said he got to know Browning through the presiding bishop's "deep compassion" and "unbelievable practical hospitality." Bruno likened the Browning administration and Browning's pastoral style to the "Harry Truman model." Said Bruno, "Power never took over Ed's heart, yet he always took responsibility and bore the brunt of other people's misdeeds." One thing in particular that Bruno said he learned from Browning was the importance of staying in relationship with clergy who are deposed or leave the church. "He taught me that 'we can get through this and still stay in communion with each other.'" Bruno saw both Ed and Patti Browning as "strong justice leaders in the church," and admitted, "To tell you the truth, I'm a little afraid of Patti. She is so determined and makes me feel like a slacker sometimes."[41]

A more public example of Browning's faithfulness to his role as pastor to bishops was his care for Clarence Pope, retired bishop of Fort Worth, and a vocal critic of the Browning administration on women's ordination, human sexuality, and other concerns. Pope and his wife left the Episcopal Church and were received into the Roman Catholic Church in January 1995. However, Pope's ministry in that church was not received as he had expected, and that, along with a cancer diagnosis, brought a call to Browning with a request to return to the Episcopal Church. The presiding bishop's response to Pope was that he had never really left the church, and Browning warmly welcomed back one of his most vocal critics. "This church is his home, his family, and with joy we welcome him home," said Browning in a letter to bishops.[42] "It is my opinion that he would come back into the house with full membership as the retired bishop of Fort Worth," said Browning.[43] "I think the whole issue spoke volumes to us about Ed Browning," said Francis C. Gray, bishop of Northern Indiana at the time. "That's been the hallmark of what Ed Browning has done for the last ten or eleven years."[44]

Arthur B. Williams, Jr., retired bishop suffragan of Ohio, worked closely with Browning as vice president of the House of Bishops from 1995 until Browning's retirement. The position of vice president is more than ceremonial. The vice president not only presides over the

House of Bishops when the presiding bishop is absent, but also participates in the highest level of decision making and influence in the church. He is a member of the presiding bishop's Council of Advice and serves on the committee that sets the daily agendas for the General Convention. The vice president often serves as a personal advisor to the presiding bishop on confidential matters. Williams said that his appointment as vice president of the House of Bishops was an example of how Browning used his authority and nominating responsibility to raise people of color to positions of power and influence. "Given three opportunities to make this nomination [for vice president of the House of Bishops] Ed chose a black member of the House and in my case broke precedent by nominating not only a black person but a suffragan to fill this position." [45]

Browning first nominated John T. Walker, bishop of Washington, who served until his death in 1989; he next nominated James Ottley, bishop of Panama; in 1995 Browning nominated Williams who served the rest of his term and beyond, until 2000. Art Williams noted that Browning also called upon black clergy to serve as resource people to the House of Bishops. Michael Curry, then rector of St. James' Episcopal Church, Baltimore, and now bishop of North Carolina, was asked to preach, and Kortright Davis, a faculty member of Howard University Divinity School, was asked to provide theological reflection. [46]

Williams noted that the priority Browning put on his role as pastor to bishops and his sense of responsibility to all the dioceses of the church was reflected in his participation in the consecration of almost all of the bishops elected during his administration. Browning traveled for the consecrations of bishops, not only as a sign of the unity of the church, but also to be a pastor to the bishops-elect and their families and to be present to the wider diocese as well. By Art Williams's calculation 125 bishops of domestic dioceses were consecrated during Browning's term as presiding bishop, and Browning was chief consecrator at 108 of them. Most of those that were delegated to other chief consecrators were in 1997 when Browning became ill. [47]

Two issues polarized the House of Bishops and the church at large during the Browning years. The first was human sexuality, specifically homosexuality, the ordination of gay and lesbian people, and same-sex blessings. The second was the ordination of women to the episcopate and the mandatory acceptance of the ordination of women in all dioceses. There were major differences of opinion on other issues, such as scriptural interpretation, Prayer Book revision, abortion, euthanasia, marriage, and divorce, but the press coverage focused largely on homosexuality and women's ordination.

Collegiality in the House of Bishops was sorely tested during the General Convention in Phoenix in 1991, where a sharp verbal dispute broke out on the floor between John Shelby Spong, bishop of Newark, and John MacNaughton, bishop of West Texas, during a discussion of human sexuality. The incident affected Browning deeply and he seriously wondered if there was a "center" in the Episcopal Church anymore. Believing that the actions displayed in the House of Bishops not only crossed the line of appropriate collegial behavior but also signaled serious underlying problems, Browning cleared the session of press and visitors and decided to take action to reconcile relationships among bishops.

During the Phoenix convention, the House of Bishops met in an unprecedented six closed sessions to repair the bishops' collegiality. After that convention the bishops held an extra "retreat" meeting each year, in addition to the annual business meeting, to nurture collegial relationships and foster constructive dialogue. "During our meeting in Phoenix, I came to the realization that we could not go on in this fashion any longer," said Browning. "I thought that we were cheating ourselves and the church by not claiming the shared leadership, the *episcope*. I did not want to go through the next six years of my time as presiding bishop trying to argue disputes and keeping order." [48]

The additional retreat of the House of Bishops was held at the Kanuga Conference Center in North Carolina. Browning appointed the Kanuga Planning Committee, "a cross section of wise bishops to plan the process." Sam Hulsey, bishop of Northwest Texas, and a "bridge person" between Province VII bishops and the Browning administration, agreed to chair the committee. "We are in a constant process of learning—including *how* to be bishops," said Hulsey. [49] Browning preferred to lead the House of Bishops collaboratively and utilize the gifts of group members to address challenges. He seldom acted unilaterally.

Shortly before the first Kanuga meeting of the House of Bishops, Ed and Patti Browning met over dinner with retired presiding bishop John Allin. Allin put things in perspective for another man in a situation only few people experience. "You know the problems in the House have been with them as long as I can remember," Allin said. "They were present in my time. They were present in John Hines's time. The difference is we never really stopped to take them out and look at them. We never dealt with them, and that is what you are doing now." [50] One of the enduring and publicly unrecognized contributions of Browning's leadership was his addressing the systemic challenges within the House of Bishops, going back for a generation, to provide a more effective and collegial episcopacy for the Episcopal Church. Browning's efforts at rebuilding relationships and restructuring the meetings of the House of Bishops held that body together so that consensus could gradually emerge and historic decisions could be made later on.

At their first Kanuga meeting in March 1992, Arthur Vogel, bishop of West Missouri, presented a paper on the episcopacy in order to set a framework for the discussion. "Because faith is of the community," wrote Vogel, "the only way the faith can be discerned is communally— dialogically within the community." [51] The bishops developed four hypotheses about their common life. Browning found the hypotheses devastating yet realistic: first, the House of Bishops, as a collective body, had not agreed upon an understanding of the episcopacy or what it means to be a community of bishops; second, there was no clear understanding on how the House of Bishops should function in leading the church; third, the House of Bishops operated in a competitive climate, leading to polarization and opposing coalitions; fourth, the House of Bishops was not structured to enable effective discussion and analysis of issues facing the church. Browning described the scene in the House of Bishops after the hypotheses were developed: "We sighed deeply—out of relief I think more than despair—because we had named the problem. We had named the problem that had existed for as long as any of us can remember." At that same meeting, the House of

Bishops crafted a purpose statement that was accepted by acclamation: "What has emerged is a commitment to a new community of relationships among bishops without which it is not possible to make decisions which manifest the gospel. We recognize that we must focus upon our communal life as a House of Bishops because it is the source of our identity. We learned that if we cannot be bishops together, we cannot be bishops alone." [52]

At the next meeting of the House of Bishops in Baltimore, not all the bishops recollected the work they had done together at Kanuga six months previously. Some had forgotten that the hypotheses were their own work, not the work of consultants. There were also time constraints, with an agenda set in advance on the authority of scripture, making it difficult for the House of Bishops to continue to reflect on how they did business. Despite the constraints, however, Browning thought the meeting was successful. "Our work on the authority of scripture showed us that we can come at things with a variety of approaches but still find a great deal of commonality, and the ability to honor, to learn from, our different approaches. I don't think we had that ability in Phoenix," said Browning. [53] He spoke of the importance of the baptismal vows in his opening address to the House of Bishops:

> I truly believe that the erosion of community and the ignoring of the baptismal vow to respect the dignity of every person are at the root of the systemic and societal ills…all around us, and that we are called to confront. A beginning of that confrontation is in our own lives—in the House of Bishops. That is why we are called to embody what community really means in the deepest sense. [54]

After the Baltimore meeting, the Kanuga Planning Committee decided to discontinue the use of outside consultants, with the exception of assistance with the process, and instead to build collegiality by using the gifts within the House of Bishops itself. Through the work of the Kanuga Planning Committee, Browning initiated the tradition of scripture study and sitting in table groups during House of Bishops meetings, altering the long-standing custom of bishops seated in rows by consecration date. The change in the physical arrangement of the room signaled a switch away from a legislative model of meeting to a collegial model of shared leadership. "The House of Bishops is an organic entity," Browning said. "It has a personality. It changes and evolves as every person does and we need to keep checking in on where we are and who were we becoming." [55]

Another change was the introduction of more spiritual content and liturgy into all House of Bishops meetings. The house was already accustomed to hearing addresses from staff and outside experts. Browning believed that for the church to become more compassionate and inclusive, issues should be addressed spiritually rather than ideologically and that the place to start was with the House of Bishops. Browning named M. Thomas Shaw, superior of the Society of Saint John the Evangelist (SSJE) and later bishop of Massachusetts, and Martin Smith, a former superior of SSJE, as chaplains to the house. Ideally, Browning wanted a chaplain to serve for a full triennium to assure continuity in the spiritual life of the House of Bishops. "Though the atmosphere was emotionally charged in the House of Bishops, he really did trust in us, and was not trying to control the agenda," said Smith. [56] Other notable figures, such as Desmond Tutu and Henri Nouwen, also enriched the spiritual life of the House of Bishops. "Even a casual look across the faces of our members would indicate that we are far, far more inclusive, and that has only come by way of compassionate leadership," wrote Bill Swing, bishop of California in 1995.[57] Shaw, who experienced the House of Bishops from the perspective of its chaplain and as a bishop, said, "I realized what a visionary Ed was from the beginning. He gradually transformed that house from debate to genuine conversations." Shaw said that while there was a lot of resistance among the bishops at first and no shortage of passive aggressive behavior and complaints about meeting in a retreat setting, it was Browning's persistence that was transformative. "Ed kept everyone's feet to the fire." Shaw believes that outside of the consecration of Bishop Barbara C. Harris, Browning's work in transforming the House of Bishops was the most important accomplishment of his administration.[58]

In September 1995, as the embezzlement scandal drew to its conclusion, Browning addressed what he identified as "mean spiritedness" in the House of Bishops. "We have to name that there is a mean spirit abroad in the church," said the presiding bishop. "I believe this spirit is intolerable and that we as a house must not tolerate it." Browning believed that negative energy was draining energies more rightly focused on the mission of church. He also commented on the attacks made against him:

> I think you are all aware of the attacks made on me as presiding bishop. I want you to know that I would have to have such a large ego that it would be pathological to have this not bother me at all. I don't have that kind of an ego. And, I will confess that some of it has been very troubling. However, I do have something else. I have faith in God's

leading me, guiding me. I believe that I have been
called to this office and, surely, I don't have to
depend on my own strength, my own wisdom. [59]

After the presiding bishop's address, bishops discussed
the "mean spiritedness" in the house in table groups. "We
acknowledged we're all responsible," said James Jelinek,
bishop of Minnesota. "We've been invited by Ed to
participate fully in the direction of this church and we
haven't always done so." "Bishops are called to model
discussions in Christian love," said John MacNaughton,
bishop of West Texas. "If we can't do it, who can?" [60]

In his address to the 1997 General Convention in
Philadelphia, his last as presiding bishop, Browning
reflected on the six years of his term during which the
House of Bishops met at Kanuga. He felt that the House
of Bishops had come to a new place. Remembering the
1991 General Convention, Browning said that "the House
of Bishops erupted into turmoil and I had to do something
I never thought I would. I closed the doors so we could
express ourselves openly and begin to work through our
anger and our hurt. But God was with us and by the
time we were ready to go home, both Houses of that
convention knew that the Holy Spirit had not deserted
us after all." [61] That was then. Six years later the sixty-five
bishops consecrated since 1992 had no experience with
the old manner of operation. Said Browning, "They have
never experienced a House of Bishops whose members
didn't even know one another, who sat in formal rows by
order of consecration, who voted after formal debate and
had little opportunity to know the mind and heart of one
another, and to build a new community of trust." [62]

The new spirit of cooperation extended beyond the
House of Bishops. By 1997, because of the intentional

collaboration between Browning and Pam Chinnis, there was a renewed sense of cooperation between the House of Bishops and the House of Deputies. Legislative committees of the two houses were working together as teams. Browning believes that the partnership between the two houses facilitated the dialogue on difficult issues. "I did not choose these issues," he said. "Nor did you. They are the challenge of this generation given to us through the God of history. I believe with all my heart that for the most part, we are responding to them out of the gospel: not some literalist gospel, or a liberal gospel or a conservative gospel, but the gospel of Jesus Christ, whom we know and love." [63]

Human Sexuality

The most persistent debate during Edmond Browning's term as presiding bishop had to do with human sexuality. Tenaciously and compassionately he steered the church through highly charged discussions. While criticized by members of the church for his support of gay men and lesbians, he was also commended by the House of Bishops in 1995 for his pastoral support for those on all sides of the debate. Although the General Convention had voted to uphold the civil rights of gays and lesbians in 1976, debate on the ordination of "practicing" homosexuals and the blessing of same-sex unions was heated during the Browning years. When several incidents of sexual misconduct became news, Browning also worked to clarify the expectations of the church in terms of clergy contact and to separate the issue of sexual misconduct from that of sexual orientation.

In 1987 the Education for Mission and Ministry unit at the Episcopal Church Center released *Sexuality: A Divine Gift,* a publication designed to facilitate the church-wide dialogue on human sexuality mandated by the General Convention in 1982. It was faulted for its lack of support for traditional church teachings. Some in the church were concerned that the resource was intended as an official statement or a position paper, rather than an educational resource designed to further the dialogue. The criticisms contributed to the publication of an additional resource, *Continuing the Dialogue,* which included authors who differed from the views presented in the first resource. Browning urged dialogue throughout the church on human sexuality. "This process of discerning God's will occurs in every generation. And I believe we are in such a period of faith discernment." [64] Two additional resources, *Human Sexuality: A Christian Perspective,* developed by Province VII, and *Human Sexuality and the Christian Church,* developed by the Evangelical Lutheran Church in America, were distributed to facilitate the dialogue on human sexuality in congregations and dioceses. The 1991 General Convention had mandated that a process of "dialogue not debate" and "open conversation take place between All Saints' Day 1992 and Easter 1993." Episcopalians were asked to fill out questionnaires that were then tabulated by province. The intention was to send the findings to the House of Bishops to assist them in preparing a pastoral teaching on human sexuality for the 1994 General Convention in Indianapolis. [65]

As a pastor, Browning saw members of the gay community not as "issues" to be voted on, but human beings and members through baptism of the Christian church. He repeatedly sought to assure the gay, lesbian, bisexual, transgender (GLBT) community of his commitment and his prayers. Many believed he was *their* pastor. "For me, Ed Browning's statement 'In this church there will be no outcasts' came at a time when both the AIDS folks and the GLBT people were the faces I needed to see as a part of the baptismal mandate to seek and serve Christ in all persons and to respect the dignity of every human being," writes Linda Privitera, an Episcopal priest now serving in Canada. "Some time ago I was able to tell Ed Browning what that statement has meant for me as a lesbian priest to know that I would not be an outcast; he was characteristically gentle and self-deprecating about the power of that statement; with those words, however, he gave me strength and an ability not to displace myself from the life and ministry of the Episcopal Church." [66]

Gene Robinson, bishop of New Hampshire, remembers meeting with Browning and other people from the gay and lesbian community in 1986, soon after he had come out as a gay man himself. "I remember thinking, 'what a risk for the new PB to be doing this,'" said Robinson. "I was newly out and thought my ordained life was over, and there was Ed acting like this was just another conversation between Christians. It clearly was not all that amazing to him." Robinson said that meeting inspired him for years though he does not recall its specific agenda. "The world has changed so much that it is almost impossible for us to remember what it was like for gay people then, and here was the new PB meeting with us. I left realizing that we were beloved by God and that we could be part of the church—it was just breathtaking!" [67] As celebrant for the Integrity Eucharist at the General Convention in Anaheim in 2009, Gene Robinson publicly reiterated this sentiment with Browning in attendance. "Ed's witness gave permission for me to come out," said Robinson. "This is all your fault," he said to Browning. The response from the crowd was great laughter and then thunderous applause for Browning, who was deeply touched to receive acclaim more than a decade after leaving public life.

Browning preached at the annual conference of Integrity, the national organization of lesbian, gay, bisexual, and transgender Episcopalians, in Houston in 1992, despite a request from the diocesan bishop that he not attend the conference. He urged Integrity members to "hang in there" and challenged those present to be reconcilers throughout the church. "Is it possible to know the pain you have known and still find it within yourself to remain in the body where so much of that pain has occurred?" [68] Fred Ellis, a past national president of Integrity, said that the power of Browning's sermon in Houston was in his challenge to the gay community to remain at the table. "He challenged us," said Ellis. "He effectively said that when all of this is over—and some day it will be over—it will be us who will be called upon to extend our hand in reconciliation to the church." [69]

Bruce Garner, a former national president of Integrity from the Diocese of Atlanta, recalls his meetings with Browning. "I always felt I had access to him," said Garner. "Others were more vocal about the issues, but I also understood that he was walking a very tight line and had to make himself available to all sides." Garner remembers fondly when Browning was invited to preach at All Saints, Atlanta, during the 1996 Olympics. "He got a five and one-half minute standing ovation," said Garner. "Not many people get that for a sermon! He brought us a long way toward full inclusion." Fred Ellis said that his relationship with Browning (and Integrity) evolved over time. Although Ellis was upset when he was asked to leave the House of Bishops' meeting in Panama—Pam Chinnis and the press were the only non-bishops allowed to stay while the house continued to discuss difficult issues— "we kept talking and remained in conversation." Ellis said Browning gave his full support when a chaplain at Fort Bragg disclosed the identity of a gay soldier to the man's commanding officers. Outraged, Integrity sought and received the support of Charles Keyser, the suffragan bishop of the Armed Forces. [70]

Browning's support of the GLBT community extended beyond the Episcopal Church. In 1993 he wrote President Clinton and protested the continuing bias against gays and lesbians in the military. In 1994 he filed an *amicus* brief at the Supreme Court to oppose Colorado's discriminatory laws against gays and lesbians. In June 1996 conservative church members took out an advertisement in *The Washington Times* refuting Browning's statement that gays and lesbians in committed relationships can serve as wholesome examples. In the same year Browning insisted that the World Council of Churches engage in dialogue about human sexuality, despite protests from the Orthodox churches. [71] Nancy Wilson, moderator of the Metropolitan Community Churches (MCC), a church formed in 1968 as a spiritual home for gays and lesbians, said that Browning "made an effort to reach out" to the newer denomination and offer his public support for the denomination's membership in the National Council of Churches and World Council of Churches. At the time other churches wished to exclude the MCC from both ecumenical bodies. "At that time it was very important that he treated me collegially. I knew that if I needed to call him, he would be accessible," said Wilson. [72]

A pivotal event in the dialogue on human sexuality occurred when the Diocese of Newark ordained a non-celibate gay man, Robert Williams, to the priesthood in December 1989. The House of Bishops had resolved in 1979 that it was "not appropriate" to ordain a practicing homosexual or any person engaging in heterosexual relations outside of marriage. Browning and his Council of Advice disassociated themselves from the Newark ordination, stating, "We believe that good order is not served when bishops, dioceses, or parishes act unilaterally." [73] They stressed that their primary concern was one of "collegiality" and that they did not intend to make a negative statement on the ordination of gay men and lesbians.

However strongly he felt about justice for gay and lesbian people, Browning knew that the issue would have to work itself out through the normal channels of church governance. In the meantime, he prayed for guidance and a resolution that would sustain the unity of the church. Not surprisingly, the House of Bishops also voted to disassociate itself from the Newark ordination. Browning was concerned that the Newark ordination would lead to a backlash against gay men and lesbians throughout the church. "It is incumbent upon each one of us to take the greatest care in how we pronounce on this matter," he said to the Executive Council, which eventually commended to the church the statement made by the presiding bishop and the Council of Advice after many hours of prayer and deliberation. David Collins, the president of the House of Deputies at the time, presided over the discussion and observed that there was "a wide variance" and fundamental differences among Executive Council members on human sexuality. "It is an issue we're going to have to deal with in this church," said Collins. "I wish we didn't have to, but we do." [74]

John Shelby Spong, bishop of Newark, denied that any member of the Diocese of Newark had acted inappropriately in ordaining Robert Williams and stated that he was shocked at the hatred and condemnation that emanated from parts of the church. But soon after the ordination, Spong asked Williams to resign from his ministry after he made inappropriate public remarks at a conference. At the request of the presiding bishop, Spong delayed the ordination to the diaconate of another noncelibate gay man, Barry Stopfel, in an effort to keep the dialogue open for the good of the church. Stopfel later wrote that he did not present himself for ordination out of deference to Browning's request and with the knowledge that the presiding bishop had pledged his support of the ordination of gay and lesbian persons. Stopfel was ordained in September 1990 by Walter Righter, assisting bishop of Newark. On the same day, Ronald Haines, bishop of Washington, ordained Elizabeth Karl, who was living in a committed lesbian relationship. Although Browning had disassociated himself from the ordination of Robert Williams, he did not separate himself from the man himself. Two years later, as Williams was dying of AIDS, the presiding bishop came to his bedside. As was the case with many of Browning's pastoral actions, the visit was not reported, yet it is was example of his compassion, even for those who caused him personal difficulties.

The House of Bishops prepared a pastoral letter on human sexuality for the General Convention in 1994. The process tested the level of collegiality within the House of Bishops, still coming to terms with its collapse in Phoenix in 1991. Called "Continuing the Dialogue: A

Pastoral Study of the House of Bishops to the Church as the Church Considers Issues of Human Sexuality," the document traced the history of the church's views on human sexuality, reviewed scriptural interpretations, discussed the discontinuities between official teaching and the experience of the church's members, and offered guidelines for further dialogue. The team preparing the draft met for three years and went through four revisions. The secrecy around the project fueled anxiety about the document's contents. Weeks before its release on the first day of the General Convention, Episcopalians United, a traditionalist group, leaked the two final drafts, an action which Browning found reprehensible and which further fueled controversy. The pastoral teaching eventually was downgraded to a "study" and was joined by two other competing documents: "An Affirmation," prepared by some Province VII bishops to uphold traditional teachings on marriage, and "Koinonia," a statement presented by John Shelby Spong, bishop of Newark, asserting that sexual orientation was "morally neutral" and upholding the ordination of non-celibate homosexuals. By the end of the convention, 106 bishops had signed "An Affirmation," and fifty-five had signed "Koinonia."[75] The House of Bishops decided to send out "Continuing the Dialogue" without either statement attached.

Throughout the many discussions on human sexuality, Browning was clear that his role was to clarify the issues and build bridges between opposing perspectives. He used all the resources of his office to foster dialogue and healing, seeking to show compassion to those on all sides of an issue, whether they recognized his support or not. "To be a bridge builder in a divided community is to reach out with *both* hands and to draw the sides together.

This is the role of the prophetic pastor, seeking out both sides and enabling them to enter into dialogue for mutual understanding and acceptance....I am called to this ministry and it is out of this I can say there will be no outcasts."[76]

Browning's perception of his role as "prophetic pastor" also meant that he did not always share his personal feelings on human sexuality, instead choosing to remain open to the pain present on all sides. Occasionally, however, Browning's own views became known. John Clinton Bradley tells the following story of a meeting with the presiding bishop at a reception at Washington National Cathedral in 1995:

> When my turn came to greet Bishop Browning, I discreetly pressed into his hand a pink triangle button superimposed with the slogan "Affirm Koinonia." This, of course, referred to the controversial "Koinonia Statement" authored by Jack Spong and signed by seventy-one other bishops in 1994. I said to Bishop Browning, "I know you can't wear this button in public, but I wanted you to have it as a token of thanks for your support of gay and lesbian equality in the church." Ed replied, "Who says I can't wear it?" and pinned it to his lapel![77]

In contrast to the dynamics of the 1991 convention in Phoenix, the debates around human sexuality and the pastoral study at the General Convention in 1994 were surprisingly civil. One area of contention was a guideline that committed bishops to ordain "only persons [they] believe to be a wholesome example to their people according to the standards and norms established by the church." The question of who was considered a "wholesome example" was much debated, including a suggestion that the decision to ordain a non-celibate homosexual should be a local option. The House of Deputies was concerned that the bishops' pastoral study not be used to sidestep other resolutions on human sexuality. Although approval by the House of Deputies was not needed to release the pastoral study, they did urge the church to study it and created a twelve-member Committee on Dialogue on Human Sexuality, made up of bishops and deputies. After failed attempts in previous conventions, both houses agreed to change the canons to ensure that no one be barred from access to the ordination process because of "race, color, ethnic origin, sex, national origin, marital status, sexual orientation, disabilities, or age," except as otherwise specified in the canons. At the same convention, the House of Bishops voted down, after two days of debate, a resolution to develop rites for same-sex blessings, instead opting for a substitute resolution calling for a study of the theological and pastoral considerations in developing "rites honoring love and commitment between persons of the same sex." A resolution calling for materials to understand and accept children's sexuality was approved, although bishops and deputies did not agree to distribute a report from the Standing Commission on Human Affairs on youth at risk, including gay and lesbian youth. [78]

Despite his attempts to support healthy and balanced dialogue about human sexuality, Browning was regularly excoriated in the press, both in the United States and abroad, for his support of the GLBT community. One well-publicized conversation occurred between Jack Iker, bishop of Fort Worth, and George Carey, archbishop of Canterbury, in a conference center hot tub during a House of Bishops meeting. Reportedly, Carey asked Iker if the presiding bishop realized how harmful it would be to the Anglican Communion (and the next Lambeth Conference) if the General Convention approved same-sex unions and the ordination of non-celibate homosexuals. Iker replied that he believed Browning was more concerned about gaining approval for the gay agenda than with any unhappiness in the rest of the Communion. Carey reportedly also asked Iker if he believed that they were "really going to make me do it," that is, accept the mandatory ordination of women, to which Iker responded that he believed the intention was to make women's ordination mandatory at all levels of the church, in every diocese. Carey replied that he believed the Church of England was dealing with it in a much better fashion and that he hoped the Episcopal Church could find another way forward. [79]

Although Browning made every effort to be hospitable to Carey on his many visits to the United States and Episcopal dioceses, he grew weary of Carey's offering opinions on human sexuality and women's ordination in public forums, not to mention private conversations with other bishops in hot tubs. Although the archbishop of Canterbury has no jurisdiction in the Episcopal Church, his office carries moral weight and Carey used it to undermine Browning's efforts to achieve mutual respect among people of differing views. Carey never gave Browning the courtesy of knowing when he was going to be in the United States or any other part of his jurisdiction. On at least one occasion Browning was in the position of having to inform Carey that if he was going to speak at a major event in the Episcopal Church, he must not offer his views on human sexuality. [80] Though Browning raised difficult issues with Carey and the primates, he sought to do so in a way that would not undermine the Anglican Communion. Browning cared about how the Episcopal Church was perceived within the Anglican Communion and worked to forge positive relationships with churches and his fellow primates.

Near the end of his term, Browning grew impatient with the ongoing divisions in the church around human sexuality. He believed most of the people in the church agreed on many of the issues, such as the sanctity of marriage and the evil of abusive relationships, but that instead of witnessing to the culture with unity and strength, the church's message was distorted. "We have been diverted by fear," he said, "and, let me name it, by hate."[81] Rather than trying to agree about what a "wholesome" relationship is and causing the church to appear "ludicrous" to others, Browning thought it was time to move past using literalistic interpretations of scripture to incite prejudice against gays and lesbians and to return to our Anglican roots:

> I'm a traditionalist. That's right. I'm a traditionalist because I treasure and believe in the ethos of Anglicanism. As Anglicans, we discern God's word through scripture, tradition, and reason. However, some have chosen to embrace biblical literalism instead of our Anglican tradition. History tells us that biblical literalism was used to support both the practice of slavery and the denigration of women. We have moved past slavery and we are moving past the oppression of women. It is time to move beyond using literalistic readings of the Bible to create prejudices against our gay and lesbian brothers and sisters. Biblical literalism may be someone's tradition, but it's not our tradition and it's time we came home to our Anglican roots.[82]

The last General Convention of the Browning administration in 1997 continued to focus on legislation pertaining to gay and lesbian church members. It extended health benefits to domestic partners, but rejected pension benefits for surviving partners of gay and lesbian clergy. At the same convention, a resolution calling for the development of rites for the blessing of same-sex relationships was rejected by one vote in each of the clergy and lay orders of the House of Deputies. Despite the lack of consensus, the convention issued an apology to lesbians and gay men for "years of rejection and maltreatment by the church," at the same time acknowledging "the diversity of opinion…on the morality of gay and lesbian relationships." Advocates of the measure, such as Louie Crew, a deputy from Newark and founder of Integrity, signed the resolution, "not because lesbians and gays need this apology, but because the church needs to apologize." [83]

The Walter Righter Presentment

Ten Episcopal bishops brought disciplinary charges against Walter Righter, assisting bishop of Newark, in January 1995, stating he had violated church doctrine and his ordination vows when he ordained Barry Stopfel, a non-celibate gay man, in 1990. Righter had acted under the authority of the bishop of Newark, John Shelby Spong. For a presentment to proceed to trial, one-fourth of the 297 members of the House of Bishops needed to consent to it. The trial was the first since 1924, when a retired bishop was found to hold doctrine contrary to the teachings of the church; two other bishops had been tried in the nineteenth century. [84] The presiding bishop was opposed to the presentment from the onset. "This presentment is not the way to go deeper into the truths of one another," said Browning. "Regardless of its merits, its worth, and what might or might not be found by invoking the legal process, this presentment will not solve anything. It will resolve nothing. When it comes my turn to vote, I cannot, and will not, consent to this presentment. And I pray that the house will realize that this is not the way." Browning pointed out to the House of Bishops that they were already embarked on another process, a community process of discerning Christian truth, before the canonical route mandated by the presentment. That process had begun during the difficult days of the General Convention in Phoenix in 1991. Knowing that the bishops who signed the presentment against Righter had a list of other charges to come, Browning raised the equally daunting possibility of presentments against bishops who did not permit women's ordination in their dioceses. "We could do all of this, yes, but what a price," he said. "Would this help us better know how God calls us? Would we find consensus? Would we better understand anything? What would we achieve? I feel certain the answer is no and no and no and nothing." [85]

Despite Browning's arguments, the necessary consents were received by a narrow margin and the case went to trial. The court, composed of a panel of nine bishops, held the hearing at the Cathedral of St. John in Wilmington, Delaware. Three months after the hearing, the charges of teaching false doctrine and the violation of ordination vows against Walter Righter were dismissed on the grounds that the trial court could find no doctrine prohibiting the ordination of non-celibate homosexuals. The court voted 7-1 to drop the charges, stating there is "no core doctrine prohibiting the ordination of a non-celibate homosexual person living in a faithful and committed sexual relationship with a person of the same sex." The judges further stated that the decision was intentionally limited in scope. "We are not deciding whether life-long, committed, same-gender relationships are or are not a wholesome example with respect to ordination vows. We are not rendering an opinion on whether a bishop and diocese should or should not ordain persons living in same-gender relationships. Rather, we are deciding the narrow issue of whether or not under Title IV a bishop is restrained from ordaining persons living in committed same-gender relationships." [86] Andrew Fairfield, bishop of North Dakota, cast the dissenting vote.

The ten bishops who brought the presentment charges against Righter found the decision "deeply flawed and erroneous" and issued a strongly worded statement after the court dismissed the charges. "In a single pronouncement," the statement said, "it has swept away two millennia of Christian teaching regarding God's purposes in creation, the nature and meaning of marriage and family, the discipleship in relation to sexuality to which we are called as followers of Jesus, the paradigm of the church as bride and Christ as bridegroom..." [87] There was no appeal, although the bishops who issued the presentment stated their intention of bringing a canon to the 1997 General Convention which would require all clergy to abstain from sexual relations outside of marriage. Other groups, such as the Episcopal Women's Caucus, applauded the decision as positive. "We especially rejoice with our lesbian sisters and gay brothers in this affirmation of the gift of their ministries in our church," the caucus said. [88] Positive and negative reactions to the decision were heard around the church, including a consensus that the issues raised by the presentment needed to be further discussed at the General Convention.

Before his hearing, Walter Righter told the House of Bishops that he was prepared to go through the presentment process if necessary. He believed the presentment was about intolerance, not heresy. "People are struggling to find out some social agreement between what's wrong and what's right," he said. "Now, to be involved in that means being on the frontlines between the past and the future, and that's scary. These people [who brought the charges] want to take us back into the past, but we really need to participate in the future." [89] Following the decision, Righter commented on the invasiveness of the presentment process to himself and his family and said he felt like a "guinea pig." The bishops issuing the presentment later indicated that Righter had been chosen to be the first from a field of bishops who had ordained non-celibate gay men and lesbians because the five-year statute of limitations would run out if a trial was delayed. After the Righter decision, Browning dismissed similar charges against Allen Bartlett, bishop of Pennsylvania, stating that the issue had already been decided by the Righter case. [90] An attempt to discipline Browning for this decision failed.

Sexual Misconduct

When Edmond Lee Browning was bishop of Hawaii, James Montgomery, bishop of Chicago, visited him as part of the search committee looking for a new presiding bishop and asked him whether, if he became presiding bishop, he would have the strength to deal with powerful bishops who misbehave. Browning answered that he thought he would. Little did he know how difficult handling such misbehavior would be, or what personal resources it would require.

It would be during the Browning administration that the Episcopal Church came to terms with clergy sexual misconduct and put in place a formal process to make the church a safer place for all its members. Browning characteristically saw it as his responsibility to lead the church through the pain and controversy ahead rather than evade the issue. "As one charged with giving comfort and fairness to the victim and to the accused, I don't think there will ever come a time when dealing with this painful issue will be easy for me," he wrote, "or for any of us." [91]

In 1988, three years after he was elected presiding bishop, Browning appointed Harold "Hoppy" Hopkins, then bishop of North Dakota, director of the House of Bishops' office of pastoral development. Hopkins immediately appointed an ad hoc committee to investigate and change the way the church deals with clergy misconduct. The work of the ad hoc committee was expanded in 1991 when the General Convention established the Committee on Sexual Exploitation. Over three years it developed a preventative educational curriculum on sexual abuse, exploitation, and harassment and proposed a code of conduct for pastoral relationships.

As the number of clergy sexual misconduct claims escalated from a handful in the 1980s to thirty-nine in 1992, the Church Insurance Corporation (CIC), the primary liability insurer for dioceses and parishes in the Episcopal Church, developed stricter guidelines for personnel management and pastoral counseling, including background checks for all staff and volunteers. The committee and the CIC worked to coordinate efforts directed at the larger church. The two groups had different perspectives. "The thing a lot of people are missing is that the Church Insurance Company is not laying out ethical and moral guidelines for the church," said Harold Hopkins. "What it is doing is saying if you want insurance coverage this is what you must do." [92] By contrast, noted Hopkins, the work of the Committee on Sexual Exploitation was to examine sexual misconduct in a systemic way and consider the impact on the victims, their families, congregations, and dioceses. Browning and Hopkins received much criticism for their handling of cases of sexual misconduct. Hopkins was sometimes referred to as the "sex cop." Some accused the presiding bishop and the CIC of being "top-down" in their approach. The fact that stricter conditions were added to obtain liability insurance drew a highly negative reaction across the church and some clergy felt they were wrongly suspect, given the low incidence of misconduct. "Many feel particularly vulnerable. They may not understand the context out of which this has arisen," said Hopkins. [93]

Cases involving bishops did not gain prominence until 1991. This coincided with Browning's appointment of a new chancellor, David Booth Beers, formerly chancellor for bishop John Walker in the Diocese of Washington. One evening Browning called Beers and Hopkins into his hotel room where the Executive Council was meeting. He asked Beers what protocol he should follow in dealing with a new charge of episcopal misconduct. After hearing a very clear outline of a rigorous process, Browning turned to Hopkins and asked, "Do I have to do this?" "Yes," said Hopkins, and Browning sighed. So began a deep partnership among the three that would guide the church through many choppy waters, sometimes quietly, sometimes very publicly. [94]

Once he knew what was required, Browning worked swiftly and decisively to address cases of sexual misconduct. This aspect of his pastoral ministry took a great deal of his time, much of it unknown to the wider church. He worked behind the scenes with both the accused and the complainants and acted to aid healing for the individuals and the dioceses involved. No victim was ever denied a personal meeting with Browning. He read everything sent to him by a complainant or an accused bishop or prepared for him by staff. He was engaged in every case. He believed that while "it is sometimes hard to make out the shadow of God's hand through the veil of tears, of this we are clear—God is present with those who suffer." [95]

David Beers later said that Browning dealt with cases of sexual misconduct discreetly and strongly. "Though at times it was tough on him, he was very strong. There was no one he was unwilling to confront if it was necessary. A series of bishops who got caught were called to his office, and they went, and he confronted them with great strength and great integrity. It's a piece of his ministry that most folk did not really understand." [96]

Among the more than twenty cases that crossed Browning's desk over a span of six years, some were publicly known and others not. They spanned all geographical regions of the church. Beers also noted that Browning dealt with bishops charged with offenses who were both liberal and conservative, those who had close personal relationships with him, and others whom he knew less well. He maintained equanimity with all of them. The cases resulted in resignations, withdrawal from ordained ministry, both voluntary and involuntary, and suspensions. Some of the bishops vigorously denied the allegations against them, leading to protracted proceedings, which consumed vast amounts of the presiding bishop's time. The cases involved both heterosexual and homosexual misconduct on the part of bishops and other clergy under Browning's jurisdiction. [97]

Beginning on January 1, 1996, the Episcopal Church put into effect uniform procedures for bringing charges against clergy accused of sexual misconduct, prosecuting the charges, and protecting the due process rights of both the accused and the complainants. The new "Title IV" clergy disciplinary canons replaced old canons dating from 1915, which focused primarily on matters of heresy and doctrine. Until the 1970s, clergy misconduct was usually handled privately, resulting in divergent ways of dealing with similar complaints across different dioceses. Despite arguments over the statutes of limitations for cases of alleged abuse, the General Convention approved the legislation in 1994.

Browning was a staunch advocate of the new disciplinary canons. Although the process of bringing the issue forward was tumultuous, he believed it was necessary if the church was to become the community he envisioned. "I have no doubt that it was time for the church to address the misconduct in our midst, and to be responsible. The impact of these cases to the people involved and to the local diocese is enormous and further diverts our energies from the mission of the church." [98]

In 1996 Browning and the rest of the Episcopal Church learned about an article in *Penthouse* magazine alleging that Episcopal priests in the Diocese of Long Island had imported Brazilian men for sex and participated in sexual acts and drug and alcohol use in Brooklyn churches. Although limited in his authority in local dioceses, Browning stated that the alleged actions were "deplorable." He was in frequent communication with the bishop of Long Island about the matter. Browning was incensed that some in the church inflamed the situation and used it to scapegoat the gay and lesbian community. "The alleged actions in Long Island are clearly outside acceptable parameters and should not be confused with our ongoing struggles about sexuality," said Browning. "Attempts to link the two bring negative attention to our church and pain to our gay and lesbian members. We must clearly differentiate between issues of sexual abuse and exploitation, and sexual orientation." [99]

Full Speed Ahead

Groups such as the Episcopal Synod of America (ESA) repeatedly requested that the presiding bishop establish a non-geographic province for traditionalists to allow them to stay in the church. Encouraged by a resolution of the Lambeth Conference 1998 stating provision should be made for those who dissent, ESA sought a structural solution for those who held to the church's "historic faith and order." [100] Their proposals never made it out of committee and onto the floor of the General Convention. The Browning administration rejected the proposals, contending that "parallel jurisdictions" were specifically rejected elsewhere in the Anglican Communion. Moreover, George Carey, archbishop of Canterbury, said he would not recognize overlapping jurisdictions in the United States. [101]

The issue of a parallel jurisdiction for traditionalists was not concluded during the Browning administration. But Browning initiated two meetings with select bishops prior to the 1997 General Convention to discuss issues "that threaten to fracture the church," namely human sexuality and mandatory acceptance of women's ordination. "In spite of endless claims about 'dialogue' in the past, this really was the first instance of genuine dialogue on either subject," said Frank T. Griswold, then bishop of Chicago. "The discussion was good, balanced, respectful, and helpful." [102]

Other bishops appreciated the dialogue yet wondered if the talks had occurred too late to have a lasting impact. Some of the primates of the Anglican Communion had already begun to seek to excommunicate the Episcopal Church, based on the concept of core doctrine and the dismissal of the charges against Walter Righter. [103] Conversations regarding the efficacy of a new province for dissenters from the Episcopal Church continued, sponsored by U.S. groups and dioceses in Nigeria, Kenya, Uganda, Rwanda, and the Southern Cone. Meanwhile, Episcopal Church leaders maintained their opposition to non-geographical structures. As one commentator wrote, "The new province, as it is now, is neither orthodox, nor a province, nor of the Anglican Communion." [104]

At the end of the 1994 General Convention in Indianapolis, Browning and Pam Chinnis had held a joint interview to reflect on the work of the convention and the days to come. Mindful that he was facing the last three years of his term as presiding bishop, Browning commented, in the euphoria of the moment, that the next three years would be "a piece of cake." Wrong. "Well, I guess my crystal ball wasn't working," he said three years later. "I have been through a great deal in these last three years, most significantly with an unparalleled embezzlement which has been one of the greatest personal challenges I have ever faced." [105]

After 1996 some believed the "unholy trinity" of events—the suicide of Massachusetts bishop David Johnson, the presentment against Walter Righter, and the Ellen Cooke embezzlement—would make it very difficult for the Browning administration to regain momentum in its last two years. Others believed the events would have a direct impact on the nomination process for the next presiding bishop, favoring those less likely to be "pastoral" or focused on social justice. Browning critics saw the events, in particular the embezzlement, as grounds to request the presiding bishop's resignation. Richard Kim, a priest who had worked with Browning in Hawaii, writing for *United Voice,* compared the Cooke embezzlement to Watergate. "Perhaps it is time for the presiding bishop, during whose watch all this is happening, to step down," said Kim. [106]

Ever the pastor, even to his detractors, Browning was known to follow up personally with some who had criticized him. Rustin Kimsey, the retired bishop of Eastern Oregon, tells the story of one such incident, when the presiding bishop called a senior warden in Texas after the man complained bitterly and threatened to leave the church. "Have I hurt you so much that you want to leave the church?" said Browning to the shocked churchman on the other line. The incident did make the detractor think again about his membership. [107]

Douglas LeBlanc, who got off to a rocky start with Ed Browning at the 1991 General Convention where he was a writer for *Convention Daily* for Episcopalians United, said that at first it was "really tempting for me to blame Bishop Browning for everything about the Episcopal Church I found disappointing." But the two forged a friendship during the three years between conventions and began to "recognize each other as fellow Christians." LeBlanc believes a lot of the vitriol between factions during the Browning administration could be described as "What are they doing to the church I grew up in?" LeBlanc suggests that human sexuality was the focus of controversy because it "touches all of us." Although LeBlanc is skeptical of much of the talk about inclusion, having experienced exclusion as an evangelical, he respects those who believe such inclusion is possible and characterizes Browning as someone who was best when speaking from his heart. "He inspired me to be as open to folks on the other side as I can be," said LeBlanc. "He is still quoted saying 'there are no outcasts.' There are, but his saying it represents a clear step forward for the forces of inclusion. He gave untold energy to Integrity and women's ordination, and that momentum has not stopped," said LeBlanc. [108]

Edmond Lee Browning believed he was called by God to be presiding bishop. It was not something he chose for himself, so he was responsible to see the commitment through. He never considered resigning after the embezzlement or during other periods of controversy. "Let us move on past hand wringing, second guessing, and fruitless exercises in twenty-twenty hindsight. Let us move on and give the full speed ahead signal to the church," he said. [109]

Chapter Eight Notes

1   "It's Not an Easy Thing to Be a Leader These Days," Episcopal News Service (hereafter cited as ENS), October 22, 1995.

2   Barbara C. Harris, interview by Sheryl Kujawa-Holbrook (hereafter cited as SKH), April 2009.

3   Edmond Lee Browning (hereafter cited as ELB), "Statement On Women Priests and Anglican Roman Catholic Relations," June 30, 1986, Browning Collection.

4   Michael Peers, interview by SKH, May 2009.

5   "Ordination Nearing of Women as Episcopal Bishops," n.d. [1986], Browning Collection.

6   "Question of Women Bishops Requires Primates' Attention," *Canadian Churchman*, March 1986.

7   Ibid.

8   Marjorie Hyer, "Bishops Back Male Substitutes for Ordained Women Leaders; Vote Called 'Negative Signal' for Episcopalians," *The Washington Post*, July 6, 1988.

9   "Massachusetts Election: Comments," *The Living Church*, October 23, 1988.

10   ELB, "Remarks to the House of Bishops," San Antonio, September 22, 1986, Browning Collection.

11   "Historic Consecration," *The Living Church,* February 26, 1989.

12   "Eames Commission Report," *The Living Church,* May 28, 1989.

13   ELB, Address to the Executive Council, June 13, 1989, Browning Collection.

14   Jane Holmes Dixon, interview by SKH, April 2009.

15   Mary Adelia McLeod, letter to SKH, April 23, 2009.

16   David Kalvelage, "What's Good for the Goose," *The Living Church,* October 29, 1995.

17   Michael Barwell, James Solheim, Jeffrey Penn, "Urging Continued Dialogue on Thorny Issues, General Convention Ends in a Fragile Peace," ENS, September 4, 1994; "Women's Victories In Both Houses," *The Witness* 77, no. 10 (October 1994): 22.

18   Jan Nunley, "Women's Ordination Mandatory, but Opponents' Right Respected," ENS, August 6, 1997.

19   Ginger Paul, interview by SKH, September 2009.

20   Eleanor Smith, interview by SKH, March 2009.

21   Ruth Nicastro, "Patti Browning Carries out Personal Ministry," *Dateline Detroit,* 1988.

22   Patricia Sparks Browning (hereafter cited as PSB), "Women in Ministry," Diocese of Oregon, October 21, 1988.

23   Ibid.

24   Mark Browning, interview by SKH, March 2009.

25   Sharon Sheridan, "Patti Browning Finds Christ," *Episcopal Life,* December 1997.

26   PSB, "Clergy and Spouses Conference," Diocese of Western New York, April 14, 1997.

27   Ibid.

28   PSB, "Speech to the Clergy Spouses," Diocese of Lexington, February 22, 1996.

29   Brian Grieves, letter to SKH, November 2009.

30 "Episcopal Bishops Strive for Firmness, Diversity," ENS, October 2, 1986.

31 Ibid.

32 Ibid.

33 "Browning Calls Bishops to Teaching Ministry," ENS, October 8, 1987.

34 Ibid.

35 George W. Cornell, "Bishop Browning Thrives In Rough Seas," Associated Press, n.d. [1995], Browning Collection.

36 Ibid.

37 ELB, *A Year of Days with The Book of Common Prayer* (New York: Ballantine Books, 1997), June 29.

38 Hays H. Rockwell, interview by SKH, March 2009.

39 Alden M. Hathaway, letter to SKH, March 2009.

40 Robert H. Johnson, interview by SKH, June 2009.

41 Jon Bruno, interview by SKH, April 2009.

42 "Bishop Pope Returns to the Episcopal Church," *The Living Church,* September 10, 1995.

43 David Kalvelage, "PB: Mean Spiritedness in the Church Must Not Be Tolerated," *The Living Church,* October 15, 1995.

44 Ibid.

45 Arthur B. Williams, Jr., letter to SKH, April 25, 2009.

46 Harold T. Lewis, *Yet With A Steady Beat: the African American Struggle for Recognition in the Episcopal Church* (Valley Forge: Trinity Press, 1996), 168.

47 Arthur B. Williams, Jr., letter to SKH, April 25, 2009; Arthur B. Williams, Jr., interview by SKH, April 2009.

48 Kalvelage, "PB: Mean Spiritedness in the Church."

49 "Episcopal Bishops Continue Journey Toward a More Collegial Style of Leadership," ENS, September 16, 1992.

50 ELB, "Remembrances and Reflections," March 1993, 7-12, Browning Collection.

51 ELB, "Remarks of the Presiding Bishop," March 1995, 3, Browning Collection.

52 Ibid.

53 Ibid.

54 ENS, "Episcopal Bishops Continue Journey."

55 Ibid.

56 Martin L. Smith, interview by SKH, February 2009.

57 William E. Swing, "The Browning of the Church," *Pacific Church News,* April/May 1995, 5.

58 M. Thomas Shaw, SSJE, interview by SKH, April 2009.

59 Kalvelage, "PB: Mean Spiritedness in the Church."

60 Ibid.

61 ELB, "Address to General Convention," August 6, 1997, Browning Collection.

62 Ibid.

63 Ibid.

64 "A Continuing Struggle to Reach Consensus," ENS, April 21,1988.

65 "Dialogue on Sexuality Planned in Many Places," *The Living Church,* January 10, 1993.

66 Linda Privitera, letter to SKH, February 6, 2009.

67 Gene Robinson, interview by SKH, March 2009.

68 "Bishop Browning to Integrity: Be Reconcilers," *The Living Church,* April 16, 1992.

69 Fred Ellis, interview by SKH, September 2009.

70 Bruce Garner, interview by SKH, September 2009; Fred Ellis, interview by SKH, September 2009.

71 Brian Grieves, ed. *No Outcasts: The Public Witness of Edmond L. Browning, the XXIVth Presiding Bishop of the Episcopal Church* (Cincinnati: Forward Movement, 1997), 88-90.

72 Nancy Wilson, interview by SKH, April 2009.

73 "1990: New Beginnings and More Controversy," *The Living Church,* January 6, 1991.

74 "Executive Council Meets," *The Living Church,* April 1, 1990.

75 David Kalvelage, "It Was a Typically Anglican Year," January 1, 1995.

76 ELB, letter to *The Witness,* July 1986, Browning Collection.

77 John Clinton Bradley, letter to SKH, February 3, 2009.

78 Michael Barwell, James Solheim, Jeffrey Penn, "Urging Continued Dialogue on Thorny Issues, General Convention Ends in Fragile Peace," ENS, September 7, 1994.

79 Louie Crew, note, "Reply to Two Bishops in a Hot Tub," October 12, 1996, Browning Collection.

80 ELB, interview by SKH, January 2009.

81 ELB, "Address to the 72nd General Convention," July 18, 1997, Browning Collection.

82 Ibid.

83 Jan Nunley, "Convention Says 'Now, No, and Not Yet' on Sexuality Issues," ENS, August 6, 1977.

84 "Trial Against Righter Will Proceed," *The Living Church,* September 10, 1995.

85 ELB, "Remarks of the Presiding Bishop," Special Meeting of the House of Bishops at Kanuga, March 3, 1995, Session on Presentment, Browning Collection.

86 "1996 in Review: For Better or Worse," *The Living Church,* January 5, 1997.

87 "Presenter Bishops Respond to Trial Court Vote," *The Living Church,* June 9, 1996.

88 Ibid.

89 "US Church Facing Schism?" *Anglican Journal,* February 1, 1996.

90 "Bishop Browning Decides Against Investigation," *The Living Church,* September 29, 1996.

91 ELB, *A Year of Days,* May 15.

92 David Skidmore, "General Convention Will Respond to Shock Waves Sent by Cases of Sexual Misconduct," ENS, June 15, 1994.

93 Ibid.

94 David Booth Beers, interview by Brian J. Grieves, December 2009.

95 "Executive Council Receives First Reports from Diocesan Visits, Grapples with Misconduct," ENS, June 23, 1993.

96 David Booth Beers, interview by SKH, March 2009.

97 Ibid.

98 ELB, interview by SKH, January 2009.

99 David Kalvelage, "'Deplorable' Situation," *The Living Church,* December 1, 1996.

100 Warren Tanghe, "Birth of a Province," New Directions 164 (January 2009). Found on Cost of Conscience's Trushare website, http://www.trushare.com/ 0164JAN2009/04%20birth_of_a_province_warren_tangh.htm (accessed January 3, 2010).

101 "Episcopal Synod Rebuffed," *The Washington Post,* May 19, 1990; "10th Episcopalian Province Sought," *The Washington Post,* August 4, 1990; "ESA Working Toward Non-Geographic Diocese," *The Living Church,* May 11, 1990.

102 Frank T. Griswold, interview by SKH, March 2009.

103 "P.B. Holds Meetings on Two Major Issues," *The Living Church,* May 11, 1997.

104 Tanghe, "Birth of a Province."

105 ELB, "Address to General Convention," August 6, 1997, Browning Collection.

106 Ibid.

107 Rustin Kimsey, letter to SKH, April 13, 2009.

108 Douglas LeBlanc, interview by SKH, March 2009.

109 ELB, "The Presiding Bishop's Address from the Chair to the Executive Council in Seattle, Washington, June 13, 1995," ENS, June 21, 1995.

Chapter 9

World Citizen
1986-1997

Mɪɴᴇ ɪs ᴀ ᴅᴇᴇᴘ ᴄᴏᴍᴍɪᴛᴍᴇɴᴛ to a worldview.
It is a commitment to the Anglican Communion,
to ecumenical councils at every level, and to the
dialogues between faiths that will lead to greater
service in ministering to a broken world. People
will believe when they see the larger church
focused together in a faith that is authentic. [1]

— Edmond Lee Browning,
Statement as Presiding Bishop Nominee,
June 1985

Tʜɪs ᴄᴇɴᴛᴜʀʏ ʜᴀs sᴇᴇɴ more religious persecution than all the early centuries, so famous for
their holy martyrs, combined. It doesn't happen
here in America, of course...But it is our business,
even if it is far away. Our souls will grow soft if
we do not engage in the struggle of our brothers
and sisters for whom these things are daily realities. If we abandon one another, each to our own
local sorrows and challenges, we lose the gift of

paradox, which is God's primary way of interact-
ing with the human. We cannot know the risen
Christ if we shrink from the crucified Christ. [2]

— Edmond Lee Browning,
Meditation on the
"Collect of a Martyr"

During his pastoral visits throughout the world, Ed
Browning encountered Jesus in unexpected places.
Having lived where Christianity is a minority religion,
he appreciated the gifts of the religions of the world and
understood the ways other religions revealed divine truth.
One such place was Myanmar, formerly known as Burma.
There he met the Nobel Peace Prize laureate and spiritual
leader of the nation's democracy movement, Aung San
Suu Kyi. She is known in her country simply as "the
Lady." She is a Buddhist and at the time of Ed and Patti
Browning's visit had been under house arrest, away from
her family, for six years because she would not abandon
the cause of democracy. "I do believe in the power of
prayer," she said. "I do not think that there is any division
between Buddhists or Christians or Muslims if we are all
working for peace and justice, and that binds us." [3] Ed and
Patti Browning went to Aung San Suu Kyi's home. "As
I listened to her, a person whose life has been in danger
more than once for her beliefs, I thought of Jesus, on his
way to Jerusalem, knowing what lay before him," said
Browning. "Now here was this tiny, courageous woman,
sitting in the semi-darkness of her bare living room and
talking softly about freedom, her country, her own death.
I had the sense of being with Jesus. He is truly Lord of all.
There is nowhere on earth where we cannot find him." [4]

Patti Browning, who had a similar spiritual experience during the visit, wrote: "I thought of Jesus…refusing to let his fear define him. Letting his obedience define him instead."[5]

Ed and Patti Browning were already inveterate travelers by the time they arrived back in New York to begin his term as presiding bishop; meeting people wherever he went had always energized Browning—even when the travel was arduous and the hours long. Patti was not always as energized, but she was always interested in the people and their stories. Ed Browning would say that his travel schedule caused him to be physically tired, yet always excited about the newness of the adventure. "There is always much to love in every place I go—loving people I would not have met had I stayed home, beauty I would not have seen," he said.[6]

The international and ecumenical accomplishments of the Browning administration were stunning, as he forged new ground on behalf of the Episcopal Church. Moreover, his partnership with Patti Browning, herself a seasoned missionary and human rights advocate, made them a powerful team. "He has the heart of a missionary," said Alden Hathaway, retired bishop of Pittsburgh and a friend and colleague of Browning's.[7] His ability as presiding bishop to represent the Episcopal Church across the world did much to bring the denomination to the world's attention, and while sometimes associated with controversy, Browning's ministry more often was a symbol of compassion, friendship, and solidarity. "He was the consummate missionary bishop," said Herbert Donovan, retired bishop of Arkansas.[8] While it is not possible to recount all the overseas tours and initiatives of the

Browning administration, this chapter highlights a portion of that important work and the relationships he built.

Browning always worked on planes and trains, often writing notes to people with a pastoral need or to thank the hosts he had just visited. On long tours Ed and Patti traveled together when possible, often saying their prayers together on the plane. At one point during a busy travel year, a visitor to the Brownings' apartment at the Episcopal Church Center in New York asked Patti where "home" was. Reportedly, she pointed to the bags lined up at the door for an impending trip. "That's my home," she said. During their term in office, neither Ed nor Patti Browning left their bags unpacked for long. "He could go anywhere and do anything," said J. Patrick Mauney, a deputy who traveled frequently with the Brownings. "Patti was a partner in the ministry and they very much worked together when on tour," he said. "[Ed Browning] brought honor to the Episcopal Church around the world." [9]

Africa

Soon after he was elected presiding bishop, Browning announced his intention to place all the authority of his office in solidarity with the people of South Africa and the struggle against apartheid. Soon after his installation he attended the enthronement of Desmond Tutu as archbishop of Cape Town. Although the Episcopal Church had been a leader in the anti-apartheid movement since 1971, Browning entered into the struggle with fervor and formed a strong friendship with Desmond Tutu that remains to this day. When Tutu's leadership was severely criticized in some sectors in the United States, Browning proclaimed his unconditional support. "God has called

Desmond Tutu to give voice and power to the desperation of his people in South Africa," said Browning to the House of Bishops. "I stand here today to give acclamation and support of his prophetic ministry." [10] Aware that the struggle against racism was not limited to South Africa, Browning challenged churches throughout the United States and the world to make clear their commitment. "The struggle against racism is dramatically engaged in South Africa, but is being fought around the world: in the Middle East, in Southeast Asia, in Sri Lanka, Central America, may I suggest even some parts of this country." [11] Although overjoyed at the release of Nelson Mandela in 1990, Browning urged the continuation of economic pressures on South Africa and the end of apartheid. "We rejoice that the walls are tumbling and that captives are being freed and the broken-hearted are given hope," Browning said to Executive Council at the time of Mandela's release. [12]

With the passage of the South African referendum in March 1992 ending apartheid, Browning appealed to the church and the U.S. government to pray for the new South African society and support it financially. Browning made several trips to South Africa during his time in office to show his solidarity and the support of the Episcopal Church. He also invited Desmond Tutu to address the General Convention. On one trip, John, the Brownings' youngest son and a college student, went along as part of the group. His final report not only describes the experience in detail, but reflects his learning process as he witnessed the impact of apartheid. John's views on the role of the church in developing nations changed as a result of his experience in South Africa. Before traveling to South Africa, John Browning wrote that he was skeptical about the role of the church in developing countries. "This trip has completely blown away all criticism. The church is alive in Mozambique and South Africa. It provides hope and courage for the people. It allows them to believe in something and gives them courage to fight against the extreme adversity they face." [13]

The Browning administration also responded to crises in other countries on the African continent through staff visits, collaborations with partner churches in the Anglican Communion, and humanitarian aid provided through the Presiding Bishop's Fund for World Relief. The struggles and joys of the people of Africa were never far from the attentions of Browning and the staff, and much progress was made behind the scenes to ameliorate human suffering there and to help African refugees who had fled to the United States. During the killing campaigns in Rwanda in 1994, when hundreds of thousands of Tutsis and Hutu moderates were killed, Browning wrote Bill Clinton to commend his efforts to work with the international community to restore Rwanda. Browning also encouraged President Clinton to ask the United Nations to intervene in the fate of 500 hostages held in a hotel in Kigali and requested that the State Department grant temporary protective status to Rwandans in the United States whose visas were about to expire. Always in communication with Anglican partners, Browning wrote to George Carey, archbishop of Canterbury, asking about the disposition of Anglican clergy and laity in the refugee camps, hopeful that Anglicans had not taken part in the killings. (Despite reports to the contrary, most of the Rwandan bishops fled the country.)

In the same year, Browning spent a week in Uganda, where the Anglican Church has played a pivotal role in rebuilding the nation after years of devastation caused by terrorism, civil war, and AIDS. The story of the Ugandan Church in the twentieth century is one of courage and service to its people. While there, Browning said a young priest took his hand and told him how much the concern of the Episcopal Church meant to the Ugandan people. "It just means everything to us," said the priest. "How could I fail to deliver that message?" said Browning to Executive Council. [14]

Asia

In the spring of 1987 Ed and Patti Browning journeyed for "forty days and forty nights" to East Asia. They participated in an Anglican Consultative Council (ACC) meeting in Singapore and centennial celebrations of the Anglican Church in Japan. Pastoral visits in Taiwan and Okinawa followed. The goal of the trip was to strengthen the bonds of friendship between the Episcopal Church and the churches in the Pacific and to share with them the priorities of the new Browning administration: "The importance of the church as family; the affirmation of unity within the Anglican Communion's diversity; the top priority of seeking peace and justice; the enrichment to the total church of the ministry of women." [15]

During the ACC meeting Browning was a key participant in a section meeting on the ordination of women. The final paper by the section was a carefully worded statement on the pros and cons of women's ordination, leading to the conclusion that the full church will eventually include women in all three orders. Only one woman participated in the section, delegate Ruth Choi, whose brief talk on ordination from a Korean perspective was the highpoint of the meeting for Browning, who was moved by her grace and courage. From Singapore, Browning flew to Taiwan, the most distant diocese of the Episcopal Church, where he visited local churches.

And then there was the Brownings' return to Okinawa. Ed and Patti had not been back to Okinawa since 1971. Arriving on the island as presiding bishop was poignant and a true homecoming. "You taught us the meaning of family," Browning said. "You taught us that the family of God—the family of the church—transcends national barriers, class barriers, racial barriers. You taught us that indeed God calls us to be one." [16] Returning to Japan was another homecoming for the Brownings. There Browning urged the Japanese church to offer a unique "vision of the kingdom of God seen through the eyes of Japanese culture." Reflecting on his conversion experience in Hiroshima in 1981, Browning affirmed the relationship between the church in Japan and in the United States. "The horrors of the most destructive war in human history could not separate us," he said. "Neither, we can be sure, will the uncertainties of today or of the future, for we are bound together in Christ, in whom all things hold together." [17] During the visit to Japan, Browning led a pilgrimage to Peace Memorial Park in Hiroshima, the site of the world's first atomic bomb attack on August 6, 1945. [18]

Also in 1987 the Brownings made a ten-day visit to the Philippine Episcopal Church. Bishop Robert L. O. Longid of the Diocese of Northern Philippines and his family were close friends of the Brownings. The trip was a profoundly moving journey, and ended with the presiding bishop convinced that the Philippine Episcopal Church was perhaps without equal among Anglican churches in its commitment to justice and peace. In the Philippines, as was the case in most of his international visitations, the

Brownings' low-key personal styles, obvious compassion for all people, and ability to act appropriately in all sorts of social situations caused friendships to develop quickly. Throughout urban centers and in small villages accessed only by unpaved roads, the Brownings were met with warmth and joy. Despite the violence perpetrated toward church leaders there—only a year earlier a priest had been hacked to death with a machete—the Philippine Episcopal Church, along with the United Church of Christ in the Philippines, took a leading role in social action and reconciliation ministries, especially among minority groups and tribal mountain people. The Brownings presented themselves as friends and a source of encouragement in the midst of conflict and strife. "Maybe it is just the ministry of presence—offering the gospel of hope," said Browning. [19]

Ed and Patti Browning also spent eight days in the People's Republic of China, hosted by the Standing Committees of the China Christian Council and Three-Self Patriotic Movement (CCC/TSPM). Browning was the first primate ever to visit China. There he learned about the "post-denominational, ecumenically-based" official Protestant church structure in China, the fastest growing Christian church in the world outside of Africa. In Shanghai, Nanjing, and Beijing, Browning visited and spoke at seminaries and local congregations and attended an ordination. At the Yanjing Theological Seminary in Beijing, Browning asked the students: "What is your hope for the church in China?" "With the guidance of the Holy Spirit, we can become as strong as the church in the West," said one student. [20] Browning invited K. H. Ting, the last Anglican bishop in China, to conduct Bible studies for the

House of Bishops at the General Convention in Detroit in 1988.

It was in January 1996 that Ed and Patti Browning visited the Anglican Church in the Province of Myanmar (Burma). Before traveling to Myanmar they met with refugee leaders in Bangkok, aided in part by an Episcopal congregation, Christ Church, Bangkok. Once in Myanmar at the invitation of Archbishop Andrew Mya Han, the Brownings learned about a church in a country that had been severely restricted and isolated from outside influences for nearly thirty years. Although some restrictions had been recently relaxed, the country was still run by a military regime and most of the people were desperately poor. Browning asked more than once for a meeting with Aung San Suu Kyi. There was some vagueness in response, but a couple of members of the archbishop's staff quietly arranged a meeting. In an exchange with Archbishop Mya Han afterwards, Suu Kyi turned to him and pointedly noted that this was the first time any Christian had visited her. "Why haven't local Christian leaders been to see me?" she asked, more as a challenge than a question. The Brownings' visit opened a door that would not have opened otherwise. [21]

In addition to the encounter with Nobel laureate Aung San Suu Kyi, the Brownings explored ways that the American Episcopal Church might further assist the struggling Anglican province. [22] The visit was further escalated as a public event when the United States Chargé d'Affaires hosted a reception for the Brownings at the U.S. Embassy.

Latin America and the Caribbean

The Executive Council of the Episcopal Church, for the first time in its history, met outside of the continental United States in 1988. The new presiding bishop made the commitment in February 1986, only a month after his installation, to hold the meeting in Latin America, pledging his support to the self-determination of the dioceses and nations of the region. In preparation for the historic meeting, Executive Council members visited fourteen dioceses in Province IX and the extra-provincial dioceses, from Puerto Rico in the Caribbean to Ecuador in South America, to learn about the diverse region and the role of the church. For most of the 1980s, the dioceses of Province IX proclaimed the gospel in grueling conditions, often amid civil unrest. "Until now, 'Edmond, our primate' has been just a phrase, but now when we pray for Edmond, we will be praying for a person," said Armando Guerra-Soria, bishop of Guatemala. Although the immersion in the region was limited due to time constraints, the churches of the region appreciated the effort made by Executive Council and the American church. They were aware that in the past they had often been viewed as marginal to the Episcopal Church—geographically and otherwise. "We have witnessed our church's mission and ministry in Latin America," said Browning. "We have visited congregations that meet regularly in people's homes. We have toured church facilities, which serve as both places of worship and community centers for education, medical care, and occupational training. This is true self-giving and should be a model to us all. We must find ways to support the mission and ministry in Latin America and affirm its aspirations." [23]

Beginning in 1989 Browning played a pivotal role in winning the release of ten church workers, nine of whom were from the Episcopal Church, arrested by the government of El Salvador, a country in the midst of civil war fueled by military aid sent by the United States. The outraged presiding bishop met with Bernard Aronson, Assistant Secretary of State for Latin America, to advocate for the prisoners' release. He argued that since El Salvador was a "domestic diocese," it was in the jurisdiction of the Episcopal Church. Thus it was Browning's *duty* as primate to protect the church of El Salvador. [24] Aronson reported to his boss, Secretary of State James Baker, who responded by writing to President Alfredo Cristiani of El Salvador with the threat to cut off U.S. military aid to his government unless the attacks on churches ceased immediately. Cristiani then withdrew troops from church properties and after several days released all the church workers, including Episcopal Volunteer for Mission, Josephine Beecher. "The situation right now is one of total terror for anyone who works in the churches in El Salvador," said Beecher after her release. Beecher had been seized in a predawn raid and taken to detention where she was blindfolded, handcuffed, beaten on the head, and threatened with death. "They [the military] are trying to destroy the Episcopal Church in El Salvador," she said. [25] In attacking the church leaders, the military was attempting to collapse the only "neutral place" in Salvadoran society. [26]

Browning also requested a meeting with James Baker. Early in January he was one of nine ecumenical and interfaith leaders who met with the Secretary of State in an effort to ensure the cooperation of the United States' government to end religious persecution in El Salvador and to end the war. The religious leaders were also concerned that the political situation in El Salvador hampered the ministry of the church there. The safety of religious workers in El Salvador was of particular concern given the murder of six Jesuits and two women in the fall of 1989 and the recent detentions and continued harassment of others. Church officials also wanted the United States government to exert pressure on the Salvadoran government either to return seized church property or make restitution so that humanitarian work could continue. Despite the release of most church workers from detention, Browning wanted to impress upon Baker that fundamental problems in El Salvador remained. "I don't think military aid is the way toward peace in El Salvador," said Browning after a "productive" thirty-five-minute meeting with Baker. "The way toward peace is human rights," he said. [27] Browning was incensed at reports suggesting churches and humanitarian organizations were fronts for Farabundo Marti Liberacion Nacional (FMLN), an opposition political party in El Salvador. "We're not in El Salvador to support political parties," said Browning. "We are there to carry out the mission of the church—to work with the poor in every way to improve their lives." [28] Baker arranged a meeting, which Browning hosted, with President Cristiani and his administration in New York, where the president apologized for attacks on the church and vowed that they would cease.

Confirming Browning's personal credibility as an advocate for peace, the leadership of FMLN asked him to carry a peace proposal to the United States government. Although the U.S. would not officially talk to the FMLN, Browning left it with Bernard Aronson, at his suggestion, on a coffee table in his office. The proposal, in a sealed envelope, was at first refused by the State Department.

Browning refused to take it back, and continued to use his communications with the FMLN through his Director of Government Relations in Washington, Robert J. Brooks, to support peace negotiations. A peace agreement was eventually negotiated through the United Nations. "Ed Browning was seen as 'the honest broker' during the peace process," said Brooks. "Ed Browning and the Episcopal Church had an integral role in the peace talks, which otherwise would not have occurred that soon."[29]

While immersed in the situation in El Salvador, the presiding bishop received the news of the invasion of Panama. In 1989 Browning had accepted the invitation of Panamanian dictator Manuel Noriega to visit his headquarters in Panama City the week before Easter and about a month before the Panamanian presidential elections. Although leery at first of accepting Noriega's invitation, Panamanian church leaders urged Browning to accept the invitation and to speak with General Noriega about the need for freedom of speech, freedom of the press, and a democratic election process in Panama. Although they pleaded their case, Noriega eventually declared the election a fraud when his candidate lost at the polls.[30] The United States invaded Panama and deposed Noriega in December. The costs of the invasion were enormous in terms of fatalities, destruction of property, and negative impact on the local economy. Browning was deeply disturbed by the invasion because of the violence to civilians and the United States government's decision "to intervene militarily and unilaterally once again in the affairs of a Western Hemisphere nation—even in the face of extreme provocation."[31]

Diane Porter tells the story of Browning going to the White House to meet with President Bush to discuss the invasion of Panama. She and Robert Brooks of the Washington Office were the two staff to accompany the presiding bishop. Sitting in the Oval Office, President Bush thumped the coffee table when Bishop Browning asked him not to invade Panama. "People so easily tell me what *not* to do! But they never tell me what I should do!" Bush then expressed some remorse for the outburst, and Porter excused herself and Brooks from the room so Browning could be a pastor to the president. [32]

As in El Salvador, both church property and the bishop and his family were endangered. At the invitation of James H. Ottley, bishop of Panama and interim bishop of El Salvador, Browning and three other Anglican primates, Orland Lindsay of the West Indies, Michael Peers of Canada, and Desmond Tutu of Southern Africa, conducted a pastoral visit to the dioceses of Panama and Nicaragua. The pastoral visit of the primates addressed human rights violations, the legitimacy of upcoming general elections, the "double oppression" experienced by the people of Panama due to United States-imposed sanctions, and the role of the church in peace and reconciliation.

While in Nicaragua, the primates, joined by James Ottley, met with people representing the entire political spectrum of the country, including human rights advocates, leading journalists, and civic and diplomatic officials in "a show of solidarity and a demonstration of faith in a loving and reconciling God." [33] The primates' action focused attention on the human rights abuses in Nicaragua and the physical devastation and poverty throughout the region. Although Browning's earlier correspondence to President Reagan in opposition to all covert aid to the right-wing Contras had been ignored, the statement by the Anglican primates addressed the ongoing seriousness of the matter and the hope that the Bush administration would bring change. "Our Nicaraguan experience has given us a new sympathy for the view of great numbers of people in the developing world that United States' administrations, in this case, the Reagan administration, have been prepared to subject entire peoples to the ravages of war to pursue their economic interests and because of objections to the ideological complexion of their governments." [34]

Following his visits to El Salvador, Panama, and Nicaragua, Browning established an informal "crisis management team" convened by his deputy for Anglican Relations, to anticipate and monitor situations throughout the world that might impact the Episcopal Church or one of its partner churches. The people of Central America were never far from Browning's pastoral reach. "Since visiting with them, I have become more intentional in my prayers for them, and my prayers for them have grown to occupy a bigger part of my prayer time." [35]

Browning was concerned about the continued use of sanctions and whether they were an effective means to end injustice and oppression. The unwillingness of the Haitian military to allow the return of the legitimately elected president, Jean Bertrand Aristide, brought U.S. sanctions which caused further suffering for an already devastated people, but not those in power. When Congressional black caucus leaders began to urge President Bill Clinton to intervene militarily in Haiti, Browning began to rethink his position on sanctions and was outraged by the CIA's attempts to undermine Aristide. As it turned out, the planned United States invasion of Haiti was halted when the military junta surrendered in September 1994.

Haiti is the most populous diocese in the Episcopal Church. Hence Browning was personally pained as a pastor by the terror perpetrated on the Haitian people and what he saw as the racist disinclination of the United States Department of State to accept refugees from Haiti. While Browning abhorred the thought of another unilateral United States invasion in Latin America or the Caribbean, he accepted the idea of a multilateral invasion if it was the only route to ending the tyranny and restoring democracy. "Until such a multilateral effort is undertaken," he said, "I beseech my government, in the name of all that is decent, to lead other nations in receiving those beleaguered Haitians who risk their lives to come to America." [36] While living in exile in the United States, President Aristide visited the presiding bishop at the Episcopal Church Center in New York. Once there he had a chance to meet privately with six Haitian staff. "I met my president today," said one of the staff, a night custodian, after meeting with Aristide. [37]

In 1996, two years after the crisis in Haiti, Ed and Patti Browning once again took on the role of reconcilers and peacemakers in the Caribbean in a visit to Cuba, the first by a presiding bishop since Henry Knox Sherrill in 1954. Pamela Chinnis was also a member of the delegation. Prior to going to Cuba the group spent several days meeting with religious leaders and diplomats in the Dominican Republic. Because travel to Cuba is restricted, the delegation had to receive special permission from the United States Treasury Department for the visit. The church in Cuba was beginning to rebuild in the midst of isolation, division, and economic dysfunction. Yet in the midst of these harsh realities, the Cuban Episcopal Church and the wider Christian community had grown tenfold as restrictions on religious groups had lessened. Despite the political divide, the Episcopal laity of Cuba appealed to Cuban clergy and laity in the United States by letter in an effort to heal old wounds. "We realize our reconciliation with God can only occur if we are first reconciled with our brothers, so we invite you to join us in recreating our identity and community," said the letter. [38]

Cuban church leaders felt abandoned by the Episcopal Church when autonomy was "imposed" on the diocese in 1967 by the House of Bishops. (The Cuban Episcopal Church did not ask for autonomy, nor were they consulted in the decision.) The move to autonomy left Cuban clergy without salaries or other means of income. "The church in the United States said, 'We will always be with you,'" said Bishop Jorge Perera Hurtado, "but the reality is that we were completely isolated." [39] Ed and Patti Browning and Pam Chinnis returned to the mainland with a renewed resolve to support dialogue among Cubans at home and in exile and to facilitate religious and cultural exchanges between the United States and Cuba. They also committed to report their experiences to government officials in the United States. In July 1996, Browning wrote President Clinton encouraging him to waive a portion of recent legislation that would have tightened the U.S. embargo on Cuba. "Thirty years of an embargo and isolation has not produced the kind of change that serves the interest of the United States or the people of Cuba," wrote Browning. "I urge you to encourage greater dialogue and peaceful change in Cuba, not further separation and antagonism between the two countries." [40]

The Persian Gulf War

Ed Browning has said that the Persian Gulf War and the Los Angeles race riots were the saddest events in his term as presiding bishop. [41] Because he worked passionately to evade war and organize the religious community for peace, the events of the Persian Gulf War were wrenching for Browning and his staff. Early in his administration he had said he would stand up to the United States government when necessary. He was also clear that he did not want the Episcopal Church to take money from the government for overseas development because of the restrictions put on that funding. Rather, he set up a reserve fund to protect the partnerships of the Episcopal Church overseas. [42] Browning believes that all Christians are commissioned in baptism to be peacemakers. Not strictly a pacifist—he believes that the military does at times serve moral purposes—Browning nonetheless abhors war and is not comfortable with traditional "just war theory." "The more I see about war and how war is conducted, the less I believe it is possible for there to be a just war." [43]

As early as 1980, five years before he was elected presiding bishop, Browning deplored the unilateral action in bombing Libya and requested the withdrawal of forces so that grievances could be addressed and terrorism ended. Browning saw peace as more than the passive absence of armed hostilities. It was to be actively pursued. "If war is something we have to learn, then perhaps we can learn peace, too. The pursuit of peace is not something we can afford to leave to the experts." [44]

In the summer of 1990 Browning began to work with staff after the invasion of Kuwait to organize the religious community. In October he released a statement to 2.5 million Episcopalians, all bishops of the church, the Episcopal Peace and Justice Network, and President Bush. "In spite of the near unanimity of the United Nations in confronting the crisis, the time is fraught with danger," stated Browning. "Lines have been drawn in the desert sands. Huge armies and armadas, led by those of our own country, face each other with the promise of unimaginable destruction and havoc."[45] Browning supported the United Nations' sanctions against Iraq as "just and sound" and urged Iraqi leaders to heed the community of nations, including other Arab states, and withdraw completely from Kuwait "while an embracing diplomatic solution is sought for the complex, interlocking problems of the Middle East as a whole."[46] Part of the "interconnected whole" Browning referred to was the Palestinian problem, "which lies at the core of Middle East unrest."[47] Browning reminded his audience of the message of Samir Kafity, the bishop of Jerusalem and the primate of the Church in Jerusalem and the Middle East, that the conflict in the Persian Gulf should not be dealt with in isolation or without considering the region's history. "Part of that history is the arbitrary and self-serving manipulation of the colonial powers seventy years ago, manipulations that still engender rage among the Arab peoples and make all talk of Western democracy and justice sound to them like sheer hypocrisy."[48]

Concerned that the crisis would ignite anti-Arab sentiments in the United States and abroad, Browning was quick to point out that the situation in the Persian Gulf was not a clash between Christianity and Islam. There is a sizable indigenous Christian community in Iraq, and the Anglican Diocese of Cyprus and the Gulf is present throughout the area. "Americans must realize that the

Saddam Hussein characterized as Adolf Hitler after his invasion of Kuwait is the same person who a few weeks earlier was being touted by the Bush administration as a possible guarantor of peace and stability in the region," he said. "Surely truth and justice are not served by stereotype and propagandistic demonization." [49]

In December 1990, immediately preceding the outbreak of the Persian Gulf War, Browning was part of a high-level delegation of religious leaders that went to the Middle East on a peace pilgrimage to meet with church and government leaders to avoid war and to address disputes in the region. The group gathered in Cyprus for two days of briefings before splitting into three teams—one going to Israel and the occupied territories, one to Beirut and Damascus, and a third to Baghdad and Amman. Browning was the head of the peace delegation that went to Baghdad and Amman. The delegation planned to appeal to both George Bush and Saddam Hussein to resolve their differences diplomatically. The peace pilgrimage emerged from a growing sense of alarm on the part of church leaders that the military build-up in the Persian Gulf was making war inevitable. The previous October, Browning had joined in a press conference in Washington, D.C., urging a peaceful solution in the Persian Gulf.

While the visits to Baghdad and Amman meant a great deal to the Christians in the two countries, the team was frustrated by attempts to make their movements difficult. First, the whole team wanted to meet with President Bush, but he would only see Ed Browning. Then the White House gave Browning a date to see the president but it required him to leave the Middle East a day earlier than planned. (He did depart early via the Concorde to make the appointment.) In the meantime, the team's plans to meet with Saddam Hussein failed to materialize. The group had flown to Baghdad with the expressed purpose of speaking to Saddam Hussein to dissuade him from a direct confrontation with the United States. The hope was that Hussein might make concessions on behalf of American religious leaders that he would not make for the American government. The delegation waited for days to meet the Iraqi president and they soon realized that he was enjoying making them wait. But they also had no doubt that Hussein had received the message that the team was strongly opposed to his occupation of Kuwait. After meetings with Iraqi religious leaders and some governmental officials, the disappointed team decided to head home for the Christmas holidays. It was demoralizing to return with the country on the brink of war and with so little accomplished. Once the group arrived at the Baghdad airport, Iraqi soldiers escorted them to a special lounge, where the soldiers watched them intently. Jim Wallis, editor-in-chief of *Sojourners* and a friend of Browning, was a member of the delegation to Baghdad. Wallis remembers this scene at the Baghdad airport:

> I spotted a picture of Saddam Hussein on the wall of the airport lounge; his photograph seemed to be on every wall we had seen throughout our visit to Iraq. Suddenly I had an idea and walked over to Ed to whisper it in his ear. "Why not give Saddam your speech right now!" I told him. "Tell him what you wanted to say and didn't get the chance to before. Now is your opportunity!" I said, smiling and nodding toward the picture on the airport wall. Browning got a twinkle in his eye and slowly got up to walk over to face the picture, with Saddam's guards eyeing him suspiciously. Speaking with a

strong and clear voice, our leader quickly got all
our attention. He began to gesture dramatically
and shake his finger at Saddam, looking directly
into the eyes of the Iraqi dictator while telling him
exactly what he really thought. Finally, Ed was
giving the speech he had been preparing for all
week. The beleaguered church leaders began to
laugh for the first time during the trip, while the
military police glared in helpless anger. What were
they going to do, shoot Ed for talking to a picture?
It was a great moment of emotional release and
effective satire at the same time. Soon we were all
doubled over, and it was the only time all week
when we felt we really had the upper hand in a
situation that had been stacked against us from
the beginning. We all went home with a smile on
our faces. [50]

Browning did meet with George Bush as soon as
he returned from Baghdad, and also spoke with him by
phone the day the war began. It was an intense conversation just before the bombing of Baghdad. Although
Bush defended the war as a "morally correct action,"
Browning seriously disagreed and pleaded with the
president to avoid military action. Bush pointed to the
list of atrocities committed by Iraqis occupying Kuwait,
as reported by Amnesty International. "I asked him not
to take us to war," said Browning about his conversations
with Bush. "I said, 'I don't believe this war is going to
serve anybody's purpose.' He said it was a matter of high
morality. I said I had to disagree, and we left it there." [51]

Browning had left the White House in December
1990 convinced that George Bush intended to lead the
country into war. [52] "He [President Bush] is focused on
a military response, yet he still has an inward struggle,"

reported Browning.[53] Later, Bush remembered the conversation and said he was moved by it, although the men disagreed. "I had nothing in my heart that felt a bitterness or a restlessness that he [Browning] didn't understand where I was coming from," said Bush.[54] He added, however, that in speaking with church leaders as president he "draws the line at the separation between church and state."[55]

While Bush did not receive support from the leader of his own church for the Persian Gulf War, he launched a religious counteroffensive and turned to theologically conservative Protestants such as evangelist Billy Graham. Graham, a close friend of the Bush family, endorsed the war at a special service for Bush and government officials in January 1991.[56] When contacted for this book, President Bush recalled his relationship with Ed Browning: "I have great respect for Bishop Browning. We did have several major differences, especially over the first Persian Gulf War. I felt it was a just war. He felt it was immoral. But I did not let these differences affect the great respect I have for him and for anyone who devotes their life to the church."[57] For his part, Browning maintained his role of pastor to the president throughout his years as presiding bishop. Bush gave Browning more access than either Ronald Reagan or Bill Clinton had given him. In addition to engagement on political issues, Browning extended his pastoral care to the Bush family, visiting the president's mother when she was ill in Greenwich, Connecticut.

In January 1991 Browning joined with religious leaders who had gone to Baghdad and released a powerful statement, "War Is Not the Answer: A Message to the American People," decrying the march to war and anticipating "a chain of human tragedies that will be with us for generations to come." [58] On January 16, 1991, millions watched the start of the Persian Gulf War—for the first time in American history on live television. Two days earlier Ed and Patti Browning had participated in a prayer vigil coordinated by the Episcopal Peace Fellowship (EPF) and joined a march to the White House with military families. Browning prayed that night for "a speedy conclusion to a great tragedy." [59]

On the morning of the attack on Baghdad, Secretary of State James A. Baker called Browning to ask him to pray with him, which Browning did from *The Book of Common Prayer.* Baker later shared the prayers with his staff. Browning ran into Baker again after their severe disagreement over the Gulf War, at the signing of the Oslo Peace Accord in 1993 at the White House, "Well, we addressed the concern you had for the Palestinians so I hope you feel good about this outcome," said Baker to Browning. [60]

In his message to the Episcopal Church at the outbreak of the war, Browning urged all to work and pray for peace. "Even in the heat of battle let us not forget that the call to peacemaking is an imperative for Christians," said Browning. "What lies ahead, only God knows. We hold in our hearts all who are caught in the agony of battle. Particularly we pray for the brave men and women of the military forces, for those who wait at home, and for all the innocent caught in horror of battle." [61] Browning instructed the Presiding Bishop's Fund for World Relief to respond to the plight of refugees and military families. He also instituted special measures to support the work of Charles Keyser, suffragan bishop for the Armed Forces, in providing for the pastoral needs of military personnel, dependents, and chaplains serving in Operation Desert

Storm. Browning also made personal telephone calls. John L. Peterson, then dean of St. George's College, Jerusalem, received such a call. "I just left a meeting with Jim Baker and the war will start soon," Browning said to Peterson. "I just want you to know how much Patti and I love you, and that you and your family are in our prayers." [62]

Unable to convince government leaders to avoid war, Browning and other members of the peace-seeking delegation turned to the World Council of Churches (WCC) General Assembly meeting in Canberra, Australia. On the last day of the Canberra meeting they succeeded in getting the WCC to adopt a statement calling for an unconditional ceasefire. "Let Christians help build a disciplined, morally based nonviolent movement in response to the war in the Gulf and in response to poverty and suffering throughout the world," read the statement. [63] However, some at the assembly were disturbed that U.S. church leaders tightly controlled the agenda of the Canberra meeting. Others accused Browning and the U.S. delegation of blatantly "hijacking" the world assembly. "From the first day to the final debate, the dominance of the war issue in sermons, executive committee statements, press briefings, and 'peace' activities precluded sustained focus on any other issue," said Stephen Swecker of the United Methodist Church. Swecker also said that Browning, along with Joan Brown Campbell, the general secretary-elect of the National Council of Churches (NCC), and Melvin G. Talbert, a United Methodist bishop of the San Francisco area, "spent moral capital on the war that was urgently needed on other issues," some of which had far-reaching consequences. [64] At the same time other participants in the assembly believed that Browning and the others had appropriately asked the global Christian community to join in the appeal for a cease-fire. "It's true that the war dominated press conferences, executive committee statements, sermons, etc. That is precisely the point: The whole world was concerned about what increasingly felt like a possible World War III," wrote Betty Thompson, public relations director of the United Methodist General Board of Global Ministries. [65]

Nancy Wilson, moderator of the Metropolitan Community Churches (MCC), attended the WCC Worldwide Assembly in Canberra and experienced some powerful moments in the actions against the Persian Gulf War. Wilson said the U.S. delegation in Canberra held a twenty-four-hour vigil focused on the war. Browning was part of the planning group that was headed by Joan Brown Campbell of the National Council of Churches. It was also the first WCC assembly where the NCC was an official observer. In preparation for the vigil, delegates decided to anoint with oil, as the war was about oil. The vigil was not planned before they arrived in Canberra, and hence they needed to find supplies. Baby oil was eventually found for anointing and scented with some frankincense one delegate had used on Epiphany. The oil was placed in empty film cannisters for the vigil. The vigil combined Psalm 133 with the anointing, "Come, Holy Spirit, renew your whole creation." The gathering also sang the spiritual "There is a balm in Gilead." Wilson was paired for the anointing with Browning, and she remembers him as "very real and absolutely fearless." The bishop of Baghdad was also there. An Eastern Catholic, he had escaped with his life, though his family was left behind. The bishop came up to Browning to be anointed and broke down sobbing. Wilson refers to that vigil as an "iconic moment."

"We had the opportunity to help at a moment; to make an experience, to break it open for people. Many said they found it very helpful." [66]

When asked if he would make the same recommendations to George H. W. Bush today, Browning said, "Absolutely. I'm only sorry I did not push harder when given the chance. When you think of all the human suffering, I do not believe that the war accomplished very much, and I have had generals who were there tell me the same thing." [67] Browning's joy at the news of a ceasefire was tempered by his belief that a broader peace was needed for the Middle East region and by his knowledge of the death and suffering endured by thousands of people, including civilians and children. Angry at media reports that he was disloyal to the president, Browning corrected the record at an Executive Council meeting in February 1991. "George Bush is a child of God and a member of this body," Browning said. "I love that man, even though I have held from the beginning that going to war was not the answer to the crisis in the Persian Gulf." Further, Browning pledged to continue "strenuous peacemaking efforts in cooperation with other religious leaders…and all who refuse to give in to despair." [68] Although he had originally supported sanctions against Iraq in the effort to force Saddam Hussein to abandon Kuwait, Browning vehemently opposed the sanctions after learning from church leaders and the king of Jordan that they caused the death of an estimated half a million children. Still haunted by the face of a child he encountered in Baghdad, Browning called on the Clinton administration to end the sanctions. Browning eventually met with Nizar Hamdoon, permanent representative of Iraq to the United Nations, to discuss the sanctions and to plead for the release of two

American prisoners. The prisoners were released, yet the sanctions continued, as U.S. and Iraqi interpretations of the UN resolutions were in conflict. [69]

Joined at the Heart

The Browning administration turned the attention of the Episcopal Church to the needs of the Palestinian people. In negotiating the complex issues of the Middle East, Browning managed both to acknowledge the right of Israel to exist and to advocate for a Palestinian state. The Brownings made several visits to Palestinian refugee camps in Gaza, the West Bank, Jordan, Lebanon, and Syria. They also met with Palestinian and Israeli leaders in an effort to better understand the issues. "To us, Palestinians," wrote Samir Kafity, retired bishop of Jerusalem and former primate of the Middle East, "Ed and Patti were a voice for the voiceless." [70]

Browning looked for a constructive role for the Episcopal Church in resolving the conflict. In 1988 he met with Mubarak E. Awad, the founder and director of the Palestinian Center for the Study of Non-Violence. Shortly afterward, Awad was deported from Israel on the grounds that his visa had expired. In the same year Browning urged the church to increase its giving to the Good Friday Offering, for the Church in Jerusalem. He also launched a special appeal through the Presiding Bishop's Fund for World Relief for the Diocese of Jerusalem, appointed a committee of distinguished Episcopalians to advise him on issues in the region, and asked staff to prepare educational materials on the Middle East for the Easter season. Also in 1988 the General Convention passed a resolution affirming Israel's right to exist within "recognized and secure borders" and also supporting "the right of Palestinians to self-determination, including the choice of their own representatives and the establishment of their own state."[71] As violence and repression against the Palestinian people escalated, Browning asked President Bush to place conditions on American aid to Israel. Billions of dollars in aid, he reasoned, "can no longer be provided unconditionally to a state that is violating the fundamental human rights of an occupied people."[72]

The Brownings also made an emergency trip to Jerusalem during the Persian Gulf War at the request of Samir Kafity. Kafity hoped that a show of solidarity from Christians from around the world might ameliorate the extreme suffering of the people. He added, "Our Jewish brothers and sisters are coming to Israel by the thousands to be in solidarity with the Israeli people. My people ask, 'Where is the Church?' " After the Allied Forces began their bombing of Iraq, Kafity reported that the Palestinians suffered more than they ever had under the Intifada. "People have no food, they have no medicine, they have no work, they have no money and very little hope. The curfews are horrendous."[73] Once in Jerusalem, Browning would not leave despite advice to the contrary. "Is my blood more important than their blood?" he asked.[74]

Convinced that a just peace was only possible through securing rights for the Palestinian people alongside security for Israel, Browning met twice with Chairman Yasser Arafat of the Palestinian Liberation Organization (PLO) to assure him of support and to encourage him to pursue negotiations with Israel. Browning was at the White House when the agreement between Arafat and Prime Minister Yitzhak Rabin of Israel, the Oslo Accord, was signed in 1993.

The support of Ed and Patti Browning for the Palestinian people was controversial, especially as the church took a more critical stance toward Israel. But the Brownings were determined to speak the truth as they saw it. They continue in active support of the Palestinian people today. "From my perspective I really give Bishop Browning credit for turning the Episcopal Church toward issues of justice, especially the Palestinian conflict," said Naim Ateek, a Palestinian priest and the head of Sabeel Ecumenical Liberation Theology Center in Jerusalem. "With Patti Browning's commitment they both opened a way that had not happened before. He was a presiding bishop who could grasp injustice and saw that he could do something about it." [75]

In addition to the political ramifications of their visits, the Brownings believed that each trip to the Middle East was a spiritual journey and a pilgrimage dedicated to peace. In addition to their solidarity with Samir Kafity and the Diocese of Jerusalem, the Brownings also visited and talked with religious and political leaders in Egypt, Syria, and Jordan. In 1994, they met with President Hosni Mubarak of Egypt and Pope Shenouda III of the Coptic Orthodox Church. In Syria they met with diplomatic officials and the patriarchs of the Oriental Orthodox Churches. In Jordan they met with King Hussein. On Good Friday the Brownings walked the narrow streets of Jerusalem's Old City with other pilgrims. At the meeting with Pope Shenouda, Kafity introduced Browning as "a man who took the risk of being our friend—especially the Palestinians; he is with us as a pilgrim who has come to pray." [76]

Several of the visits the Brownings made to Jerusalem were ecumenical. Browning and Herbert Chilstrom, the retired former presiding bishop of the Evangelical Lutheran Church in America, both returned to the Middle East in 2000 in retirement, as part of an ecumenical group from the United States. The visit coincided with the second Intifada. "I recall vividly the warm and personal relationship Ed had with Yasser Arafat. They had met before and Arafat seemed to have a clear recollection of the passion the Brownings had for the Palestinian cause," wrote Chilstrom. [77] Again the religious leaders listened to both sides, prayed, and urged a peaceful resolution to the conflict. "Most poignant from that visit is the memory of marching with Ed and others in a torchlight parade through the streets of Bethlehem," said Chilstrom. "Both Arab Christians and Muslims marched with us. Once more, Ed's passion for the cause of the Palestinians was apparent to everyone." [78]

Patti Browning's own passion to alleviate the suffering and bring justice to the Palestinian people was a driving force during the Browning administration, and it continues as a major focus of her ministry today. She has been referred to as "the most dangerous woman in the Middle East." [79] The Israeli Minister for Religious Affairs has also referred to Patti Browning in exasperated tones as "that woman!" Beginning in 1962 when Ed and Patti Browning first visited the region as missionaries on furlough, Patti has been to Jerusalem more than twenty times. Although Ed Browning has his own commitment to a lasting peace for the Palestinian people, many say that his position intensified through Patti's ongoing advocacy. Her ministry raised the consciousness of thousands to the plight of the Palestinians. "When it has come to the Palestinian cause, Ed was the one with the supportive role," said John L. Peterson, the former secretary general of the worldwide

Anglican Communion. "There in Jerusalem Ed Browning would say, 'I am Patti's husband.' Patti is a powerful advocate for the church in Jerusalem," said Peterson. [80] While in Jerusalem Patti Browning reached out to women and children, and her compassion moved them to speak intimately with her about their struggles and faith.

John L. Peterson tells a story of an encounter Patti Browning had while visiting St. Luke's Hospital in Nablus, in the Occupied West Bank, a hospital run by the Episcopal Church. Since 1987 when the first Intifada began, the people of Nablus have suffered enormously. As Patti Browning visited patients she could hear shooting and demonstrations going on outside: "One Palestinian woman had just, within the hour, given birth. As she held her baby for Mrs. Browning to see, Patti asked the baby's name. She was told, through the translator, that the child would be called Salaam (Peace). What a moving, eloquent prayer. In the midst of shootings and demonstrations outside her hospital window, a mother named her child, 'Salaam,' 'Peace.'" [81] Patti Browning believed "God was waiting" for her in Nablus in the person of the woman and her newborn son as well as the doctor who continued to treat her patients amidst gunfire. "And now, with my understanding of these icons, God was urging me to be an instrument of teaching, reconciliation, healing, peacemaking, and bridge-building," she said. "I was being called to help others to see past and through their icons, and with God's help, I will." [82]

During Ed Browning's years as presiding bishop, Patti took groups to Jerusalem annually, a practice that began with provincial leaders, with the idea that they would be able to go back home and engage more people. "I am not a one-issue person," said Patti, "but I am a staunch advocate for human rights and the Palestinians' suffering seemed so endless." [83] Patti knew the Palestinian people wanted and needed help and that, as the wife of the presiding bishop, she could share the story in a way that could get a lot of attention for the cause. Yet she struggled with public speaking. "I was terrified of standing in front of people, let alone public speaking." [84] But on a long flight Patti happened to open an airline magazine to an article about the fear of public speaking. The article said that if we do not speak about our experiences, we deprive others of what they need to know. Patti realized that she needed to share the truth as she witnessed it. She soon started speaking regularly. Ed Browning knew of the potential for violence on Patti's many trips, yet he also knew that he could not ask her to stop. "My wife is passionate about a great many things, but Patti prays and works for the healing of the brokeness of the land where Jesus lived harder than she prays for anything else....I want her to be home where she's safe. But I know that her destiny, like my destiny and like yours, is not always about being safe." [85]

Patti Browning traveled to Jerusalem as often as possible, sometimes on crutches. She visited hospitals, churches, families, and government officials. She took as many people along as she could. "I went to Jerusalem with Patti in 1990 and 1991, and it was a conversion experience for me," said Gene Robinson, bishop of New Hampshire. "It was a real wake-up call and totally changed the way we talk about issues there," he said. "It was Patti's work with Palestinian women that really captured me, lit a spark in me," said Ann Struthers Coburn. "I am now deeply involved in Sabeel." [86] Patti Browning reflected on her experience of God's call after a trip to Jerusalem, shortly after Ed Browning's election as presiding bishop:

> As we lived and worshiped and visited among the Palestinian people, God again was effecting a conversion in my life....God met me in the human fear, suffering, and death of the men, women, and children of the Holy Land. God held up for me an icon of the tortured, bleeding, thirsty, dying person of the cross. The image is not one of hate and retribution—it is of forgiveness and reconciliation. [87]

Throughout the Browning administration Patti Browning worked to make the Episcopal Church "a bridge of reconciliation of the children of Abraham." Traumatized in particular at violence aimed at children and youth, "of bed after bed with young people bandaged and bleeding," Patti Browning worked assiduously to keep the needs of the Palestinian people in front of the Episcopal Church and to provide what relief she could manage "of my heart, my soul, my waking and sleeping hours," she said. [88] She said that the deplorable conditions, devastating starvation, and unremitting violence surrounding the Palestinian people broke her heart—and yet it was her broken heart that kept her going, "because my broken heart allows me to access Christ's heart that bleeds for all the world yet keeps on beating...And that is what discipleship has come to mean to me: not working for Christ, but as one with Christ, joined at the heart—same body, same blood, same knowing that peace is here and meant to be no matter how far away it seems." [89]

Toward the end of his term as presiding bishop, the Palestinian Authority presented Ed Browning with the Palestinian Medal of Jerusalem in appreciation for his advocacy. The Diocese of Jerusalem also dedicated the library at St. George's College in Jerusalem to Ed and Patti Browning, to honor them for their tireless advocacy for the region. "They will forever be engrained in the Diocese of Jerusalem," said John L. Peterson. [90] "There is nothing we believe in more than the ministry of the church in this place," said Ed Browning at the library dedication. [91] In retirement, profits from Ed and Patti Browning's blueberry crop are designated for Sabeel, an international peace movement initiated by Palestinian Christians.

Europe

Ed Browning engaged the Clinton administration on war and peace in Bosnia in 1994-1995. Browning believed the conflict presented a special challenge to churches "because religion itself was a major contributor to the suffering." In his struggle to determine the moral position, Browning eventually admitted that while armed intervention might escalate the violence, to oppose such intervention "remains virtually certain to condemn further innocent people to death—or to survival on brutal terms." Despite his typical opposition to armed intervention, Browning's statement in February 1994 announced that he could not "oppose NATO air strikes against military targets as long as they hold the promise of ending the despicable siege against the civilian population of Sarajevo." Unlike the Gulf War, Browning believed that an end to the human suffering in Sarajevo might have been achievable only through armed intervention. His decision not to oppose the air strikes was predicated on the availability of humanitarian relief for the people of Sarajevo. He also called for every Episcopal congregation, at every public service, to pray for the people of Bosnia. [92] Browning sent an emissary to the Orthodox Patriarch of Moscow, whom he had met both in New York and in Moscow, with a request that the patriarch use his influence with the Serbian Orthodox Church to end the violence and bloodshed in the region. In response the patriarch called for an end to the violence. Although Browning was widely applauded for providing decisive leadership, many in the American Serbian community criticized him. [93]

Browning appreciated President Clinton's work as peacemaker in Bosnia and in Northern Ireland. He felt the president's actions to end the violence reflected high moral values and furthered U.S. interests. "I can think of no greater mantle for the president of the United States to wear than that of peacemaker," said Browning. "It brings honor to him and to the United States. And it is my prayer that such will be his legacy. Our country has been searching for its proper role in the wake of the end of the Cold War, and I think the president has discovered part of that role." [94] Relieved that the troops sent to Bosnia were to engage in peacekeeping rather than combat, Browning hoped for "a deep and enduring reconciliation." However, he also asserted that lasting peace would ultimately require the removal of outside forces so that the parties to the conflict "maintain the peace from within their hearts and through their inner resolve." [95]

The Anglican Communion

As referenced elsewhere in this book, Ed Browning played a key role among the primates of the Anglican Communion. "He does not have a pretentious bone in his body," said John L. Peterson, then secretary general of the worldwide Anglican Communion. "He did not have to let people always know he was the presiding bishop; he was always known as 'Ed.'" Peterson noted that Browning took his role as "chief pastor" very seriously. "He wanted to hold different sides together in tension and wanted to make sure all sides were represented at the table," said Peterson. [96]

Michael Peers, retired primate of the Anglican Church of Canada, was elected just six months after Ed Browning. They were part of the distinguished primates class of 1986 that also included Desmond Tutu and Brian Davis of Aotearoa, New Zealand, and Polynesia. Peers and Browning first met in Nigeria in 1975 when Browning was at the Episcopal Church Center; their second meeting was as primates at Desmond Tutu's enthronement in Cape Town. There had been little connection between the Anglican Church of Canada and the Episcopal Church, and the two men worked to create new structures for collaboration. During the Browning administration, a designated member of the Executive Council served as a liaison to the Anglican Church of Canada and attended meetings of the General Synod there, and vice versa. The collaboration strengthened relationships in both churches and fostered friendships and the sharing of resources. Michael Peers believes that Browning's earlier experiences as a missionary made him particularly effective as a primate in the global Anglican Communion. "When Ed was elected he really knew more about the church outside the lower forty-eight," said Michael Peers. "He was a world citizen and had a world mindset." [97]

As a friend and as a primate, Peers had the opportunity to observe Browning in action at primates' meetings around the world. Browning reported what was happening in the Episcopal Church without value judgment, in a clear style that was appreciated by the other primates and that unaggressively outlined the options. "He was almost unassailable," said Peers. "He did not want to mislead people or hide anything, and that went a long way." Browning's popularity around the world came from his ability to speak to people "on the footing of equality." When asked about Browning's contribution, Peers summed it up with the words "reality and grace." [98]

Judith Conley, a lay delegate from the Episcopal Church to the Anglican Consultative Council, worked with Browning over several years. "People throughout the Anglican Communion clearly had a high regard for him," observed Conley. Others looked to him for his counsel and advice and he clearly put the Episcopal Church in a good place." [99] Although he brought unpopular positions to the table, such as the ordination of women to the episcopacy, Browning's ability to reach out to other perspectives ameliorated the level of conflict. Also, the fact that there was no Internet at that time meant that instant dissemination of opinions and accusations could not magnify differences and fuel controversy. "If it had not been Ed Browning, it would have been worse," believed John L. Peterson. Because there had been a higher level of civility at primates' meetings when he began his term than when he ended it, Browning felt compelled, at his last primates' meeting in 1997, to challenge the primates to listen to each other. "He eloquently let them have it about being so divisive and told them that they could not be chief pastors if they did not include everyone." [100]

Historic Ecumenical Relationships

Early in his term, Ed Browning emphasized the importance of ecumenism both at home and abroad. After his first year in office, Browning's alacrity in ecumenical affairs was further fueled by what he called the "deep desire of the people for Christian unity."[101] William Norgren, ecumenical officer of the Episcopal Church, said that fostering ecumenical relationships between the Episcopal Church, a relatively small church, and other churches brought "moments of great seriousness and great hilarity."[102]

Browning's first extensive ecumenical tour in January 1987 took him through Istanbul, the Holy Land, Rome, and Geneva. It ended in London with a briefing by Robert Runcie, then archbishop of Canterbury. In addition, Browning also met with Muslim scholars and made a quick visit to Hagia Sophia in Istanbul, a holy site for both Christians and Muslims. Although the Anglican-Orthodox Dialogue was stalled due to differences over theology and the ordination of women, Browning found common ground in discussing clergy training and the revival of the diaconate. While in Rome, Browning was one of more than two dozen Anglican, Protestant, and Orthodox church leaders who met with Pope John Paul II. Although the group was brought together by the pope, Browning believed that the meeting was a sign of community and had hoped the churches in the United States could get past differences and "do more on such urgent issues as justice, peace, and human rights, especially religious freedom."[103] Browning had an off-the-record opportunity to speak to John Paul II about women's ordination. While the pope admitted that it was possible to make a credible theological justification for women's ordination, he did not see how it could be worked out practically and believed that the Orthodox churches would never tolerate movements in that direction. [104]

In the same year, at the celebration of the one hundredth anniversary of the Chicago-Lambeth Quadrilateral, Browning gave his assessment of the state of the ecumenical movement: "One of the questions often asked of me is if the ecumenical movement has run out of steam," he said. "The truth is that a lot of steam goes into cultivation of newly developed linkages between families of churches and the multitude of fresh and demanding issues in our world....In the midst of all this," he suggested, "it is difficult to escape the conclusion that God is at work, urging us through our very frustrations to renew our vision of the church's life and mission." [105]

Relations between the Episcopal Church and the Russian Orthodox Church reached a new level during the Browning administration. Ed and Patti Browning traveled to the Soviet Union for three weeks in September 1989 for the meeting of the Central Committee of the World Council of Churches and then, as guests of the Russian Orthodox Church, visited Ukraine, Georgia, Armenia, and Latvia. It was an exciting time for the church in the Soviet Union when, after seventy years of persecution, sanctions on its ministry were lifted. Although committed to responding to the needs of Russian society, the Russian Orthodox Church was also challenged to put training, education, and service programs in place for the first time in over two generations. It was the policy of the Episcopal Church, rather than to evangelize in Russia, to help build up the Russian Orthodox Church. Moved by the suffering of the people and the tremendous challenges facing the

Russian Orthodox Church, Browning was determined to find ways that the Episcopal Church could effectively partner with Christians in Eastern Europe to make the church a symbol of hope throughout the world. He secured a large grant from the Presiding Bishop's Fund for World Relief to aid earthquake victims in Armenia. While in Ukraine, Browning met with Metropolitan Filaret, patriarch of the Ukranian Orthodox Church, who told him that of the 5,000 Orthodox congregations in the region, more than 2,000 had reopened in an eighteen-month period. "Perestroika for us," he said, "means repairing and replacing the churches." [106] In Latvia, Browning was interviewed by a reporter from TASS, the Soviet news agency, and asked about President Bush and President Gorbachev:

> I told her [the reporter] that what I hear from both men is that there is something more than national security. There is mutual security, global security. We are coming out of a period when, given the tension between our two nations, national security was an obsession with both of us, causing serious problems throughout the world, as well as within our two nations. I said that it is my great hope that we are also coming into a period when the question will not be, "What is in my best interest?" but rather, "What is in the best interest of all God's people?" [107]

After an encouraging three visits with Patriarch Alexsy II of the Russian Orthodox Church, Browning set up a Joint Coordinating Committee to work on questions dividing the two churches. Despite the theological differences between Alexsy II and Browning, the two formed a friendship. (Alexsy II reportedly kept a photograph of Browning in his private quarters.) Browning was moved by the human suffering in formerly Soviet-dominated countries after the collapse of communism and saw a supportive role for the Episcopal Church in rebuilding the church in those places. Although bluntly opposed to "the extreme feminist views and other radical ideas" of the Episcopal Church and other churches in the Anglican Communion, Alexsy II was a moderate and committed to ecumenism. [108]

J. Robert Wright, professor at the General Theological Seminary and a theological consultant to the ecumenical office, said he was concerned when he first learned he was to accompany Browning to Russia to meet with church leaders there. "I did not know Ed very well," said Wright. "I wondered about putting a liberal Protestant into an Orthodox ethos. Did he understand Russian Orthodox expectations? They have ways of showing respect for holy things and holy places, making signs of the cross, reverencing icons. I was worried that he was not sufficiently coached." Wright said that William Norgren, the ecumenical officer of the Episcopal Church, simply said, "Let him do what he is inclined to do." Wright was pleasantly surprised when Browning fit into the scene as if born to it. "He knew *exactly* what to do, instinctively," said Wright, "and Patti would follow suit." Wright said that Ed and Patti Browning always conducted themselves as "public representatives of the church." They prayed the Office on the plane and wrote personal thank you notes. "I tried to carry his bags, but he reached out his hand and said, 'I am still a deacon you know.'" He never wanted to appear pompous. Wright said that Alexsy II considered the relationship with the Episcopal Church an example of "good ecumenism," largely due to Ed Browning. "For the patriarch of Moscow to get up in front of an assembly of monk bishops and say 'these people are our friends' is *remarkable.*" [109]

The ecumenical breakthrough with the most far-reaching implications was the Concordat of Agreement between the Episcopal Church and the Evangelical Lutheran Church in America (ELCA) whereby the two churches entered into full communion. After almost thirty years of official dialogues between the Episcopal Church and Lutherans, the Concordat offered both churches new possibilities for joint ministries. In 1988, the founding year of the ELCA and two years after the start of the Browning administration, the Episcopal Church and the ELCA released *Implications of the Gospel,* a document addressing common concerns, including liturgical renewal, education, shared leadership, and evangelism. In 1990 Ed and Patti Browning went on an ecumenical pilgrimage to Canterbury, Oslo, Stockholm, Helsinki, and Copenhagen with Herbert Chilstrom, the first presiding bishop of the ELCA, and his wife Corinne. "It was December and, especially in Scandinavia, we were impressed by how believers in those parts of the world fought the darkness by incorporating light into every conceivable setting," recollected Chilstrom. "In both England and Scandinavia we and the Brownings learned much about the ancestral roots of our respective churches." [110]

In 1991 both churches released details of an unprecedented proposal for full communion to allow them to "become interdependent while remaining autonomous." [111] While acknowledging the catholicity and apostolicity of both the Episcopal Church and the ELCA, a key sticking point was the historic episcopate, considered unnecessary by Lutherans yet important to Episcopalians, especially if the goal was for complete interchangeability of clergy.

By the third round of talks, some ELCA clergy and laity were feeling overburdened with the demands on the fairly new denomination, while others objected for doctrinal reasons. This delayed official consideration of the proposals for two years, until 1993. Although this reaction from the ELCA was not unexpected, Browning felt it important not to lose the momentum. In a letter to Browning, Herbert Chilstrom reported that he had received substantial reaction from members of his church and "almost all of it has been quite negative."[112]

Although lingering reservations, especially among Lutherans, continued throughout the study process, momentum for the agreement gradually emerged. Browning kept in contact both with Chilstrom and his successor, George H. Anderson. A pivotal five-day meeting in 1996 between more than two hundred Episcopal and ELCA bishops managed to allay most of the fears and move the two churches closer together. "It was the most intensive negotiation of my life," said William Norgren.[113] Despite the ecumenical importance of the Concordat, the response among many in the Episcopal Church was tepid, even in dioceses that had engaged in years of dialogue. "We face a crucial challenge of educating people in our church about the implications of this decision before the General Convention votes," said David W. Perry, then the church's ecumenical officer.[114]

Hailed by J. Robert Wright, a principal author of the Concordat, as "the most important ecumenical decision our church will make this century," the vote at the General Convention in 1997 was overwhelmingly positive.[115] To the disappointment of many, the ELCA voted down the proposal by only six votes, committing itself to two years of further study. Yet Browning remained hopeful for a deeper relationship between the two churches. "The unity in Christ which has always existed, and which awaits our acceptance, will be reestablished whenever God's people want it and claim it." [116]

In 1999, the Churchwide Assembly of the ELCA passed an amended version of the Concordat of Agreement. Although Browning had retired at the time of the final passage of the Concordat, much of its eventual success is due to his unwavering commitment to ecumenism and his tenacity in the face of setbacks. He believed that the Concordat of Agreement was the single most important piece of legislation to come before the General Convention in 1997. "Presiding bishops get elected and serve and retire," he said. "We come and we go. But the chance for a new expression of the unity of our two churches, for our mission together, is a God-given opportunity. This is truly a *kairos* moment for Christendom." [117]

Chapter Nine Notes

1   John Paul Engelcke, "Interview with Bishop Edmond Lee Browning," *The Living Church,* June 2, 1985.

2   Edmond Lee Browning (hereafter cited as ELB), *A Year of Days with The Book of Common Prayer* (New York: Ballantine Books, 1997), May 27.

3   "Burmese Nobel Laureate Vows to Continue Struggle for Democracy," Episcopal News Service (hereafter cited as ENS), February 8, 1996.

4   ELB, *A Year of Days,* June 30.

5   Patricia Sparks Browning (hereafter cited as PSB), "Speech to the Clergy Spouses," Diocese of Lexington, February 22, 1996, Browning Collection.

6   ELB, *A Year of Days,* February 26.

7   Alden Hathaway, interview by Sheryl Kujawa-Holbrook (hereafter cited as SKH), March 2009.

8   Hebert Donovan, interview by SKH, March 2009. Donovan said at the time of his interview, "I stole the phrase from Ian Douglas!"

9   J. Patrick Mauney, interview by SKH, March 2009.

10   ELB, Sermon to the House of Bishops, September 1986, Browning Collection.

11   "Bishops Strive for Firmness, Diversity," ENS, October 2, 1986.

12   ELB, "Address from the Chair," ENS, March 14, 1990.

13   John Browning, "South Africa," n.d., Browning Collection.

14   Brian J. Grieves, ed., *No Outcasts: the Public Witness of Edmond L. Browning, XXIVth Presiding Bishop of the Episcopal Church* (Cincinnati: Forward Movement, 1997), 143-144.

15   "Browning Trip Renews, Strengthens East Asia Ties," ENS, May 28, 2987.

16   Ibid.

17   Ibid.

18   "Browning Leads Pilgrims to Hiroshima Memorial," ENS, May 21, 1987.

19   "Browning in Philippines: 'Visitation of a Friend,'" ENS, December 17, 1987.

20   Richard Henshaw, Jr., "Presiding Bishop Makes Historic Visit to China," January 7, 1988.

21   Brian J. Grieves, interview by SKH, November 2009.

22   "Presiding Bishop Takes Message of Hope to Myanmar," ENS, February 8, 1996.

23   "Browning Challenge: Model Selfless Giving," ENS, March 4, 1988.

24   Robert Brooks, interview by SKH, April 2009.

25   Robert Brooks, interview; "Episcopal Church Volunteer Reports on Deliberate Campaign of Terror Against Churches in El Salvador," ENS, December 8, 1989.

26   Robert Brooks, interview.

27   "Religious Leaders Put U.S. Secretary of State on Alert," ENS, January 25, 1990.

28   Ibid.

29   Robert Brooks, interview.

30   Melanie Hirsch, "Mission in Central America: Episcopal Bishop Goes to Panama," *The Post-Standard,* June 10, 2989.

31   ELB, "Statement on Panama at the Time of the U.S. Invasion," December 21, 1989, in *No Outcasts,* 187.

32 Diane M. Porter, interview by SKH, March 2009; Brian J. Grieves, written statement, October 2009.

33 "Statement of Anglican Bishops and Archbishops on Nicaragua," March 18, 1989, in *No Outcasts*, 180-181.

34 Ibid.

35 ELB, *A Year of Days*, November 14.

36 ELB, "Statement on Haiti," in *No Outcasts*, 190.

37 Quoted in Grieves, *No Outcasts*, 188.

38 "The Letter from Cuba," *Episcopal Life*, May 1996, 4.

39 Nan Cobbey, "Leaders' Visit Offers Cuba Reconciliation," *Episcopal Life*, May 1996, 4.

40 ELB, "Letter to President Clinton," July 9, 1996, in Grieves, *No Outcasts*, 191.

41 Grieves, *No Outcasts*, 161.

42 Bruce Woodcock, interview by SKH, September 2009.

43 Adam Nagourney, "A Just War? Not So, Say Some Theologians," *Honolulu Star-Bulletin*, January 29, 1991.

44 ELB, *A Year of Days*, July 15.

45 "Browning Calls for Creative Solutions to Gulf Crisis, Reexamination of National Priorities," ENS, October 10, 1990.

46 "A Statement to Episcopalians by Presiding Bishop Edmond L. Browning on the Persian Gulf Crisis," ENS, October 5, 1990.

47 Ibid.

48 Ibid.

49 Ibid.

50 Jim Wallis, letter to SKH, April 13, 2009. Also see Jim Wallis, *Faith Works: Lessons from the Life of an Activist Preacher* (New York: Random House, 2000), 274-275.

51 ELB, interview by SKH, January 2009.

52 Ibid.

53 John Dart, "Bishop Browning Says Bush Is Struggling Inwardly Over Iraq," *Los Angeles Times*, n.d. [1991], Browning Collection.

54 "Bush Soul-searching Religion and Public Policy," ENS, April 29, 1991.

55 Stephen L. Swecker, "Bush: No Ill Will Toward Religious Critics of War," *The United Methodist Reporter*, April 5, 1991.

56 John Dart, "Episcopalian Bush Opens Religious Counteroffensive for a 'Just War,'" *The New York Times*, February 2, 1991.

57 George H.W. Bush, letter to SKH, September 24, 2009.

58 "War Is Not the Answer: A Message to the American People," ENS, January 11, 1991.

59 "As War Breaks Out, Episcopalians Join National Outpouring of Prayer and Protest," ENS, January 25, 1991.

60 Brian J. Grieves, statement, September 24, 2009.

61 "Presiding Bishop Responds to Outbreak of War with Call for Peacemaking," ENS, January 25, 1991.

62 John L. Peterson, interview by SKH, April 2009.

63 "A Call to the Churches," ENS, February 14, 1991.

64 Diane Huie Balay, "Was WCC 'Hijacked'?" *The United Methodist Reporter,* March 8, 1991.

65 Betty Thompson, " 'Hijack' Image Distorted WCC Reality," *The United Methodist Reporter,* March 8, 1991.

66 Nancy Wilson, interview by SKH, April 2009.

67 ELB, interview.

68 "Executive Council Responds to Gulf War, Forges Ahead on Environmental Policy," February 14, 1991, Browning Collection.

69 Ibid.

70 Samir Kafity, letter to SKH, March 24, 2009.

71 "Episcopalians Witness Ministries in Middle East," ENS, July 6, 1989.

72 "Presiding Bishop Condemns Violence, Asks President Bush to Place Conditions on American Aid to Israel," ENS, June 21, 1990.

73 "Bishop Samir Kafity Appeals for Solidarity Visit to Jerusalem," ENS, February 14, 1991.

74 John L. Peterson, interview.

75 Naim Ateek, interview by SKH, March 2009.

76 "Brownings Join with People in the Middle East in Prayers for Peace," ENS, April 7, 1994.

77 Herbert W. Chilstrom, letter to SKH, April 3, 2009.

78 Ibid.

79 Jim Solheim, interview by SKH, March 2009.

80 John L. Peterson, interview.

81 Ibid.

82 PSB, "Breaking the Other Icon," *The Living Church,* October 1, 1989.

83 PSB with Sandra J. Bright, "A Lifelong Commitment...to a People and the Soul of a Country," *The Witness* 84, no. 9 (September 2001).

84 PSB and Bright, "A Lifelong Commitment."

85 ELB, *A Year of Days,* May 13.

86 Ann Struthers Coburn, interview by SKH, March 2009.

87 PSB, "Breaking the Other Icon."

88 PSB, "Address to the Episcopal Peace Fellowship, the General Convention, 1997," Browning Collection.

89 Ibid.

90 John L. Peterson, interview.

91 ENS, "Brownings Join with People."

92 "Browning Would Not Oppose Air Strikes If They Lead to Peace in Bosnia," ENS, February 24, 1995.

93 Grieves, *No Outcasts,* 204.

94 ELB, "Presiding Bishop's Statement on President Clinton's Peace Initiatives in Ireland and Bosnia," ENS, December 12, 1995.

95 Ibid.

96 John L. Peterson, interview.

97 Michael Peers, interview by SKH, May 2009.

98 Ibid.

99   Judith Conley, interview by SKH, September 2009.

100 John L. Peterson, interview.

101 "Browning Begins Ecumenical Tour," ENS, January 15, 1987.

102 William Norgren, interview by SKH, April 2009.

103 "Browning Joins Ecumenical Meeting With Pope," ENS, September 24, 1987.

104 ELB, interview.

105 "Bishops Attend Centenary of Chicago Quadrilateral," ENS, October 8, 1987.

106 Quoted in "News," *The Living Church,* January 7, 1990.

107 Grieves, *No Outcasts,* 209.

108 "Russian Orthodox Patriarch Brings Message of Hope to Meetings with Episcopalians," ENS, November 21, 1991.

109 J. Robert Wright, interview by SKH, April 2009.

110 Herbert W. Chilstrom, letter to SKH, April 3, 2009.

111 "Lutherans and Episcopalians End Dialogues, Propose Steps Toward Full Communion," ENS, January 25, 1991.

112 "Lutherans Propose Delay in Consideration of Full Communion with Episcopal Church," ENS, April 29,1991.

113 William Norgren, interview.

114 "Episcopal Church Facing Major Ecumenical Decisions – In a Climate of Indifference," ENS, December 12, 1995.

115 "Episcopal Church Approves Historic Ecumenical Agreement, Awaits Lutheran Response," ENS, August 6, 1997.

116 "Lutherans Approve Full Communion with Reformed but Not with Episcopal Church—Yet," ENS, September 26, 1997.

117 ELB, "Presiding Bishop's Address from the Chair to the Executive Council," ENS, June 26, 1996.

A Work of the Heart
1997-2010

I MAY FAIL some of you as a prophetic voice. I pray never to fail you as a pastor. [1]

> — Edmond Lee Browning,
> Installation Address,
> Washington, D.C.
> January 11, 1986

SOMEONE ASKED ME how I want to be remembered. I hope I am remembered not just for what I professed, but because I worked for a church where there is respect and room for everyone. [2]

> — Edmond Lee Browning,
> Address to the
> General Convention,
> August 6, 1997

I DON'T FEEL myself as a powerful person. Sometimes I feel very powerless....Maybe, hopefully, I will have sown seeds. That's my one hope. Whatever will happen is in God's hands. [3]

> — Patricia Sparks Browning,
> December, 1997

Barbara Harris tells a story about her retirement party in the Diocese of Massachusetts in 2002. Edmond Lee Browning, retired presiding bishop, was among the evening's speakers and commented to the dinner guests: "So many people have told me how good I look. When I retired, I must have looked like hell!" [4]

Last Official Moments

"I have been thinking about this day for a long time. I stand before you intensely aware that this is the moment—my last official moment—to tell you what is on my heart," said Browning in his farewell address at the General Convention in Philadelphia in 1997, the one that was to elect his successor. Browning spoke with candor to a joint session of both houses, and again stressed his unswerving commitment to the vision of a more compassionate and inclusive church that he had vowed to strive for at the time of his election. "There are serious differences present in this hall today," he said. "Sadly, I know that there are those who wonder if they have a home in the Episcopal Church any more. But hear me again: For the sake of the gospel, we must stay in fellowship, read scripture together, pray together, break bread together, and discern God's will for us, together." [5] Although some took offense at parts of the address, including a comment against biblical literalism, others applauded the speech as "vintage Browning." At the same convention, Browning admitted that at the time he delivered the challenge to become a church with "no outcasts," he did not really know what he was asking of the church or of himself, nor did he know the costs to Patti and their family. He did not realize the extent to which his challenge would become empowering to some and painful to others—yet he stood before the 1997 General Convention with a "thankful heart" for his years as presiding bishop. "Responding to the challenge to become more compassionate, more inclusive, to become more than we are, has not been easy, for any of us," said Browning. "But hear this: If I had it to do over, I'd do it all again." [6]

Probably no two people at the 1997 General Convention were anticipating with more enthusiasm the election of a new presiding bishop than Ed and Patti Browning. A pastor to the very end, Browning thanked the church for all his experiences as presiding bishop: "I carry a heart full of thanksgiving today...And know this. I am thankful today not just for *most* of you, but for *all* of you, because together, as the baptized, we are more than a legislative body. We are the Body of Christ, walking in unity, though not uniformity." [7] Three years earlier the General Convention had reduced the term of office for the presiding bishop from twelve years to nine, a move affirmed by Browning. "Twelve years is too long—for the church, but also for the person who is asked to do the job," he said at the time. [8] The change in the length of term also increased the number of available candidates for the job.

Although he supported all the nominees for presiding bishop in 1997, Browning was delighted when Frank T. Griswold, bishop of Chicago, was elected the twenty-fifth presiding bishop. Griswold had worked closely with Browning on liturgy for the House of Bishops' meetings. "We have done a good thing today," said Browning after the election. [9] For his part, Griswold felt that he had learned much from his predecessor. "Ed always was *my* presiding bishop," he said. [10] Later, in December 1997, in a town hall meeting in the Diocese of Chicago, Browning spoke of his hope in the church of the future, his fears that there would be more conflict, and his confidence in his successor: "Frank will have to find ways to allow profound disagreement within the body to stay together in love, if not in harmony." [11]

Browning called his years as presiding bishop "hard, but good." "I wouldn't have traded it for anything," he wrote. [12] *The Living Church* commended Browning for his "grace and thoughtfulness," as well as "a pastoral presence even his opponents could admire." [13] In the same magazine, Richard S. O. Chang, bishop of Hawaii, wrote of Browning as "a pastor with a deep personal faith, possessing love for all people, and committed to peace and justice in the name of God." [14] Although preparing for retirement, Ed and Patti continued major tours during 1997, including a visit to the Church of Bangladesh, the Church of North India, and the Church of South India. Once there, in a remote village several hours drive from Madras, the Brownings joined hands with those considered untouchables, pledging to do all in their power to root out racism. [15]

In the final weeks of his term, Browning went on a pilgrimage for peace and reconciliation with officials of the Japanese government and preached at Coventry Cathedral in England. The historic Coventry Cathedral had been destroyed by the Nazis during World War II and was rebuilt from the ashes as a center of peace and reconciliation in 1958. There Browning prayed the Coventry Litany of Reconciliation with representatives of the Japanese government, in both Japanese and English. "Many communities almost destroyed by hate have found strength to carry on through this cathedral: Hiroshima, Ireland, South Africa, many places that have become watchwords for human misunderstanding and division. Life is hard in the human community," he said. "But God is good and, by God's grace, healing happens where no one ever thought it would." [16]

During his last year in office, Browning's ministry took on a more reflective tone. Although he never shirked his responsibilities or the issues of the day, he and Patti slowly moved west toward retirement. Both grew tired with accumulated stress and each had health concerns. During their last few years in New York, Patti Browning had numerous orthopedic surgeries, often appearing in public while in pain and on crutches. She bore in her bones much of the stress faced by her husband and their family in his years as presiding bishop. "One aspect of this ministry that has been difficult for me is dealing with criticism of Ed," said Patti to a group of clergy spouses in the Diocese of Western New York in 1997. "I don't mean having people disagree with him; you expect that. I mean the certain nastiness that sometimes happens. This is hard for me and it has been terribly hard for our children." [17] Still, Patti believed in the importance of sharing to benefit others. A report dated December 1997 noted that Patti Browning had the saying "All that is not given is lost" affixed to her mirror. [18]

Although usually healthy, Browning arrived in Tokyo in May 1997 with a case of the flu, probably caught at the Executive Council meeting in Honolulu where others came down with the same malady. He managed to attend a reception in his honor at the Four Seasons Hotel, but was barely coherent. What was thought to be the flu and the lack of food was in reality pneumonia and the first signs of hyperglycemic shock. Unable to rouse him during the night, Patti called for help, an ambulance was dispatched, and Browning was taken to St. Luke's Hospital for treatment. The Brownings' physician in New York, Dr. Harvey Goldberg, was called and upon hearing that the presiding bishop was nonresponsive, said, "Oy veh!" [19] The doctors in Tokyo quickly diagnosed the situation and Browning responded to treatment. He was mystified to wake up in the hospital, where he stayed for a week. There was no lasting damage, but for the first time in his administration, Browning was not able to do everything on his calendar, including the consecrations of new bishops. [20] Browning's illness caused him to miss a trip to Okinawa, although Paul Nakamura, bishop of Okinawa, flew to Tokyo to meet with Browning in the hospital. "His plan to return to Okinawa was not just a sentimental journey," said Nakamura. "He wanted to come to be in solidarity with the churches and to support the Okinawan people in their appeal to get the military bases out of Okinawa. When the Okinawa people are ignored, Bishop Browning listens to us." [21]

A More Balanced Life

To those who worked closely with Ed and Patti Browning, it was clear by 1997 that they were ready to move on. "All the things they stood for—love, compassion, hope, inclusivity—they gave and were spent many times over," said a longtime friend. [22] "It was painful to see him the last years in office; it damn near killed the man," said Mary Miller of the Episcopal Peace Fellowship. [23] "Ed's call for compassion was so prophetic and he was leading from it when it was not the thing to do. In some sense Ed was too good to be PB, just as Jimmy Carter was too good to be president. He was too decent and too Christian to do the job. Some said without guile that he was not hardened enough to make it through," said Gene Robinson. "But Ed was more successful, and he did make it through, and we didn't deserve him, but that's God for you. I was so honored when he was one of my co-consecrators. It was like the embodiment of 'there will be no outcasts.'" [24]

Ed and Patti Browning bought their retirement home in Dee, Oregon, a few years before their actual retirement. The property sits outside of Hood River, a city at the fork of the Hood and Columbia rivers, and is surrounded by pear orchards. The house is simple and elegant, situated to take in a magnificent view of Mt. Hood.

Douglas LeBlanc visited the Brownings at their home in Dee after a meeting in Portland. "It was good to see him without the weight of office," said LeBlanc. [25] Some friends were at first concerned about the remote location and wondered whether the Brownings were isolating themselves. But others who visited them saw how nurturing they found the solitude and that they remained in relationship with family and friends. "I went out there to their place so I could say 'thank you' to them. It is remote and they are so happy there. They have not turned their backs on anyone," said Ann Struthers Coburn. [26]

The Brownings delight in entertaining friends and family at their home in Dee, doing daily chores, and sharing meals together. Downstairs is the "presidential bathroom," filled with signed photos and news clippings of Ed Browning with presidents Reagan, Bush, and Clinton, along with an archbishop of Canterbury thrown in for good measure. The Brownings' home and two outlying cabins are roomy enough to accommodate their children, children's spouses, and thirteen grandchildren for the annual "Camp Browning." The summer gathering of the clan is part of Ed and Patti's commitment to get to know their grandchildren better in retirement. The yearly gathering has also brought together the youngest generation of Brownings, and the cousins stay in touch via e-mail during the rest of the year. In his home community Ed is sometimes known as "Mr. Blueberry," a reference to the large blueberry field he tends along with some migrant workers. The profits go to Sabeel. [27]

"I don't believe that my meaning depends on being the presiding bishop," said Browning near the end of his term. "It depends on my relationship with my Maker, my relationship with the person who has been my partner for the last forty-four years, my relationship with my children and grandchildren, and my relationship with the new community into which I am now moving." [28] The Browning children have all taken on lives of service in adulthood. Mark Browning is a family court judge in Honolulu; Paige Browning is a reading teacher and artist and works with horses in Hood River; Philip Browning is an obstetrician and gynecologist in Honolulu; Peter Browning is vicar of St. Andrew's Episcopal Church and Children's Center in Irvine, California; and John Browning is head men's tennis coach at Emory University in Atlanta. Patti said at the time of Ed's election as presiding bishop that their children were the ones with the "empty nest syndrome," with mixed feelings about the geographical distances that sometime separate the family. Now Ed and Patti once again have quality time with their children and grandchildren.

In retirement, the Brownings have gathered a menagerie of chickens, ducks, horses, and three amorous and rambunctious dogs. Webster was the first dog to arrive, a standard poodle, with a mass of appropriately colored red hair. Then came Benson, another standard poodle, and after him came Cedric, a schnauzer. The original retirement plan did not call for three dogs, but then the Brownings did not really *plan* on having five children, either. Ed and Patti's love for God's creatures is expansive and thus it is not a surprise to see the twenty-fourth presiding bishop with a standard poodle on his lap. "In the morning, when he seems to be all tail, so glad to be walking with me, and we secure the perimeter together in companionable silence, I surprise myself with how much I love this dog—how much a part of me Webster has become—how much I delight in his guileless happiness," writes Browning. He likens his experience of finding and falling in love with his dog to his experience as presiding bishop:

> Just about every new thing that happened in our church when I was presiding bishop was like that. The introduction of the controversial new Prayer Book into our lives, a new hymnal, the growth in the number of ordained women and their integration into the episcopate, the continuing candor with which African American voices, Latino voices, Asian American voices, gay and lesbian voices among us spoke their mind—I can't imagine us now without them. That is why I am not the least afraid of the future and its controversies: we have demonstrated again and again the elasticity human beings need in order to embrace change and grow in response to it. [29]

The Brownings stayed away from New York for the first couple of years of retirement, to have some time "to heal and recover." [30] Although Browning scheduled occasional speaking engagements, both he and Patti were physically and emotionally exhausted. He was ending a twenty-nine-year episcopal ministry. His life-threatening illness in Japan caused him to step back from some of his duties as presiding bishop and let go, "to find a deeper meaning in life."[31] The years of travel and stress also hit Patti hard, and there were few structural supports in place for spouses in retirement. "Given how hard they have worked, how much suffering and need they have seen, how much they have borne and for so many people, their hearts could have become hard or heavy or sad," said a family friend. "I think, rather, their hearts were broken open to God's love for themselves and for so many, many people."[32] Blessed with the precious gift of time in retirement, the Brownings have used the rich solitude of their beloved home as a source of refreshment and renewal, the same gifts they so freely gave to so many people around the world.

The People of Palestine

A great amount of the public ministry of Ed and Patti Browning in retirement has focused on the Middle East, and they continue to use their position to advocate for peace and justice for the Palestinian people and for oppressed people throughout the world. "Friends, we of the Christian nonviolent tradition hold a vision that is an open invitation to all people," preached Browning in Jerusalem in 2004. "It is not limited to one group, or one race, or even one religion. God's reign includes us all. As Jews, Muslims, and Christians, as Israelis and Palestinians, as citizens from many lands, we cannot let extremism prevail, whatever the source."[33]

Patti Browning's deep love and hope for the Palestinian people is undiminished in retirement.[34] The

Diocese of Washington honored Patti Browning with its 1999 Peacemakers award for her efforts to bring peace to the Israeli-Palestinian conflict. Although in retirement the Brownings have not been able to take their annual trips to the Middle East, they carry the people there in their hearts and in their prayers daily. It is through the struggle for the rights of the Palestinians that Patti Browning found her calling and the focus of her discipleship: "I remember that I am working as one with Jesus, hooked together, and that no matter the absence of visible results for me, the effort Christ and I are making together is godly and worthwhile: peace and justice are of God and belong to God's own earth." [35]

When the Intifada began in September 2000, the Brownings joined an ecumenical group to assess the conditions. At the time, the movement of individual Palestinians was restricted and the people found themselves separated from their families, their jobs, and their hospitals. Although heartbroken and bone-tired on their return from Palestine, Patti Browning felt the need to return once again and do something more for the people there. She decided to attend the Sabeel Conference in February 2001 on her own. She wrote:

> When I arrived in Jerusalem the breeze was so invigorating that I was ready to step into its life with both feet. I felt like I was home again. I really could live there. I think I can truly say I feel at-one there, rooted in years of getting to know and love the people: laughing with them, weeping with them, learning and sharing their story, and valuing its truth at the core of my soul. I don't believe I will ever rest until there is peace in the City of Peace,

Jerusalem, our Jerusalem: the Christian Jerusalem,
the Jewish Jerusalem, the Muslim Jerusalem. [36]

After her return from Jerusalem in 2001, Patti
Browning spoke in several venues about the situation in the
Middle East, against the expansionist policies of the state
of Israel, and in support of Mordechai Vanunu. Vanunu,
an Israeli nuclear scientist, had revealed to the world in
1986 the extent of the Israeli nuclear arms build-up. He
was later kidnapped by the Israeli government in Italy and
returned to Israel and imprisoned. (Vanunu was a convert
to Anglicanism.) In 2004, Patti and Ed were present in
Israel for Mordechai Vanunu's release after eighteen years
in prison, twelve of them spent in solitary confinement.

Reflecting on the Middle East, Patti said, "I lie
in bed and hear the radio, I weep to think that we are
bombing to avenge bombing. I think of my children and
grandchildren and weep for the young people…especially
for the young people of that part of the world: young
people brought up to desire a fiery death, young people
defending a regime that has done nothing but oppress
them, young people far from home fighting in a war for
our country, the country we love even with all its errors
and deceptions. War affects the young most of all." [37]
Although Patti Browning believes peace and justice are
values to be embraced by all humanity, she sees a special
role for women as activists for human rights and peace:
"As women make gains as decision-makers in the councils
of the world, the human race will move closer to building
a world community based on peace and justice." [38]

In retirement, Ed and Patti Browning remain active
on many fronts. In addition to the Palestinian cause
and the work of the organization Sabeel, the Brownings

support the National Episcopal AIDS Coalition (NEAC) and the Episcopal Peace Fellowship (EPF). Ed Browning appeared at Barbara C. Harris's retirement in 2002, and was on hand to see his friend Michael Peers, primate of the Anglican Church in Canada, into retirement in 2004. A year earlier, he was presented with Integrity's Louie Crew Award. He continues to serve the church as pastor to several bishops and has participated in a number of episcopal consecrations, including those of Carol J. Gallagher, the first indigenous woman bishop, and Gene Robinson, the first openly gay bishop living in a committed relationship. In 2007 Browning signed a letter, along with presiding bishop Katharine Jefferts Schori and retired presiding bishop Frank T. Griswold, expressing "deep concern" for the situation in Iraq and outlining the need for a "just peace in the region." [39]

In 2009, at the 76th General Convention in Anaheim, California, both Ed and Patti Browning were presented with the John Nevin Sayre Peace Award by the Episcopal Peace Fellowship, for their ministries as "living examples of Christ's prophetic witness." Although initially reticent to attend yet another General Convention, the Brownings' spirits were boosted by the warm welcome they received and the abiding respect many in the Episcopal Church hold for them. In an historic moment, Ed Browning and Frank Griswold served as concelebrants at the convention's main eucharist with the twenty-sixth presiding bishop, Katharine Jefferts Schori, receiving warm applause as they processed out of the liturgy.

A Work of the Heart

Christian spirituality is a work of the heart. It is the heart that urges us to look beyond the biological and the institutional and to see the world through the eyes of God. It is what lifts religion above the realms of the legalistic and the mechanical and grows the soul. Without a spirituality of the heart, there is no true conversion, no spiritual encounter, no Christian presence in the world. Rather, religion becomes adherence to inherited patterns of behavior, to rules and rituals rather than an awareness of God's love and action in the world. Edmond Lee Browning is incapable of separating his heart from his religion. His ministry has always been about seeing the world through God's eyes and accepting the challenges that presents. As one who also believes profoundly in the mission of the institutional church, Browning always knew that the Episcopal Church could move beyond inherited patterns of behavior to become a work of the heart, to embody compassion in its structures and its actions in the world. "As long as you continue to tell the truth, others will be inspired to do that, too," Browning said several years after retirement. "Whether she knows it or not, that's what the church needs. No matter what you know the church to be, tell your truth, and the church will be a better place for it. And if the church is a better place, the whole world cannot help but benefit." [40]

One reason Ed Browning's ministry as presiding bishop was remarkable is that he was utterly consistent. He believed that the church could be the one place on earth with "no outcasts" and all his pastoral action arose from that belief. Institutions, including churches, tend not to be as extravagant with justice as Ed Browning.

Rather, churches often partition justice, work through the issues slowly, and make some wait for full inclusion. Browning's belief in "no outcasts," a phrase recollected by most of those interviewed for this book, was his challenge to Episcopalians to find their hearts, to find that center of tolerance, decency, and compassion, and then through that center to address the pain of the world. At his retirement celebration at the General Convention in 1997, Michael Peers, then primate of Canada, remarked how Ed Browning turned even the hardest realities of the worst year of his ministry in 1995, his *annus horribilus,* into an *annus profundus,* or a year of profound spiritual growth. [41] "We know that justice is more important than the approval of others," wrote Browning. "We owe it to ourselves to map out a moral plan for our lives and to pray for the courage to stay on that map." [42]

As someone who has been a bishop for a long time and whose ministry was almost always supported by national church structures, Ed Browning knows well the historic limitations of the church and the pace of change tolerated by the tradition. Yet Ed and Patti Browning believe the Episcopal Church can be something more, that its members can expand their hearts and move ecclesiastical structures to respond with greater compassion to the world. At great personal cost, Browning consistently held up the ideal of "no outcasts" to the church during bitter controversies, in the face of opposition and betrayal, and as some who disagreed declared themselves to be outcasts. Despite criticism that he spent too much time on his detractors, Browning sought to expand the heart of the Episcopal Church and hold it together in tension as it found its way through the controversies of the day. In his installation address Browning referred to baptism "as the sacrament of inclusion," and promised to respect both those who affirmed his personal positions and those who did not, and although sorely tested by the response to issues such as the ordination of women to the episcopate and the full inclusion of gay and lesbian people in the life of church, he did not stray from that position.

Edmond Lee Browning refuses to see another human being as an enemy; even in the face of fierce opposition he embraces friend and foe alike. He was and is content to leave judgments about the worth of individuals to God.

As presiding bishop, Browning made an indelible impact on the Episcopal Church. Whether the church was ready for the challenge is open to question, and yet as the number of women serving in all orders of ministry expands and as the church becomes more open to the full inclusion of the GLBT community, it appears that Browning's instincts to hold the church together as consensus emerged were on target. "To become a bishop today is a little like being drafted," Browning said in 2007. "You find yourself centrally located in the midst of conflict you didn't start but through which you must lead." [43] Throughout his ministry as presiding bishop, Browning opened the church to a deeper sense of baptism as the source of authority for all ministry in the world.

Ed and Patti Browning together worked to make the office of the presiding bishop a matter of the heart, and with open hearts they served the church and the world. As chief pastor, Ed Browning transformed the culture of the House of Bishops as a spiritual community and forged a new level of partnership with the "senior" House of Deputies. As a missionary presiding bishop, he expanded the ministry of the Episcopal Church to wherever there was pain and suffering in the world. Together with the passionate ministry of Patti Browning, the presiding bishop opened the hearts of the people of the Episcopal Church in solidarity with their sisters and brothers throughout the world, in a spirit of justice and peace. As a prophetic pastor, he reached beyond the church itself as a moral voice, challenging lawmakers to legislate compassionately and those in privileged positions to use their power and resources for the good of all. "I cannot imagine a question which would frighten the Holy Spirit away from us," he wrote. "God is just not that small." [44] Most of all, with the heart of a pastor, Edmond Lee Browning taught that God is always present, that the church should be above all a compassionate community, and that the face of Christ can be seen throughout the world.

Back cover photo: Ed and Patti Browning, just prior to their retirement in 1997, visited the annual gathering of the Convocation of American Churches in Europe, in Paris. *Courtesy of David W. Perry.*

Chapter Ten Notes

1   Edmond Lee Browning (hereafter cited as ELB), "Installation Address," Washington, D.C., January 11, 1986, Browning Collection.

2   ELB, "Address to General Convention," August 6, 1997, Browning Collection.

3   Patricia Sparks Browning (hereafter cited as PSB), interview by Episcopal Women's Ministries, December 1997, Browning Collection.

4   Barbara Harris, interview by Sheryl Kujawa-Holbrook (hereafter cited as SKH), April 2009.

5   David Skidmore, *Episcopal Life Convention Daily,* Saturday, July 19, 1997.

6   ELB, "Address to General Convention."

7   Ibid.

8   ELB, "Presiding Bishop Reflects on an Inclusive Church—and Challenges for the Future," ENS, December 14, 1994.

9   Michael Peers, interview by SKH, May 2009.

10 Frank T. Griswold, interview by SKH, March 2009.

11 Patricia Nakamura, "Looking Back and Ahead," *The Living Church,* December 14, 1997.

12 ELB, *A Year of Days with The Book of Common Prayer* (New York: Ballantine Books, 1997), July 7.

13 "Bishop Browning: Grace and Thoughtfulness," *The Living Church,* December 28, 1997.

14 Richard S. O. Chang, "Vision for Diversity," *The Living Church,* September 26, 1999.

15 Barbara Braver, "Visit Forges Links with Indian Subcontinent," *Episcopal Life,* April 1997.

16 Jim Solheim, "Browning Preaches Reconciliation at Coventry Cathedral," Episcopal News Service (hereafter cited as ENS), November 13, 1997.

17 PSB, "Clergy and Spouse Conference," Diocese of Western New York, April 14, 1997.

18 Sharon Sheridan, "Patti Browning Finds Christ," *Episcopal Life,* December 1997.

19 Brian J. Grieves, letter to SKH, November 17, 2009.

20 Brian J. Grieves, statement, August 2009.

21 "Bishop Browning Hospitalized with Pneumonia," ENS, May 25, 1997.

22 Anonymous, interview by SKH, March 2009.

23 Mary Miller, interview by SKH, March 2009.

24 Gene Robinson, interview by SKH, March 2009.

25 Douglas LeBlanc, interview by SKH, March 2009.

26 Ann Struthers Coburn, interview by SKH, March 2009.

27 Elizabeth Kaeton, "The Blueberry Man," *The Witness* 86, no. 4 (April 15, 2003).

28 Jerry Hames, "Browning Looks Toward Retirement," *Episcopal Life,* December 1997.

29 ELB, "New in Our Lives," *The Vintage Voice,* The Church Pension Fund.

30 Kaeton, "The Blueberry Man."

31 Hames, "Browning Looks Toward Retirement."

32 Anonymous, interview by SKH, March 2009.

33 ELB, "Homily," Notre Dame, Jerusalem, April 18, 2004, Browning Collection.

34 PSB, and Sandra J. Bright, "A Lifelong Commitment…to a People and the Soul of a Country," *The Witness* 84, no. 9 (September 2001).

35 PSB, "Address to the Episcopal Peace Fellowship, General Convention, 1997," Browning Collection.

36 PSB and Bright, "A Lifelong Commitment."

37 PSB, "Manifest Destiny in Israel," All Saints, Pasadena, November 2001, as reprinted in *The Witness*.

38 PSB, "Jubilee Reflections on Mordechai Vanunu and Samuel Day," Diocese of Ohio, Jubilee Day 2001, St. Paul's Episcopal Church, Akron, Ohio, April 28, 2001, as reprinted in *The Witness*.

39 "Iraq's Future Requires Careful, Reasoned Debate, Bishops Say in Letter to Congress," ENS, May 16, 2007.

40 Kaeton, "The Blueberry Man."

41 *An Evening to Celebrate,* video. (New York: Communications Department, Episcopal Church Center, July 20, 1997).

42 ELB, *A Year of Days*, October 14.

43 "Quote of the Week," *The Living Church,* April 29, 2007.

44 ELB, *A Year of Days,* May 29.

Selected Bibliography

Primary Source Material

The official papers of Edmond Lee Browning are held in the Archives of the Episcopal Church in Austin, Texas. As is the case of the papers of a presiding bishop, they are closed for thirty years from the end of his administration. Thus, this book has utilized other forms of primary source material:

The Browning Collection contains a wealth of newspaper clippings, correspondence, sermons, speeches, and photos collected by Edmond Lee Browning and Patricia Sparks Browning over the course of their ministry. The collection is privately held in their home. Many of the documents are available from other sources. Researchers interested in materials in the Browning Collection should consult the Archives of the Episcopal Church in Austin, Texas, or look online in its digital archive.

Digital and hardcopy editions of the following publications were also used: Diocesan Press Service, *Episcopal Life,* Episcopal News Service, *The Episcopalian, The Living Church,* and various diocesan and local newspapers.

Digital resources from Ancestry.com and Highbeam Research provided family history information and articles from the national and international press.

Books

Alexander, Robert H. *The Purple Pilgrim: A Manual for the Education of the Pledges of the Fraternity of Phi Gamma Delta.* Washington, D.C.: Phi Gamma Delta, 1965.

Anderson, Owanah. *400 Years: Anglican/Episcopal Missions Among American Indians.* Cincinnati: Forward Movement, 1997.

Anderson, Owanah. *Jamestown Commitment: The Episcopal Church and the American Indian.* Cincinnati: Forward Movement, 1988.

Armentrout, Don S., and Robert Slocum. *Documents of Witness: A History of the Episcopal Church, 1782-1985.* New York: Church Hymnal Corporation, 1994.

Bayne, Stephen F., Jr. *Christian Living.* Greenwich, Conn.: Seabury Press, 1957.

Bayne, Stephen F., Jr. *Mutual Responsibility and Interdependence in the Body of Christ.* New York: Seabury Press, 1963.

Borsch, Frederick Houk. *Outrage and Hope: A Bishop's Reflections in Times of Change and Challenge.* Valley Forge: Trinity Press International, 1996.

Brown, Leo Maxwell, William Davidson, and Allen Brown. *Vision Fulfilling: The Story of the Rural and Small Community Work of the Episcopal Church during the Twentieth Century.* Harrisburg: Morehouse, 1997.

Browning, Edmond Lee. *A Year of Days with the Book of Common Prayer.* New York: Ballantine Books, a division of Random House, Inc., 1997.

Buddenbaum, Judith M., and Debra L. Mason, eds. *Readings on Religion as News.* Ames: Iowa State University Press, 2000.

Butt, William, and William Strode. *Sewanee: The University of the South.* Louisville: Harmony House, 1984.

Carpenter, Humphrey. *Robert Runcie: The Reluctant Archbishop.* London: Sceptre, 1996.

Cazneau, William. *Eagle Pass: Life On The Border.* Austin: Pemberton Press, 1966.

Darling, Pamela W., ed. *Decently and In Order: Selected Reflections of Pamela P. Chinnis.* Cincinnati: Forward Movement, 2000.

Darling, Pamela W. *New Wine: The Story of Women Transforming Leadership and Power in the Episcopal Church.* Cambridge: Cowley Publications, 1994.

DeMille, George E. *The Episcopal Church Since 1900: A Brief History.* New York: Morehouse-Gorham Company, 1955.

Duggan, Margaret. *Runcie: The Making of An Archbishop.* London: Hodder and Stoughton, 1983.

Foster, Roland. *The Role of the Presiding Bishop.* Cincinnati: Forward Movement, 1982.

Selected Bibliography

Grieves, Brian J., ed. *No Outcasts: The Public Witness of Edmond L. Browning, XXIVth Presiding Bishop of the Episcopal Church*. Cincinnati: Forward Movement, 1997.

Harrison, Robert. *John Walker: A Man for the 21st Century*. Cincinnati: Forward Movement, 2004.

Holmes, David L. *A Brief History of the Episcopal Church*. Valley Forge: Trinity Press, 1993.

Hood, Robert E. *Social Teachings in the Episcopal Church: A Source Book*. Harrisburg: Morehouse, 1997.

Hook, Donald D. *The Plight of the Church Traditionalist: A Last Apology*. Louisville: The Prayer Book Society Publishing Company, 1991.

Kesselus, Kenneth. *John E. Hines: Granite on Fire*. Austin: Episcopal Theological Seminary of the Southwest, 1995.

Kew, Richard, and Roger White. *New Millennium, New Church: Trends Shaping the Episcopal Church for the 21st Century*. Cambridge, Mass.: Cowley Publications, 1992.

Kew, Richard, and Roger White. *Toward 2015: A Church Odyssey*. Cambridge, Mass.: Cowley Publications, 1997.

Leckie, Will, and Barry Stopfel. *Courage to Love: A Gay Priest Stands Up for His Beliefs*. New York: Doubleday, 1997.

Lewis, Harold T. *Yet With a Steady Beat: The African American Struggle for Recognition in the Episcopal Church*. Valley Forge: Trinity Press, 1996.

Lichtenberger, Arthur. *The Day Is at Hand*. New York: Seabury Press, 1964.

Murray, DuBose. *A Short History of the Protestant Episcopal Church in Texas*. Dallas: Turner Company, 1935.

Pierce, Nathaniel W., and Paul L. Ward. *The Voice of Conscience: A Loud and Unusual Noise? The Episcopal Peace Fellowship 1939-1989*. Charlestown, Mass.: Charles River Publishing, 1989.

Restarick, Henry Bond. *Hawaii, 1778-1920, From the Viewpoint of a Bishop; Being the story of English and American churchmen in Hawaii with historical sidelights*. Honolulu: Paradise of the Pacific, 1924.

Sachs, William L., and Thomas Holland. *Restoring the Ties That Bind: The Grassroots Transformation of the Episcopal Church*. New York: Church Publishing, 2003.

Shattuck, Gardiner H., Jr., *Episcopalians and Race: Civil War to Civil Rights*. Lexington: University Press of Kentucky, 2000.

Stough, Furman C., and Urban T. Holmes III, eds. *Realities and Visions: the Church's Mission Today*. New York: Seabury Press, 1976.

Sumner, David E. *The Episcopal Church's History, 1945-1985.* Wilton, Conn.: Morehouse-Barlow, 1987.

Wallis, Jim. *Faith Works: Lessons from the Life of An Activist Preacher.* New York: Random House, 2000.

Ward, Hortense Warner. *A Century of Missionary Effort: The Church of the Good Shepherd, 1860-1960.* Austin: Von Boeckman-Jones Co., 1960.

Williamson, Samuel R., Jr. *Sewanee Sesquicentennial History: the Making of the University of the South.* Sewanee: University of the South, 2008.

Winter, Gibson. *America in Search of Its Soul.* Harrisburg: Morehouse, 1996.

Articles and Documents

Armentrout, Don S. "Episcopal Splinter Groups: Schisms in the Episcopal Church, 1963-1985," *Historical Magazine of the Protestant Episcopal Church* 55 (1986): 295-320.

Browning, Edmond Lee. "A Voice in the World." In *The Past Speaks to the Future: 50 Years of the Protestant Hour,* 131-135. Nashville: Abingdon Press, 1995.

But We See Jesus: A Pastoral Letter from the Black Episcopal Bishops to Black Clergy and Laity in the Episcopal Church. New York: Office of Black Ministries, June 25,1990.

Crew, Louie. "Lessons Learned in the Struggle to Reduce Institutional Heterosexism in the Episcopal Church." In *Overcoming Heterosexism and Homophobia,* edited by James T. Sears and Walter L. Williams, 341-353. New York: Columbia University Press, 1997.

Dennis, Walter D. "A Personal Prospectus on the Episcopal Church in the 1990s," *St. Luke's Journal of Theology* 35, no. 1 (December 1990): 8-18.

Vogel, Arthur A. "The Role of the Presiding Bishop," *The Living Church* (April 14, 1985): 9.

Sources and Permissions

Interviews

All interviews conducted by Sheryl A. Kujawa-Holbrook unless otherwise noted.

Aguilar, Richard, September 23, 2009

Almquist, Curtis, ssje, March 12, 2009

Anderson, Owanah, April 3, 2009

Ateek, Naim, March 4, 2009

Bartlett, Allen, April 20, 2009

Beers, David Booth, March 29, 2009;
    December 2009 (Interview by Brian J. Grieves)

Borsch, Frederick H., April 20, 2009

Braver, Barbara, March 24, 2009

Brooks, Robert, April 15, 2009

Bruno, Jon, April 30, 2009

Browning, Edmond Lee, January, March, May, and June 2009

Browning, John, March 23, 2009

Browning, Mark, March 27, 2009

Browning, Paige, March 29, 2009
Browning, Patricia Sparks, January, March, May, and June 2009
Browning, Peter, March 25, 2009
Browning, Philip, March 30, 2009
Browning, Robert, March 27, 2009
Cesaretti, Charles, March 30, 2009
Chang, Richard S. O., March 6, 2009
Coburn, Ann Struthers, March 4, 2009
Coburn, John Bowen, February 17, 2009
Conley, Judith, September 30, 2009
Crew, Louie, April 22, 2009
Darling, Pamela W., March 24, 2009
Dixon, Jane Holmes, April 15, 2009
Donovan, Herbert, March 23, 2009
Douglas, Ian T., April 15, 2009
Ellis, Fred, September 25, 2009
Faramelli, Norman, October 6, 2009
Frazier, Jeanette, May 6, 2009
    (Interviewed by Monna S. MacLellan)
Gallander, Cathleen, April 25, 2009
Garland, James, March 30, 2009
Garner, Bruce, September 23, 2009
Granfield, Nancy, March 31, 2009
Griswold, Frank T., March 23, 2009
Harris, Barbara C., April 1, 2009
Hathaway, Alden, March 24, 2009
Honaman, William Frederick, March 24, 2009, April 1, 2009
Hopkins, Harold, April 3, 2009
Hulsey, Sam, April 3, 2009
Johnson, Robert, June 9, 2009
Jones, Clyde, March 30, 2009

Jones, Norma, March 30, 2009

Keyser, Charles, March 12, 2009

Kimsey, Rustin, March 24, 2009

Knight, Hollinshead T., September 24, 2009

LaPiere, Virginia, February 16, 2009

LeBlanc, Douglas, March 18, 2009

Lee, Edward, March 4, 2009

Lewis, Harold T., April 1, 2009

Lockwood, John, April 4, 2009

MacLellan, Monna, March 6, 2009

Matsuda, Keiko,
(Interviewed by Laurence E. Kirchner, Sr., Spring 2009)

Mathews, Judy, March 24, 2009

Mauney, J. Patrick, March 13, 2009

McAllister, Gerald, March 17, 2009

McAllister, Helen, March 17, 2009

McNutt, Charlie, March 25, 2009

Miyagi, Yoshiko,
(Interviewed by Laurence E. Kirchner, Sr., Spring 2009)

Miller, Mary, March 19, 2009

Norgren, William, April 3, 2009

Palmore, Russell Vaughn, Jr., October 8, 2009

Paul, Ginger, September 23, 2009

Peers, Michael, May 20, 2009

Peterson, John L., April 2, 2009

Porter, Diane Marie, March 19, 2009

Robinson, Gene, March 25, 2009

Rockwell, Hays, March 6, 2009

Rodman, Edward W., February 17, 2009

Rudinoff, Jan, March 16, 2009

Rudinoff, Paula, March 16, 2009

Shaw, M. Thomas III, ssje, April 1, 2009

Shoemaker, Jack, March 30, 2009
Shoemaker, Roxanne, March 30, 2009
Smith, Eleanor, March 16, 2009
Smith, Martin L., February 20, 2009
Solheim, James, March 31, 2009
Surrett, Janet, April 22, 2009
Tederstrom, John, April 15, 2009
Van Culin, Samuel, March 26, 2009
Williams, Arthur B., Jr., April 15, 2009
Wilson, Nancy, April 23, 2009
Woodcock, Bruce, September 30, 2009
Wright, J. Robert, April 1, 2009

Written Statements and Stories

Almquist, Curtis ssje, March 12, 2009
Anderson, Jerry, February 3, 2009
Anderson, Owanah, May 4, 2009
Bradley, John Clinton, February 3 2009
Bush, George H. W., September 24, 2009
Chibana, Yasuhito, May 30, 2009
Chilstrom, Herbert W., April 3, 2009
Creasy, James A., February 3, 2009
Crumbaugh, Frank Boyd III, March 3, 2009
Fowler, Anne C., March 3, 2009
Frazier, Jeanette, May 6, 2009
Grieves, Brian J., August 19, 2009
Hoover, Judy, March 23, 2009
Horton, Carol, May 5, 2009
Kaeton, Elizabeth, March 3, 2009
Kafity, Samir, March 24, 2009
Kimsey, Rustin, April 13, 2009

MacLellan, Monna, January 24, 2009
McGaughy, Patsy Thomson, March 20, 2009
McLaughlin, Kay Collier, July 20, 2009
McLeod, Mary Adelia R., April 23, 2009
Peterson, John L., April 2, 2009
Privitera, Linda, February 6, 2009
Shoemaker, Jack, January 25, 2009
Surrett, Janet, April 23, 2009
Van Culin, Thomas, February 3, 2009
Vesely-Flad, Ethan, March 5, 2009
Wallis, Jim, April 13, 2009
Williams, Arthur B., Jr., April 25, 2009

Acknowledgements and Permissions

Archival and photographic assistance provided by the Archives of the Episcopal Church, Mark Duffy, Brian J. Grieves, Margaret Larom, J. Patrick Mauney, Harriet Murrell, David Perry, and Jim Solheim.

Browning photos provided by the Archives of the Episcopal Church, Austin, Texas; the Episcopal Church Center, New York, New York; Jennings Photography, Hood River, Oregon; J. Patrick Mauney; and David Perry. Used with permission.

Interviews in Hawaii and draft Chapter 4 by Brian J. Grieves. Interviews in Okinawa by Laurence Kirchner, Sr.

Excerpt from *Faith Works* by Jim Wallis, copyright © 2000 by Jim Wallis. Used by permission of Random House, Inc.

Excerpts from *A Year of Days with The Book of Common Prayer* by Bishop Edmond Lee Browning, copyright © 1997 by Bishop Edmond Lee Browning. Used by permission of Ballantine Books, a division of Random House, Inc.

About the Author

Sheryl A. Kujawa-Holbrook is a priest of the Diocese of Los Angeles, historian, educator, and practical theologian. She is currently professor of practical theology and religious education at Claremont School of Theology and professor of Anglican Studies at the Episcopal Theological School at Claremont, also known as Bloy House. She is the former academic dean and Suzanne Radley Hiatt professor of feminist pastoral theology and church history at the Episcopal Divinity School, Cambridge, Massachusetts. The author of numerous books and articles, Kujawa-Holbrook worked in the Browning administration for ten years from 1988-1998 as the Youth Ministries Coordinator and Program Director for Ministries with Young People. She lives in California with her husband Paul, daughter Rachel, and two cats, Moosie and Tasha.

Index